The Liberated Entrepreneur

Building a Business That Works for You

Roger Best

Contents

Introduction: The Liberated Entrepreneur

The Entrepreneurial Dream vs. Reality

WHEN I FIRST IMAGINED life as an entrepreneur, it looked like something off a postcard. You know the one - sunlit cafés, neatly foamed cappuccinos, and me, effortlessly brilliant, sketching grand ideas into a pristine notebook. There are no bosses or mandatory meetings where someone says, "Let's circle back" with a straight face. Just freedom, flexibility, and a smug, deeply satisfying sense that I was now the undisputed master of my own destiny.

Six months later, there I was—hunched over a laptop that hummed like it, too, was on the verge of a nervous breakdown, surrounded by a graveyard of empty coffee mugs and wearing sweatpants so disheveled they could've testified against me in court. My "freedom" had come with a bonus pack of never-ending deadlines, late-night emails, and the unshakable feeling that my to-do list was breeding like rabbits when I wasn't looking.

If entrepreneurship were a vacation, it would be the kind where you book a luxurious beachfront resort, only to arrive and discover your room faces a loading dock. The ocean? Oh, it's there—just past the dumpster and a particularly vengeful-looking seagull.

This, my friends, is the entrepreneurial paradox. We leap into business ownership chasing freedom and purpose, believing the stories about autonomy and meaningful work. But somewhere along the way, our businesses shapeshift into ravenous, unrelenting beasts—eating our time, energy, and occasionally our will to live. What was meant to be our liberation starts demanding more attention than a toddler hopped up on candy.

And so, the question becomes: how do we wrestle back the dream? How do we build businesses that support our lives, rather than hijack them entirely? That's what this book is all about—untangling the chaos, rethinking what success actually means, and rediscovering the joy and excitement that made us want to leap into entrepreneurship in the first place.

But first, for the love of all that is clean and holy, let's deal with the sweatpants. At least a rinse cycle. This is going to be fun. I promise.

Why This Book Exists: Escaping the Hamster Wheel of Success

The Common Trap: Dreams of Autonomy, Reality of Exhaustion

When we first set out on the grand adventure of entrepreneurship, we envision ourselves as heroic captains of sleek, nimble ships. Calm seas, golden sunsets, and horizons shimmering with promise—wealth, freedom, and an enviable tan. There's no one waving memos at us about the "synergy initiative" (what does that even mean?), no cheery supervisors holding soul-crushing quarterly reviews. Just us, the salty breeze of autonomy in our hair, confidently steering toward lives of balance, purpose, and casual genius.

At least, that's the brochure.

Reality, as it turns out, is more *Gilligan's Island* than *Master and Commander*. Instead of calmly sipping espresso while jotting down brilliant ideas in an attractive leather notebook, you're hunched over your desk at midnight, muttering choice words while Googling *"Why does my Wi-Fi hate me?"* and *"Invoice templates for people who have no idea what they're doing."* Your to-do list, once a cheerful cluster of manageable tasks, has grown into a sprawling beast with demands so incessant you half-expect it to lurch to life and start growling.

And then there are the hours. Glorious, flexible hours that have expanded to fit *all of them*. You escape the 9-to-5 only to find yourself neck-deep in the 5-to-9—5 a.m. to 9 p.m., that is, on a good day. The supposed boundary between "work" and "life" vanishes entirely. You're answering client emails with a forkful of dinner poised mid-air and drafting marketing ideas in the shower, with shampoo foam sliding into your ears.

But the real kicker is the mantra we all know too well: *Just one more thing.* It starts innocently enough—an email here, a quick tweak there. Next thing you know, it's 2 a.m., and you're sitting in a wasteland of coffee mugs, snack wrappers, and glasses of water you've abandoned like a trail of tiny, hydration-related regrets. You don't even remember if dinner happened, though an empty cereal bowl suggests something occurred.

And somehow, you're not entirely sure how you ended up here. It's as if someone left a perfectly lovely trap wide open, sprinkled it with your hopes and dreams, and gently coaxed you inside. You wanted autonomy but got a business that now keeps you on a very short leash. You longed for wealth but discovered that chasing overdue invoices is less glamorous than Instagram suggested.

This, dear reader, is the paradox of entrepreneurship. It is not a personal failing or a cosmic joke (though it sometimes feels like one). It's merely an initiation, a rite of passage into the world of being your own boss—a bit like being tossed into the deep end of the pool, only to discover you've been handed a snorkel made of paper.

But here's the hopeful part: it doesn't have to stay this way. You can untangle the mess, reclaim your freedom, and build a business that works *for* you, instead of vice versa.

First, though, we must take a moment to admit where we are: firmly stuck in the hamster wheel, spinning away. Let's laugh about it, shall we? Because if we can't find the humor in working 16-hour days to escape a 40-hour workweek, then we've truly lost the plot.

The Pivot Toward Liberation: Breaking Free to Rediscover Joy

Here's the curious thing about the entrepreneurial trap: at first, it feels almost cozy. Comfortable, even. Sure, you're swamped—so much so that your inbox looks like a black hole actively consuming time—but there's a peculiar pride in wearing "busy" like a merit badge. After all, aren't you just doing what the *greats* did? Hustling, grinding, heroically sacrificing sleep to build something extraordinary.

And then one day—somewhere between your fiftieth late-night email and that *one last* meeting you swore you'd never schedule—it dawns on you. This isn't the dream you signed up for. It's the evil twin of the dream—slightly familiar but with shifty eyes and questionable intentions. Your days, once fueled by purpose, have turned into a relentless blur of urgent tasks that feel less like empire-building and more like trying to tread water while clutching a cinderblock labeled **"Immediate Attention Required."**

This is where so many of us get stuck: caught in the absurd irony of chasing freedom only to feel more trapped than ever. And it's not just the hours—though, let's be honest, those hours are starting to feel personal. It's the creeping realization that the joy, the spark, the sense of *why* that set you on this journey has been drowned out by the clamor of deadlines, spreadsheets, and, inexplicably, twelve tabs of project management tools you've forgotten how to close.

Which brings us to this book. Don't worry—I'm not here to wag a disapproving finger and bark, "Work less!" as though that bit of wisdom alone will change your life. (If it were that easy, I suspect you'd be lounging on a beach already, not frantically looking for Wi-Fi.) Instead, this book is here to show you something infinitely better: another way to approach your business—a path toward liberation.

Now, when I say "pivot," I don't mean the kind of frantic, panic-induced pivot startups love to brag about right before they run out of cash. No, this is a thoughtful, deliberate pivot—a shift toward clarity and purpose. A chance to pause, breathe, and ask the truly big questions: *What actually matters? What's worth my energy? And how do I get my business to serve me, instead of the other way around?*

Here's the kicker: this isn't just about working less or outsourcing tasks to someone with a better grip on Excel (though we'll get there, I promise). It's about creating a life where balance, fulfillment, and—dare I say it—joy aren't fleeting visitors but full-time, rent-paying residents. It's about finding your rhythm, the one that makes you feel alive, and silencing that dreadful little voice in your head whispering, *"You should be doing more."*

Let me be clear: this journey isn't going to tell you to set your ambitions aside. Quite the opposite—it's going to nudge you toward a version of success that doesn't just *look* impressive but *feels* extraordinary. It's about reclaiming your time, your energy, and—if we're being bold—your weekends. Because life's too short to spend it staring at spreadsheets in yesterday's pajamas, wondering where the joy disappeared to.

So let's do this. Let's pivot toward liberation, one intentional step at a time. The destination? A business that thrives, a life that fulfills, and a version of you who, for the first time in ages, looks up from the to-do list and says, *"Ah, there it is. Freedom."*

A Lighthearted Yet Practical Guide

If the words *"business manual"* send an involuntary shudder down your spine, I get it. You're probably imagining something heavy with jargon, bulging with bullet points, and as thrilling as the instruction manual for a toaster oven—only with far less clarity. Fear not. This is not that book. I wouldn't dream of writing one of *those* books.

Instead, think of this as your co-pilot for the slightly wobbly, always unpredictable rollercoaster that is entrepreneurship. The kind of co-pilot who points out the breathtaking views, casually offers life-saving tips when the seatbelt starts to feel suspiciously loose, and fully supports impromptu detours for snacks.

Here's the thing: we're going to tackle big, meaningful ideas, but we're going to do it with a healthy dose of levity. Why? Because if you can't laugh at the absurdity of filing quarterly taxes, deciphering cryptic printer errors, or pretending to understand the latest TikTok trend, then what are we even doing here? Humor, you see, is the spoonful of sugar that makes the reality of running a business slightly less indigestible. And let's be honest, sometimes we all need a little help choking down the hard bits.

Now, don't mistake this for fluff. This book is practical—frighteningly so, at times. You'll find actual strategies, tools, and frameworks that you can use right away. No abstract concepts here, the kind that sound *profound* but turn out to be about as useful as a chocolate teapot. Instead, it's actionable advice, gift-wrapped in relatable stories and delivered with a wink—like a friend sneaking you a cheat sheet for life's tougher exams.

And yes, there will be digressions. Delightful, slightly irreverent digressions. Because life is messy, ridiculous, and sometimes downright baffling. Why pretend otherwise? So, don't be surprised if we meander into a tangent about the virtues of coffee, the perils of group emails, or the enduring mystery of why printers can detect low toner levels but cannot, apparently, print a simple PDF without existential angst.

Most importantly, this is a book for real people. People with bad days, cluttered desks, and an ever-growing stash of half-filled notebooks labeled things like *"BIG IDEAS"* and *"Do This Someday (Maybe)"*. It's for those of us who sometimes (frequently) feel like we're winging it, despite outward appearances of competence.

So, settle in. You don't need a highlighter, a spreadsheet, or a master's degree in sticky-note management to get through this book—though feel free to bring any of the above if it makes you feel more professional. All you really need is an open mind, a willingness to laugh (especially at yourself), and a decent cup of coffee. Or tea, if that's more your speed. I'm not here to judge your beverage choices.

Let's make this fun, shall we? Because, yes, entrepreneurship is a serious business—but that doesn't mean we can't enjoy the ride. After all, if you're going to hurtle down the tracks at breakneck speed, you might as well do it with your hands in the air and a grin on your face.

Who This Book Is For: Calling All Overworked Dreamers

If you've ever found yourself staring blankly at your computer screen at midnight, wondering how your once-glorious entrepreneurial dream devolved into something resembling a frantic circus act, then congratulations—you're in the right place. You may feel like you're juggling flaming chainsaws while teetering on a fraying tightrope suspended over a pit of particularly irritable alligators. Or worse, you hear that description and think, *Chainsaws? Tightrope? Honestly, that sounds easier than my current workload.*

You, dear reader, are what I affectionately call an *overworked dreamer*: the plucky entrepreneur who set out with stars in your eyes and visions of freedom dancing in your head, only to discover that being your own boss often means reporting to the world's most demanding, unreasonable supervisor—yourself.

Let's pause for a quick self-diagnosis, shall we? I know I promised this book wouldn't bulge with bullet points, but occasionally, they serve a higher purpose—like diagnosing an affliction. If you recognize yourself in even one or two of these, well, welcome aboard:

- **You've forgotten what weekends are for.** Were they always meant for catching up on emails? Or are weekends, like unicorns and "inbox zero," charming myths that no one actually encounters in real life?

- **You're haunted by work-related dreams.** Or, more accurately, *nightmares.* You've probably woken up in a cold sweat at 3 a.m., convinced you missed a deadline or that you accidentally sent a client an email starting with, *"Hi NAME, great to connect!"*

- **Your family refers to your laptop as "the third child."** Bonus points if your actual children have plastered it with stickers and periodically question whether it receives more love and attention than they do. (Spoiler: they might have a point.)

Sound familiar? If so, take heart. You're not alone—far from it, in fact. Entrepreneurs everywhere, even the ones who look perpetually polished and serene on social media, are grappling with the same challenges. The Instagram filter may hide the bags under their eyes, but trust me, they're there.

Here's what you need to know: You're not failing. You're not broken. And you're certainly not doomed to spend the rest of your days chained to your business, subsisting on caffeine and blind optimism. There's a better way—a saner, healthier, infinitely more fulfilling way—to run your business and live your life.

This book exists to help you put down the chainsaws (metaphorically, though if you're holding actual chainsaws, please *really* put them down), step off the tightrope, and reimagine what entrepreneurship can look like. Because no one launches a business dreaming of exhaustion. No one says, *"You know what sounds great? Answering emails in my pajamas at 2 a.m."*

It's time to wake up—figuratively and, let's be honest, sometimes literally—and reclaim the life you deserve. You don't need to do *more*; you need to do *better*. And here's the good news: you're already in the perfect spot to make that happen.

So, roll up your sleeves, grab a fresh cup of coffee, and let's get to work. This isn't just about survival—it's about building a life you actually *enjoy*. After all, you didn't come this far just to spend your days glued to a laptop wondering where the joy went, did you?

What This Book Will Teach You: From Stressed-Out Founder to Liberated Entrepreneur

Freedom Over Frenzy

Let's begin with a small, painful truth: the entrepreneurial life has a tendency to sprint off the rails. What starts as a dream of freedom—a noble escape from bosses, commutes, and company "synergy meetings"—can quickly morph into something far less inspiring. Suddenly, your business feels like an overexcited Labrador dragging you through a park teeming with squirrels, while you flail along behind it, gasping for breath and wondering where it all went wrong.

This book is here to help you take back the leash. To guide you toward building a business that supports your life, rather than eating it for breakfast. Picture, if you will, a world where your work fits neatly into your days—leaving room for family dinners that don't involve multitasking, hobbies that don't involve feeling guilty, and perhaps even the rare but glorious nap. Remarkable, isn't it?

Now, I'm not promising perfection—because, let's face it, perfection is a fairy tale told to us by productivity apps and people who iron their socks. What I am promising is progress: toward a business that doesn't just make money but gives you back your peace of mind.

Practical Strategies

Ah yes, strategies. As comforting as big-picture pep talks are, they won't get you very far without a little practicality. That's where this book shines—or at the very least, where it flickers brightly like a flashlight in a storm.

You'll find actionable advice—tips you can actually use—to streamline operations, clarify priorities, and break that particularly destructive habit of saying "yes" to everything (including tasks you resent and meetings you suspect could've been an email). We'll dive into the art of delegation, the genius of automation, and the sheer relief of stepping back and discovering that, yes, the world does keep spinning when you're not micromanaging.

But we're going deeper than time-blocking and to-do lists (though those have their moments of glory). This book is about rediscovering *why* you started this journey in the first place. It's about finding the joy and purpose that inspired you to leap into entrepreneurship—before you were knee-deep in late-night emails and existential printer battles. Because tools and hacks are lovely, but they're meaningless unless they serve a greater purpose. *Your* purpose.

The Bigger Picture

And that brings us to the heart of it all: legacy. Now, before you roll your eyes and assume I'm about to wax poetic about leaving behind a foundation or commissioning a tasteful bronze statue in your honor, stay with me. This isn't about grand gestures (unless you're into those, in which case, by all means—bronze away).

It's about crafting a life that feels fulfilling. A life that reflects your values, nurtures your relationships, and leaves behind something meaningful—whether that's a thriving community, more time for your family, or just the satisfaction of knowing you've built a business that didn't chew you up and spit you out.

Your business isn't just a profit machine; it's a vessel. A vessel for income, yes, but also for impact. So what do you want it to stand for? How do you want it to shape your corner of the world—whether that's your industry, your neighborhood, or just the face that looks back at you in the mirror?

This book will nudge you—gently but firmly—toward thinking beyond the chaos of your day-to-day grind. To consider the long game. Because, trust me, the long game is where the good stuff lives.

A Dash of Humor

Now, I should clarify: this isn't some solemn, soul-searching pilgrimage that requires you to sit cross-legged on a mountaintop contemplating existence (though if that's your thing, I salute you). No, this is more like a cheerful road trip with a co-pilot who cracks jokes, hands you snacks, and occasionally slaps your hand away from the horn when you get impatient.

There will be humor—because, let's be honest, what's life without it? And there will be plenty of moments that make you stop mid-sentence and think, *Good grief, that's me.*

So, if you're ready to swap stress for strategy, chaos for clarity, and those flaming chainsaws of overwhelm for something resembling peace, you're in the right place. By the time you've turned the last page, you'll be well on your way to becoming a *liberated entrepreneur*—one who's not just getting by but genuinely thriving.

Shall we begin?

The Road Ahead: What to Expect (Spoiler: It's Fun)

A Journey Through Mindset and Strategy

Picture this book as a road trip—one of those scenic drives where you roll down the window, enjoy the view, and feel vaguely superior to everyone stuck on the highway of mediocrity. We'll pass through some glorious vistas: rediscovering your purpose, reclaiming your time, and carving out moments for the good stuff—family dinners, hobbies, or staring meaningfully into the middle distance while clutching a cup of tea.

There will be potholes, of course. At times, we'll confront truths you'd rather not examine—like that unfortunate habit of saying "yes" to things you hate or believing your to-do list will eventually just *sort itself out*. But not to worry: I've packed plenty of snacks (humor, anecdotes, and the occasional friendly nudge) to keep things moving and, dare I say, enjoyable.

We'll begin by exploring why so many of us wind up spinning furiously on the hamster wheel of overwork, convinced that speed equals progress. From there, we'll move to the nitty-gritty—streamlining operations, building systems that work for *you,* and creating a business that feels less like a chaotic beast and more like a loyal, well-trained golden retriever. Finally, we'll zoom out and focus on legacy: how to build something that doesn't just bring in revenue now but leaves an impact you can be proud of.

It's mindset and strategy, rolled into one, like a Swiss Army knife for the overworked entrepreneur. And like any worthwhile road trip, it's not just about reaching the destination. It's about the stops, the detours, and the occasional "I can't believe that just happened" moment along the way.

The Role of Humor

Now, let's address the obvious: burnout, overwork, and entrepreneurial chaos are *serious* topics. But learning doesn't have to feel like chewing through a cardboard sandwich of advice. You know as well as I do that no one absorbs wisdom while grimacing through paragraphs of earnest finger-wagging.

That's why humor is your co-pilot here. There will be misadventures—mine, mostly, but perhaps a few of yours will come to mind as well. Expect playful analogies, the occasional irreverent tangent, and a gentle reminder that printers and Wi-Fi networks are plotting against us all. Because laughter doesn't just make the medicine go down—it makes the journey worth taking.

An Invitation to Reflect

As you turn these pages, I encourage you to bring a little curiosity and a willingness to laugh—at the challenges, the unexpected detours, and, most importantly, at yourself. Entrepreneurship, after all, is a glorious experiment, full of triumphs, mistakes, and moments that make you go, *"Well, that didn't work."*

We'll embrace the stumbles and celebrate the victories, however small. Because you're here for a reason—you're ready to make a change, to build a life and business that actually fit together, like two puzzle pieces rather than two awkwardly shaped spoons. And that, my friend, is no small thing.

So grab your metaphorical map (this book), dust off your sense of humor, and settle in. The road ahead promises a few challenges, some breakthrough moments, and—if we're lucky—a couple of epiphanies worth scribbling in the margins. But more than anything, it promises *progress*.

Welcome to the Journey

If you've made it this far, let me offer my heartfelt congratulations. Whether you're teetering on the brink of burnout, staring down an endless string of 60-hour weeks, or just wondering why your business feels like a particularly cranky toddler who skipped nap time, you're exactly where you need to be.

Entrepreneurship, as you well know, is not for the faint of heart. It's exhilarating and exasperating—like riding a rollercoaster you built yourself, one that occasionally makes ominous creaking noises. But here you are, ready to recalibrate, rethink, and take back the reins. That's no small thing—it's a declaration of sorts.

This isn't just about putting bandages on burnout or slapping duct tape on what's broken. It's about rediscovering the joy and purpose that brought you to entrepreneurship in the first place. It's about stepping off the squeaky hamster wheel and—if I may be so bold—replacing it with something more rewarding. A hammock, perhaps. Or at the very least, a quieter, more well-oiled wheel.

Together, we'll tackle the traps, unravel the mess, and rebuild your business into something that works *for* you, rather than holding you hostage. Along the way, I hope you'll find yourself smiling—at the absurdities, at my stories, and maybe even at your own entrepreneurial quirks.

So take a breath. You don't have to figure it all out today, and you certainly don't have to do it alone. This book is your guide, your cheerleader, and—when necessary—your comic relief.

Let's get started, shall we? The hammock's waiting. Or at the very least, a sturdier, quieter wheel.

Chapter One

The Entreprenuerial Freedom Paradox

Introduction: Welcome to the Great Escape (or So You Thought)

LET'S BEGIN, IF WE may, with a scene. Picture yourself—an ambitious, bright-eyed entrepreneur—seated at a charming, sunlit café, sipping an artfully crafted espresso while jotting down the world's next great business idea into a pristine notebook. Your face glows with purpose, your thoughts hum with creativity, and, if we're being honest, your hair probably looks pretty good, too. After all, you're the captain of your own ship, the master of your destiny, the proud architect of a life unshackled by corporate overlords and mind-numbing meetings about "synergy" and "key takeaways."

This, my friends, is the dream we all sign up for—the glossy brochure version of entrepreneurship. A life brimming with freedom, flexibility, and a smug sort of satisfaction that comes from knowing you're *doing it your way.*

Now let's fast-forward, oh, about six months. Same you, different scene. You're hunched over your laptop at 11:53 p.m., surrounded by coffee mugs so stained they've essentially become part of your kitchen decor. Your hair—if you remember to check—has taken on a life of its own, and your "brilliant business idea" is somewhere underneath the growing pile of responsibilities, which now looks suspiciously like a medieval scroll. Your to-do list stretches longer than the Nile, your inbox has learned to reproduce emails at an alarming rate (I swear they're mating in there), and you've forgotten what weekends used to be for. Relaxation? Leisure? You seem to recall these concepts, but only as vague, mythological constructs.

And this is where we find ourselves—a paradox of epic proportions. The entrepreneurial dream, which was supposed to look like sipping espresso while your well-oiled business machine purrs quietly in the background, has somehow shapeshifted into a perpetual game of *whack-a-mole*. Every task you finish seems to spawn three more, each more urgent and vaguely resentful than the last.

It's a bit like quicksand, really. You take one step forward, bravely tackling your inbox or invoicing or whatever other beast demands your attention that day, and before you know it, you're sinking faster—ankle-deep, waist-deep—into the murky abyss of your own responsibilities. You may find yourself looking up at the sky (or your ceiling fan) and wondering how this happened. How, exactly, did the dream of freedom mutate into a 16-hour workday filled with tasks that have names like "TPS Reports" and "Annual Budget Analysis" and "Deal With That Angry Client Who Used Caps Lock Too Liberally"?

Here's the tricky bit: we entrepreneurs are often tethered to our businesses by invisible cords—cords of our own making, no less. Some of these cords are forged from good intentions. We want to be hands-on, in control, to ensure everything runs smoothly. Others are tied with knots of fear—fear that something will fall apart without us, that a competitor will outshine us, or, worst of all, that if we take a breath and step back for even a moment, someone might discover we're just *winging it*.

This book, dear reader, is here to address that peculiar entrepreneurial predicament. We're going to laugh about it, of course, because laughter is both necessary and medicinal when your inbox has 372 unread emails and the phrase "work-life balance" sounds like the name of an indie band you used to like. But we're also going to work on it—unraveling those invisible cords, examining the traps we've set for ourselves, and, ultimately, charting a course back to the freedom we so eagerly pursued in the first place.

So, if you've found yourself in this entrepreneurial quicksand—overworked, overcommitted, and perhaps slightly over-caffeinated—you're in good company. There's no judgment here, only a firm promise: this book will help you untangle the mess, rediscover the joy, and maybe—just maybe—find yourself back at that sunlit café, sipping espresso with a satisfied grin, while your business hums happily along.

For now, though, let's just focus on getting you out of the quicksand. This is going to be fun, I promise.

The Golden Cage of Entrepreneurship

Let's begin with the pitch. The siren song of entrepreneurship that has lured so many of us from the safety of steady paychecks into the wild and unpredictable waters of "being your own boss." You know the one:

"Imagine this—no more answering to supervisors who insist on calling themselves 'team leaders.' No more commutes spent muttering darkly at traffic lights or enduring Karen from Accounting's opinions on office fridge etiquette. Instead, you'll be free. Free to set your own hours, work from anywhere, and—best of all—chase unlimited potential. The world is your oyster, and you are the intrepid pearl diver of your destiny."

It's a pitch so seductive you can practically hear the violins swelling. In your mind, you're already seated on a tropical balcony, laptop open, cash rolling in while you sip something with a miniature umbrella poking out. Maybe you'll work three hours a day and spend the rest practicing yoga, writing that novel you always said you'd write, or heroically catching up on Netflix series that *deserve* your attention.

Then, reality arrives. Slowly at first, like an overcast morning, and then all at once, like a foghorn to the face.

The tropical balcony? Turns out it's your kitchen table, which you haven't left in 14 hours. The laptop? It's a glowing portal of despair, home to 47 unread Slack messages and 200 emails, many of which involve phrases like *"ASAP"* and *"circling back."* You are now the boss, yes, but your new boss—you—turns out to be *completely unhinged*. The hours you set for yourself? Those were *adorable*.

Worse still, the business you lovingly built, the one that was meant to carry you to freedom, now teeters like an especially wobbly Jenga tower anytime you so much as think about stepping away. You tell yourself it's only temporary—just until things stabilize. But then, weeks become months, and months turn into you Googling *"how long can humans survive without sleep?"* at 2 a.m.

This, my friends, is what we call the Golden Cage of Entrepreneurship.

How the Cage Forms

Now, you may wonder: how did we get here? How did that dream of a hammock by the sea turn into the equivalent of a shiny but inescapable cage? It's a slow and subtle process, much like accidentally locking yourself in your own house.

At first, you're thrilled to be in charge—*finally*, things will be done correctly. But then perfectionism sets in. You look at every task, every email, every pixel on your website, and think: "No one can do this as well as I can." Which may be true for about 10 minutes, but before you know it, you've spent four hours adjusting the spacing on your logo while the rest of your business burns quietly in the background.

Then there's the charming beast that is *fear of delegation*. Letting someone else take over feels as reckless as handing a toddler a chainsaw. "What if they mess it up?" you think, clutching every task like it's a priceless relic. So you hold on. You say, *"It's fine, I'll do it myself,"* which is the entrepreneur's version of *"I don't need directions."* Spoiler: you do.

And here's where things take a particularly tragic turn. The very qualities that make entrepreneurs so brilliantly suited for business—drive, adaptability, the ability to spin a dozen plates without breaking a sweat—are the same ones that forge the bars of the cage. The drive becomes an inability to rest. The adaptability morphs into frantic plate-spinning. And the plates? Oh, they're fine. They're *fine*. Except you've forgotten that plates aren't *supposed* to spin; they're supposed to hold snacks.

It's like this: imagine a hamster who dreams of exploring the world. This hamster is clever, resourceful, full of big plans. But instead of charting new lands, he inadvertently invents the hamster wheel. "This is brilliant!" he thinks at first, scampering along happily. "I'm moving so quickly!" Hours later, he pauses, wheezing slightly, and realizes two things: one, he hasn't actually gone anywhere, and two, he's now stuck with the wheel because, well, he built it.

That's us—ingenious little hamsters, trapped on wheels of our own making, sprinting furiously and congratulating ourselves on our pace.

But here's the good news: the hamster wheel, while maddening, is not irreversible. Neither is the golden cage. The bars are real, yes, but they're also self-constructed, which means they can be dismantled. The first step is recognizing the cage for what it is—a place where your brilliant intentions have accidentally trapped you—and deciding you'd rather build a hammock. A very sturdy, very comfortable hammock.

And that's what we'll tackle next: how to reclaim your freedom, one thoughtfully dismantled bar at a time.

Freedom vs. Control – A Love-Hate Relationship

Fear of Letting Go

Let's talk about fear, shall we? Not the spine-tingling, campfire kind of fear—no masked villains or spooky attics here. No, this is the quieter, far more insidious fear that plagues many an entrepreneur: the fear of letting go. It's the kind of fear that doesn't announce itself with a shriek but rather settles in slowly, like a houseguest who "just needs a place to crash for a few nights" and somehow ends up permanently parked on your sofa.

Picture, if you will, an entrepreneur clutching a battered briefcase full of tasks. This is no ordinary briefcase. It's heavy with responsibilities—spreadsheets, emails, that overdue quarterly report, and a Post-it note that says something mysterious like *"Follow up on Jeff."* The entrepreneur grips it so tightly their knuckles have gone a shade of white that would make copy paper jealous. If you look closely, you might even see them muttering things like, *"If I let go of this, everything will fall apart."*

And that's the root of it, isn't it? This fear of letting go is predicated on one simple, dreadful thought: *What if someone else messes it up?*

Entrepreneurs are, by nature, people who like control. It's part of the job description—be your own boss, call the shots, keep things running smoothly. And while control has its benefits, it can quickly veer into paranoia, like a captain who refuses to let anyone else near the ship's wheel for fear the vessel will somehow end up parked on a sand dune.

The fear takes many forms.

First, there's the fear of **mistakes**. "If I don't do it myself," you think, "someone will mess up. A client will notice, sales will tank, and I'll have to explain that it wasn't *me*, it was Gary." Poor Gary.

Then there's the fear of **losing quality**. No one else will care as much as you do. No one else will understand the nuances, the fine details, or the inexplicably specific way you like your invoices filed. And so, you hold onto tasks—tasks that, frankly, you shouldn't be doing—because you've convinced yourself that letting go is tantamount to a slow, inevitable slide into chaos.

And finally, perhaps the most terrifying fear of all: the fear of **being exposed**. Letting go means delegating tasks to others, as the professionals call it. But what if, in doing so, someone realizes that you don't actually have everything under control? That you don't, in fact, know *everything* about accounting software, marketing funnels, or the mysterious ways of IT support? It's a scary thought: being seen as less than the all-knowing oracle of your business.

And so you hold on. You keep the tasks close, like a toddler clutching a blanket that's 60% fabric and 40% unidentified grime. "It's fine," you say through gritted teeth as you edit yet another email at 1:00 a.m., while everyone else is soundly asleep or doing whatever people do who have free time (knitting? dancing? solving world hunger?).

But here's the thing. Holding on out of fear doesn't make you more in control—it makes you *less* free. You end up buried under the weight of tasks, unable to see past the briefcase (backpack is probably more appropriate these days) that's always in your hand. And while you're busy micromanaging every detail of your business, you're also busy suffocating your own potential.

Because the truth—the uncomfortable, mildly inconvenient truth—is that freedom requires trust. Trust that someone else can do it. Trust that mistakes, if they happen, won't set fire to your entire empire. And trust that letting go, far from being a catastrophe, is the very thing that will allow you to step back, breathe, and maybe—just maybe—start living that dream you signed up for in the first place.

So loosen the grip. Let go of the briefcase, one task at a time. You'll be amazed at how much lighter you'll feel when you're no longer clinging to the weight of everything. And who knows? You might just discover that Gary's actually pretty great at his job.

Perfectionism: The Frenemy of Freedom

Ah, perfectionism. On paper, it sounds noble, doesn't it? The relentless pursuit of doing things *right*. Not just "good enough" or "functional" but "so meticulously correct it could bring a tear to the eye of a German engineer." It's the trait we entrepreneurs wear like a badge of honor, as though our refusal to accept imperfection somehow makes us guardians of quality and custodians of all things precise.

But here's the problem: perfectionism is a double agent. It presents itself as a friend—helpful, dependable, here to make sure your business shines. But, left unchecked, it has a nasty habit of turning on you, shackling you to endless hours of unnecessary tweaks, revisions, and fussing over details that no one—not a single human being—cares about except you.

Let me illustrate. Imagine, if you will, an entrepreneur (it could be anyone, but let's just say it's you). You've been tasked with sending out a simple report—a perfectly routine document that a reasonable person could finish in 20 minutes. But you're not a reasonable person, are you? No, you're *an entrepreneur*. And so the quest for perfection begins.

It starts innocently enough. "I'll just tidy this up," you think, adjusting the margins and maybe choosing a cleaner font because *Helvetica just doesn't feel inspiring today*. Then you notice that the bullet points are slightly uneven, so you spend another 30 minutes ensuring they align with military precision, each one as sharp and uniform as a row of Buckingham Palace guards.

But wait—should the section headers be in bold, or maybe bold italics? Or what about a tasteful splash of color? You dive into this rabbit hole with the zeal of an archaeologist unearthing an ancient temple, and before you know it, two hours have passed. Two. Entire. Hours. And you have emerged triumphant, holding what is, undeniably, the single most well-formatted report in the history of reports.

And here's the kicker: no one notices. Not a soul. Your client or colleague or mildly disinterested business partner opens it, skims past your beautifully indented bullet points, and mutters, "Looks good." Two hours of your life traded for *"Looks good."*

This, my friends, is the curse of perfectionism. It tricks you into believing that every tiny detail matters, when in reality, most people are too busy managing their own chaos to notice whether your font choice was Garamond or Calibri. The gap between "great" and "perfect" is minuscule, yet perfectionists will willingly hurl themselves into it, sacrificing time, energy, and sanity in the process.

And let's not forget the underlying belief that fuels all this: *"No one else can do it as well as I can."* It's an intoxicating thought, isn't it? On the surface, it feels like a compliment to yourself—proof that you're the one holding this whole operation together. But in reality, it's a prison sentence disguised as a pep talk. If no one else can do it, that means you'll *always* be the one doing it. Forever. Just you and your perfectionism, locked in a vicious cycle of formatting reports and tweaking websites until the end of time.

The tragedy is that perfectionism doesn't lead to freedom; it leads to exhaustion. Instead of outsourcing, delegating, or accepting "good enough" and moving on to something that actually matters—like, oh, I don't know, growing your business or reclaiming your personal life—you get bogged down in minutiae. Perfectionism robs you of the very freedom you set out to achieve when you started this whole entrepreneurial escapade in the first place.

Now, don't get me wrong. I'm not advocating for shoddy work or half-baked efforts. No one's suggesting you slap a few typos on a page and call it a day. But there's a sweet spot—somewhere between *"chaotic mess"* and *"inspected by NASA scientists"*—where your work is excellent, and you still have time to eat dinner at a normal hour.

The first step is admitting the truth: perfectionism isn't your ally; it's your captor. And while there's a certain charm to a beautifully aligned bullet point, there's also a certain charm to *not losing your mind* over things that no one else will notice.

So let it go—just a little. Outsource the formatting. Delegate the smaller tasks. Allow yourself to aim for "excellent" instead of "flawless." Because the real secret to freedom isn't doing everything perfectly; it's knowing when to stop fussing and trust that "good enough" is, in fact, *good enough.*

And here's the surprise: once you let go of perfectionism, you'll find a strange and wonderful thing happens. Life gets a little lighter. Work gets a little easier. And—most shockingly of all—no one complains about the bullet points.

How Control Undermines Freedom

Control, as far as entrepreneurial habits go, is a lot like chocolate cake: tempting, addictive, and seemingly harmless in small doses. But when indulged in excess, it can leave you sluggish, regretful, and wondering why you thought consuming the entire thing by yourself was a good idea.

You see, control feels comforting—necessary, even. After all, you're the captain of this entrepreneurial ship, and what kind of captain would you be if you didn't monitor every knob, lever, and rusty bolt? So, you tighten your grip. You oversee every decision, review every task, tweak every project, and even insist on approving the "out of office" messages your team sets when they take a day off.

But here's the problem: the more control you try to exert, the less actual control you have. It's a bit like watching a dog chase its tail—endearing at first, until you realize it's a perfect metaphor for entrepreneurial micromanagement.

Picture this dog. It starts innocently enough, spotting its tail out of the corner of its eye. "Aha!" thinks the dog. "There it is! I must catch it!" And so the chase begins. The dog spins, faster and faster, a whirl of fur and determination. In its mind, it's mere moments from victory, one decisive snap of the jaws away from triumph.

But, of course, the tail remains stubbornly out of reach. The faster the dog spins, the more the tail eludes it, until finally, the dog collapses in an exhausted, panting heap, realizing—if dogs have such epiphanies—that it has achieved nothing except a mild sense of dizziness.

Entrepreneurs, my dear reader, are often that dog. The tail is control—those stubborn details, tasks, and responsibilities you refuse to let go of—and the chase is the frantic cycle of overwork it creates. You're convinced that if you just work harder, spin faster, and keep a tighter grip, you'll get it all under control. But what actually happens is far less triumphant.

The more you try to micromanage, the more freedom slips through your fingers. You become overwhelmed, exhausted, and—here's the kicker—far less effective. Tasks that once seemed straightforward start to pile up like unopened bills. You end up buried in minutiae: tweaking font sizes, rewording perfectly acceptable emails, or double-checking someone else's work because *"I'll just do it faster myself."*

And while you're busy chasing control, two rather unfortunate things happen.

First, your team—assuming you have one—begins to feel slightly under-whelmed. Nothing crushes morale quite like a boss who insists on redoing every-thing because *"it's not quite right."* It sends a subtle but clear message: "I don't trust you to do this properly." Before long, they stop taking initiative altogether. Why bother, when the boss is going to swoop in and redo it anyway?

Second, and perhaps more tragically, you start to lose sight of the big picture. The strategic, creative work that could grow your business—the very work you, as the founder, should be focusing on—gets sidelined in favor of fiddling with a PowerPoint presentation or triple-checking the budget you've already approved. Instead of leading your business, you're stuck *in* your business, chasing your tail, wondering why freedom feels further away than ever.

And this is the paradox: control feels like the answer to chaos, but it's actually the cause. The tighter your grip, the more everything slips through your fingers, like sand in a clenched fist.

But here's the good news: unlike the dog, you don't have to keep spinning. The tail—the illusion of control—doesn't need chasing. You can let go. You can trust your team to handle tasks without your constant oversight. You can delegate, automate, and (brace yourself) accept that not everything needs to be done *your* way to be done well.

Will mistakes happen? Of course. But here's the thing: mistakes are survivable. You'll survive them. Your business will survive them. And in the end, letting go of control is the only way to gain the freedom you were chasing in the first place.

So stop spinning. Take a breath. Step back. Your tail—like your business—will still be there when you're ready to walk forward.

And who knows? You might even find that life is a lot better when you're not busy chasing yourself in circles.

Breaking Free – From Frenzied Hamster to Chill Architect

If you've been following along so far—and let's assume you have, unless you skipped ahead because you're just *that* overwhelmed—then you're probably ready for a bit of hope. After all, no one sets out to become a hamster, let alone a frenzied one, sprinting furiously on a wheel of their own design. And yet here we are, breathless and bewildered, muttering things like *"Just one more email, and then I'll stop,"* while the wheel spins merrily beneath us.

But here's the good news: there's a way off the wheel.

Now, before we get to the practical bits, let's pause to consider the hamster. The hamster, bless its tiny heart, doesn't realize it's trapped. From its perspective, it's moving very quickly. It feels productive. It's going places. This, of course, is exactly how overworked entrepreneurs feel as they sprint from task to task, mistaking motion for progress. But if the hamster could step back—perhaps sip a tiny espresso and review its situation—it might see that all its frantic effort has led it precisely nowhere.

You are not a hamster. I repeat: *You are not a hamster.* You have a brain, opposable thumbs, and remarkable decision-making ability. And it's time to trade in that hamster wheel for something better—something more deliberate, elegant, and altogether more satisfying.

It's time to become the **Chill Architect** of your life and business.

Let me explain. The Chill Architect is someone who steps back, surveys the landscape, and starts making intentional choices about how their business is built. They don't panic. They don't sprint. And they certainly don't get sidetracked formatting bullet points at 2 a.m. (see: perfectionism, previous section). Instead, they design systems, delegate tasks, and focus on the big picture—the parts of their business that only they can do.

If you're wondering how to get from Frenzied Hamster to Chill Architect, here's the first step: stop sprinting long enough to think. I know, I know—thinking feels counterproductive when you've got 734 tasks screaming for your attention. But this pause is critical, because until you recognize that you're trapped in a cycle of overwork, you'll keep running faster and faster, convinced that momentum alone will save you.

Spoiler: It won't.

Once you've paused—and possibly inhaled a calming beverage—it's time to make a shift. Instead of frantically trying to do *everything*, ask yourself: *What would this look like if it were easier?* Imagine for a moment that you're not scrambling to meet deadlines or micromanaging a dozen half-finished projects. Imagine that your business runs smoothly, with systems and processes that make life simpler for you and everyone else.

Because that's the goal. The Chill Architect builds systems that work—systems that allow you to step back, reclaim your time, and, dare I say it, breathe. And while the idea of "systems" might sound suspiciously boring—like something involving flowcharts and pie charts and other things with "chart" in the name—it's actually liberating. Systems allow you to let go without things falling apart. They mean trusting that your business can run without you hovering over it like a particularly anxious chaperone.

Of course, this transformation won't happen overnight. You're not going to go from Hamster to Architect in the time it takes to finish this chapter. But the journey begins with small, deliberate steps: handing off tasks, creating processes that don't require your constant input, and learning to accept *"good enough"* where perfection used to reign.

And here's the kicker: when you start to let go—when you release the need to do everything yourself—you'll discover something extraordinary. Your business won't implode. The sky won't fall. And freedom, that elusive treasure you've been chasing all along, will start to creep back into your days.

You'll find space for creativity, time for the things that matter, and maybe even the occasional nap (though let's call it "strategic rest" to sound impressive).

Because here's the truth: entrepreneurs are meant to build, not sprint. You're not here to endlessly spin on a wheel. You're here to design, to create, to lead—like the Chill Architect you're about to become. So step back, breathe, and pick up your metaphorical blueprint.

The wheel stops here.

The Big Aha Moment

Now, let's pause for a moment. Not just a casual, "Hmm, interesting," kind of pause but a full-on *"stare out the window like a 19th-century poet contemplating the meaning of life"* pause. Take a breath, sip your beverage of choice, and ask yourself this:

Is your business serving your life, or has it somehow become the other way around?

This question, while seemingly straightforward, has a way of sneaking up on you. It's like suddenly realizing you've driven 50 miles in the wrong direction because you were too busy fiddling with the radio to notice the signs. You started out with a clear destination in mind—freedom, fulfillment, maybe a boatload of success—and yet here you are, neck-deep in endless tasks, frantic schedules, and the vague suspicion that you're not so much running your business as being dragged along behind it like a particularly bewildered water-skier.

It's the great entrepreneurial paradox: you set out to steer the ship, to chart a glorious course across uncharted waters, only to find yourself swabbing the deck, patching holes in the hull, and arguing with the seagulls. And somewhere along the way, you forgot where the ship was supposed to go in the first place.

Picture it: a ship's captain standing proudly at the helm. The wind is in their hair, the horizon beckons, and they have a clear, determined look in their eyes that says, *"I am in control."* Fast-forward a few months, and that same captain is now knee-deep in ropes, muttering under their breath while frantically bailing water out of the ship with a saucepan. The course? Forgotten. The horizon? Obscured. The destination? "I don't know, just keep it afloat!"

And this, dear reader, is what happens when your business stops serving your life and starts devouring it. You get so caught up in the daily chaos—the emails, the invoices, the terrifying spreadsheets that stare back at you like unsolvable riddles—that you lose sight of why you started the journey at all. You're no longer captaining the ship; you're simply trying to keep it from sinking.

But here's the thing about aha moments: they don't arrive with a dramatic thunderclap or a choir of angels. No one bursts through your door to announce, *"Good news! You've been doing it all wrong, but now it's clear!"* Instead, they sneak up quietly, usually when you're already half-broken from exhaustion, and whisper, *"Hey, maybe it's time to rethink this."*

So, here's your invitation. Stop bailing water for just a moment. Put down the saucepan. Look up. Ask yourself:

- What was the dream when I started this business?

- Where is my ship supposed to go?

- And am I, right now, on course to get there?

If your answers range anywhere from "I have no idea" to "I think I accidentally sailed into a whirlpool," don't panic. You're not alone. A lot of us captains end up slightly off-course because, well, life happens. But the beauty of being the captain is this: you get to reset the course. You get to decide where the ship goes next.

So let this be your big aha moment. Maybe even write it down somewhere so you can't forget it: *Your business is supposed to serve you—not the other way around.*

If you find yourself bailing water while staring at the deck, it's time to look back up at the horizon. It's time to remember where you're going and, more importantly, *why.*

Because the point of this journey isn't just to keep the ship afloat. It's to sail somewhere magnificent.

Practical Escape Plans

Now that you've had your *aha moment* and realized you've been bailing water instead of charting a course, it's time to build yourself an escape plan. Not an escape like slipping out the back door in the dead of night and starting a new life in the mountains (tempting though that may be), but a practical, thoughtful plan to liberate yourself from the grind.

Here's where it gets tricky. Creating freedom in your business—true, glorious freedom—is a bit like assembling IKEA furniture. You start with good intentions, a shiny set of instructions, and a vague optimism that this won't be so bad. Four hours later, you're surrounded by hex wrenches, sweating profusely, and screaming at a wooden dowel that *definitely wasn't in the diagram.*

But then—then—something miraculous happens. The final piece clicks into place. The chaos recedes. And there, in front of you, is a perfectly functional (if slightly wobbly) bookshelf. That, my friends, is what implementing these strategies will feel like: mildly infuriating at first, immensely satisfying when it works.

Intentional Delegation: Handing Off the Wrench

Let's start with delegation, because if you're anything like most entrepreneurs, this is where you clutch your metaphorical hex wrench and shout, *"No one else can do it properly!"* I get it. Delegation feels risky—like handing the wrench to someone who may or may not accidentally bolt the bookshelf to the ceiling. But here's the truth: you cannot, and should not, do everything yourself.

Imagine a surgeon who insists on prepping the operating room, scrubbing the floors, and personally stitching the patient's gown before performing surgery. Would you want them to be your doctor? Probably not. You'd want them focused on what only they can do: saving your life, ideally without distractions. The same applies to you.

Start by identifying the tasks that someone else—anyone else—could handle. Email replies? Bookkeeping? Calendar management? Hand them off. Yes, mistakes might happen, but you'll survive them, and your team will get better. In fact, you'll be shocked at how competent people are when you let them try. Delegate like your sanity depends on it—because, spoiler alert, it does.

Time-Blocking: Scheduling Like a Swedish Genius

Now that you're delegating, let's move to time-blocking. Time-blocking is the art of breaking your day into focused, intentional segments—like sorting your tasks into tidy compartments so they stop sprawling all over your life like an overfed Labrador.

It's a little like setting boundaries for yourself and your workday, which, if you're not careful, tends to ooze into every available crack of time—mornings, evenings, and even those five minutes between brushing your teeth and staring longingly out the window. Time-blocking says, "From 9 to 11 a.m., I shall focus on Strategy. From 1 to 2 p.m., I shall deal with emails. And from 2 to 3, I shall reclaim my mental sanity with a break."

Of course, sticking to time blocks requires discipline. You'll be tempted to cheat—just a "quick" peek at Slack, just one tiny email. Don't do it. Treat your time blocks like they're sacred. After all, you wouldn't interrupt an architect while they're sketching blueprints to ask if they've seen the stapler, would you? Exactly.

Prioritization: Deciding What Really Matters

Finally, we come to prioritization, which is basically deciding which tasks are worthy of your time and which can be flung, with great ceremony, onto someone else's desk or into the abyss.

Most entrepreneurs approach their day like someone who's been handed 38 IKEA boxes and told, "Assemble them all. Simultaneously." The problem is that not everything needs to happen right now. Not every task deserves equal attention. You wouldn't build the tiny side table before the large dining room hutch, right? The hutch matters. Start there.

To prioritize effectively, ask yourself:

- *Does this need to be done today?*

- *Does it need to be done by me?*

- *Will the world end if this waits until next week?*

If the answer to all three is no, then set it aside. Life is too short to waste on tasks that have the importance of a lint roller when you're trying to build an empire.

The Final Click of Freedom

Here's the best part: when you combine intentional delegation, time-blocking, and prioritization, something incredible happens. Tasks that used to take up your entire day start to shrink. Chaos begins to recede. And you, dear reader, start to find pockets of freedom where previously there were only to-do lists.

It won't happen overnight, and there may be moments—much like assembling IKEA furniture—when you feel frustrated, confused, and convinced the instructions are in ancient Swedish. But stick with it. Piece by piece, the business you're building will start to serve you, rather than enslave you.

And when you finally take a step back and look at the result, you'll see something glorious: a business that works without you micromanaging every bolt and bracket.

Now, doesn't that sound worth the effort?

Tools for Intentional Leadership

Let's start with a confession: most entrepreneurs begin their leadership journeys not as serene architects designing an elegant, life-first business, but as glorified firefighters sprinting around, extinguishing flaming chaos with a damp napkin. Emails, client emergencies, staffing hiccups—everything seems to catch fire simultaneously, and you're there with your little extinguisher, muttering, *"It's fine. I'm fine. Everything's fine."*

But here's the thing about firefighting: while it makes you feel heroic—productive, even—it's exhausting, reactive, and, frankly, unsustainable. You never see an architect designing a building while frantically waving their arms and shouting, *"Quick! Somebody get me a hose!"* That's because architects operate intentionally. They plan, they design, and—this is key—they build systems to ensure things work smoothly from the start.

It's time to transition from firefighter to architect. From frantic to focused. From harried manager to intentional leader. And you don't need a drafting table or a degree in structural engineering to get there—just a few practical tools (and, of course, a sense of humor).

1. Start with the Blueprint (Your Vision)

Every architect begins with a blueprint—a clear idea of what they're building and why. Without it, they'd just be slapping walls together and hoping for the best. Yet, far too many entrepreneurs run their businesses without a blueprint. They're so busy putting out fires that they lose sight of what they're building in the first place.

So ask yourself: *What does a "life-first" business look like for me?* Maybe it's a business that gives you Fridays off, pays for that dream trip to Italy, or simply lets you sleep eight uninterrupted hours at night (a truly decadent luxury, I know). Whatever it is, write it down. This vision will become your North Star, the guiding principle for every decision you make.

And don't worry—no one expects the blueprint to be perfect. It's fine if your North Star starts as, *"Stop working 16-hour days and eat dinner with my family more than twice a week."* That's a solid first draft.

2. Stop Doing Everyone Else's Job (The Art of Delegation)

Ah yes, delegation—every architect's secret weapon and every overworked entrepreneur's greatest challenge. If you're still spending half your day fixing typos, scheduling meetings, or manually updating spreadsheets, you're essentially building the skyscraper while trying to mop the floors. It's time to stop.

Think of yourself as the conductor of an orchestra. You wouldn't expect the conductor to sprint back and forth, playing the violin, the timpani, and the trumpet while simultaneously waving the baton and yelling, *"I'll do it all myself!"* That would be madness. Your job is to lead, not to play every instrument.

Here's a quick rule of thumb: If someone else can do it *80% as well as you can,* delegate it. Will it be perfect? Maybe not. Will it be good enough? Absolutely. And more importantly, you'll have time to focus on what actually matters—like strategy, growth, and, dare I dream, rest.

Start small if you must: hand off your inbox to an assistant, delegate some bookkeeping, or let someone else format that PowerPoint presentation. When you see that the world doesn't implode without you, you'll wonder why you didn't do it sooner.

3. Design Systems That Work Without You

Here's a delightful truth: the more systems you build, the less you need to firefight. Systems are like well-designed plumbing—unseen, uncelebrated, but utterly essential. A system is what ensures your invoices go out on time, your team knows what to do without a five-page memo, and you don't wake up in a cold sweat because *"Did I forget to follow up with Jeff?"*

Systems don't need to be fancy, either. Start with a simple checklist for repetitive tasks. Automate reminders for follow-ups. Create templates for emails you send over and over again (goodbye, typing *"Per my last email"* for the 900th time). Build processes so clear and reliable that things keep moving even when you're sipping piña coladas on a beach—without your phone.

It might feel tedious at first—like drawing pipes on a blueprint when you'd rather be sketching the rooftop garden—but trust me, your future self will thank you.

4. Block Time Like Your Sanity Depends on It

Firefighters are always on call. Architects? Not so much. Architects plan their days with intent, focusing on what matters most. You, my friend, must do the same.

Time-blocking is the deceptively simple act of scheduling chunks of time for specific tasks: big, important, strategic tasks that move the needle. I know this sounds obvious, but you'd be surprised how many entrepreneurs approach their days like contestants on a game show, randomly grabbing at tasks as they spin past.

Here's the secret: when you block out time for meaningful work, you start leading proactively instead of reacting frantically. Treat your time blocks as sacred—yes, even if Gary from Accounting comes knocking with a "quick question."

5. Trust the Process (and Yourself)

The shift from firefighter to architect doesn't happen overnight. You'll feel uncomfortable at first. There will be moments when you'll want to run back to the flames, shouting, *"It's fine! I'll do it myself!"* But trust me: the more you step back, delegate, and design, the more your business will begin to work as it should.

Your team will step up. Systems will carry the load. And you'll finally find yourself with space to think, create, and—imagine this—enjoy the life you built.

Because, in the end, being an intentional leader is about more than running a business. It's about building a life. And a life-first business doesn't just happen by accident—it's designed, one deliberate decision at a time.

So put down the hose, pick up the blueprint, and start building something magnificent.

Reframing Success – Redefining Freedom on Your Terms

Success. Just the word alone feels loaded, doesn't it? It conjures up images of shiny things: skyscrapers with your name on them, cars that beep when you look at them wrong, and Instagram-perfect vacations that you'd actually enjoy if you weren't too busy taking photos of them.

For most of us, success starts out as someone else's definition. It's inherited, like an old family recipe that you follow without questioning, even though you're pretty sure Great Aunt Mildred's "secret ingredient" was just too much salt. It's a default setting we rarely stop to examine, because who has time to question success when you're sprinting after it?

But here's the thing: success isn't a one-size-fits-all concept. What looks dazzling on paper—corner offices, impressive titles, 16-hour workdays that come with a personalized parking space—might not feel all that fulfilling when you finally get there.

It's like buying a shirt that looks incredible on the mannequin but feels scratchy and slightly ridiculous when you put it on. And yet, because society insists that the shirt *looks good*, you convince yourself that it must be right.

But what if we redefined success? What if, instead of squeezing ourselves into an ill-fitting mold, we designed success on our own terms—comfortable, tailored, and uniquely ours?

Freedom as a Metric

Here's a radical idea: what if freedom—not profit, not prestige, not the number of LinkedIn followers you have—was the ultimate measure of success?

Freedom to do work that lights you up. Freedom to spend time with the people you love. Freedom to take a Tuesday afternoon off just because you feel like it. Doesn't that sound better than chasing someone else's version of success, only to find out you're allergic to it?

Now, before you start imagining freedom as some idyllic, hammock-filled utopia where money rains from the sky and you never have to answer an email again, let's get real. Freedom doesn't mean abandoning responsibility or living in a constant state of Zen. It means having the power to shape your life and business in a way that supports your values, your goals, and, yes, your happiness.

From Hustle to Harmony

If you're like most entrepreneurs, you were probably raised on a steady diet of hustle culture—the idea that success is earned through relentless effort, sleepless nights, and a willingness to sacrifice everything short of your favorite coffee mug.

Hustle has its place, sure. It can fuel ambition and drive results. But hustle without balance? That's just burnout with a better marketing strategy.

The goal isn't to hustle harder; it's to hustle smarter. To create a life where work and rest coexist, where ambition doesn't come at the expense of your well-being, and where success feels as good as it looks.

Your Success, Your Terms

Redefining success starts with asking yourself some tough but essential questions:

- What does freedom mean to me?

- How do I want my days to look?

- What am I willing to let go of to make room for what truly matters?

The answers won't come all at once, and they'll probably evolve over time. That's okay. What matters is that you're steering the ship now—not society, not comparison, not the pressure to keep up with whoever seems to have it all figured out (spoiler: they don't).

The Courage to Redefine

Redefining success is an act of courage. It means stepping away from the hamster wheel, ignoring the noise, and embracing the fact that your version of freedom might look different from someone else's. It means being okay with saying, *"No, I don't need to work 80 hours a week to feel accomplished,"* or, *"Actually, my dream isn't a seven-figure business—it's being able to coach my kid's soccer team."*

And guess what? That's still success. Beautiful, meaningful, tailor-made success.

So, let's reframe the narrative. Instead of striving for someone else's definition of success, let's start designing a version that feels right for you. A life where work serves your goals, not the other way around. A life that reflects what truly matters to you, not what looks impressive to others.

Because at the end of the day, success isn't about how it looks from the outside. It's about how it feels when you wake up each morning and think, *"This—this is the life I want to be living."*

So grab that metaphorical tailor's tape, start sketching your vision, and let's create a version of success that fits you perfectly—no scratchy shirts allowed.

Success Isn't One-Size-Fits-All

If success were an outfit, society seems convinced it's a sleek, one-size-fits-all jumpsuit. The kind that looks amazing on mannequins, works perfectly in theory, and somehow fits absolutely no one in real life.

Yet, for reasons beyond logic, we all seem to buy into this idea that success has a universal definition. It's loud and flashy—complete with a corner office, an eye-watering bank balance, and a calendar so packed it makes a game of Tetris look leisurely.

But here's the truth: success is much more like sourdough—it's meant to be personalized, nurtured, and occasionally left to rest while it figures itself out. What works for one person might look completely unappealing, or downright impractical, for another.

Take financial independence, for instance. For some, it's the pinnacle of freedom—a life where money flows with enough ease to make Scrooge McDuck's vault look quaint. For others, financial independence is merely one part of the equation, sharing space with flexible hours, time for hobbies, or the ability to step away from work without breaking into a cold sweat.

And then there are the dreamers among us who define success by something as delightfully specific as having Tuesday afternoons free to perfect their sourdough starter. That's their North Star, their version of *"I've made it."* No judgment here—if a tangy, perfectly blistered loaf is your idea of freedom, more power to you.

The point is, success isn't one-size-fits-all. It's not about checking off a generic list of achievements; it's about building a life that aligns with your values, priorities, and quirks.

Your Version of Freedom

Freedom, like success, is deeply personal. For one entrepreneur, it might mean having the financial cushion to take a sabbatical every few years and travel the world. For another, it could mean never having to set an alarm again—because mornings, frankly, are overrated.

Some might dream of the classic entrepreneurial goal: scaling their business until it practically runs itself, allowing them to spend their days mentoring others, pursuing passion projects, or orchestrating impromptu beach cleanups. Others might crave a quieter life: a steady business that provides enough income to support their family and the occasional spontaneous trip to Disneyland.

Neither version is "better" or "more right" than the other. The only wrong answer is chasing someone else's definition of freedom and wondering why it doesn't feel fulfilling when you finally get there.

Permission to Choose

Here's the good news: you get to choose what success looks like for you. You can toss the societal blueprint out the window and draw your own—complete with flexible work hours, long lunches, or an official "no emails after 7 p.m." policy. You have permission to design a life that fits your needs, not one that impresses strangers on the internet.

And the best part? Your definition of success doesn't have to be static. What freedom looks like today might change in a few years, and that's perfectly okay. Life evolves. Goals shift. What matters is that you keep checking in with yourself, making sure your idea of success still fits—like a favorite pair of jeans that makes you feel fantastic every time you put them on.

So, whether your dream is to build a business empire, master the art of sourdough, or simply reclaim your evenings to watch movies with your family, know this: your version of freedom is valid. Your success is valid. And the moment you stop chasing someone else's jumpsuit and start designing your own life, you've already won.

The Freedom Formula

Let's talk about freedom—not in the abstract, grandiose way where it's draped in flags and backed by stirring music, but in the personal, practical, *everyday* way. The kind of freedom that makes you wake up and think, *"This—this is the life I want to be living."*

For most of us, freedom is a slippery concept. We want it, we crave it, but when pressed to define it, we're often left fumbling for words. It's a bit like trying to describe your favorite food—delicious, yes, but *why*? And what does it actually look like on the plate?

That's where the Freedom Formula comes in. Think of it as a way to get specific, to paint a clear picture of what freedom means for you. Because once you know what you're aiming for, it becomes infinitely easier to build your life and business around it.

Step 1: Imagine Your Perfect Day

If the phrase "perfect day" makes you immediately think of beaches, hammocks, and an endless supply of margaritas, that's fine—but let's dig a little deeper. Perfect days don't have to be vacations (though, let's be honest, they're tempting). They can be ordinary days, designed to suit your version of extraordinary.

Close your eyes—well, not literally, because you're reading—and picture it. What does a perfect day in your life-first business look like? Maybe it's waking up without an alarm, sipping coffee while watching the sunrise, and diving into creative work that excites you. Maybe it's having a leisurely lunch with your partner, taking a mid-afternoon yoga class, and logging off at 5 p.m. sharp to cook dinner with your kids.

Be specific. What time do you wake up? What tasks are you doing (or not doing)? Who are you spending time with? How much of your day is work, and how much is play? The more vivid your vision, the clearer your target becomes.

Step 2: Write Your Freedom Statement

Once you've imagined your perfect day, it's time to distill it into words. Think of this as your personal freedom manifesto—a short, powerful statement that captures what you're striving for.

For example:

- *Freedom means spending my mornings on creative projects and my afternoons with family.*

- *Freedom means running a business that works without me, so I can focus on mentoring others.*

- *Freedom means being able to take Fridays off to explore new hobbies or simply do nothing at all.*

It doesn't have to be fancy or poetic. It just has to resonate with you. This is your North Star, your reminder of what you're building and why.

Step 3: Identify Your Freedom Metrics

Now that you've defined your perfect day and written your freedom statement, it's time to break it down into actionable steps. Think of these as your Freedom Metrics—the measurable indicators that tell you you're on track.

For instance:

- If freedom means flexible hours, your metric might be limiting your workday to six hours.

- If freedom means financial independence, your metric might be earning enough passive income to cover your living expenses.

- If freedom means spending more time with loved ones, your metric might be scheduling at least three family dinners a week.

Metrics give your vision structure. They help you track progress and make adjustments along the way.

Step 4: Design Your Life Around It

This is the fun part—taking your vision and turning it into reality. Start small. Look at your current schedule, habits, and responsibilities, and ask yourself: *What can I change today to move closer to my perfect day?*

It might be delegating one task, blocking off a free afternoon, or saying "no" to a meeting that doesn't align with your priorities. Bit by bit, these changes add up, and before you know it, you're living a life that looks a lot more like freedom and a lot less like survival mode.

A Work in Progress

Remember, your Freedom Formula isn't set in stone. It's a living, breathing thing, meant to evolve as your life and priorities change. What matters is that you're designing with intention, building a life that serves you instead of the other way around.

So take a moment, grab a notebook (or the nearest napkin), and start defining your version of freedom. Because the only wrong way to do this is not to do it at all.

And if your perfect day involves sourdough, hammocks, or Tuesday afternoons off, all I can say is: excellent choice.

Closing Encouragement

If you've made it this far, let me offer my hearty congratulations. The entrepreneurial journey is not for the faint of heart—or the faint of caffeine, for that matter—and here you are, still standing (or sitting, or possibly reclining in something vaguely ergonomic).

Let's be honest: entrepreneurship often feels like a circus act. You're the ringmaster, juggling flaming torches, tightrope walking over a pit of "urgent" emails, and occasionally trying to tame a lion labeled *"unexpected expenses."* It's thrilling, sure, but also exhausting, and every now and then, you might wonder if you accidentally signed up for the wrong show.

But here's the good news: you don't have to keep running the circus solo. The tools to reclaim your autonomy, balance, and yes, even your joy, are well within reach. They're not flashy or complicated; they're simple shifts in mindset and strategy—intentional delegation, time-blocking, prioritization, and a little less obsessing over perfectly formatted bullet points.

Think of this process like trading in a hamster wheel for a hammock. The wheel, with all its frantic spinning, was fine for a time—it got you moving, after all. But you've outgrown it. Now, it's time to step off, stretch your legs, and start building something sturdier, something calmer, something that supports you instead of spinning you into oblivion.

The hammock, in case you're wondering, isn't just a metaphor. It's a way of life—a reminder that success doesn't have to mean nonstop hustle. It can mean balance, fulfillment, and the ability to enjoy the life you've worked so hard to create.

So, here's my final nudge: give yourself permission to pause. To breathe. To laugh at the absurdities and embrace the imperfections. Reclaiming your freedom isn't about doing everything perfectly; it's about making progress, one small, intentional step at a time.

You've got this. The tools are in your hands, the hammock is waiting, and your best days as a liberated entrepreneur are ahead. Now go forth, and may your journey be filled with purpose, progress, and just the right amount of hammock time.

Chapter Two

Beyond Success

Defining Personal Fulfillment

Chasing the Golden Carrot

There's a moment in every entrepreneur's journey when the golden carrot of financial success dangles tantalizingly close. Maybe it's the allure of hitting a six-figure month, the promise of a dream vacation, or the gleam of a brand-new sports car—a gleam that practically whispers, *"You've made it."*

For many, that sports car becomes the ultimate symbol of "arriving." So, let's imagine for a moment: you've done it. After years of hustle, sweat, and not-so-occasional tears, you're finally standing in your driveway, keys in hand, gazing lovingly at your shiny new convertible. It's sleek. It's fast. It's the kind of car that makes teenagers and retirees alike stop and stare.

And then, reality strikes.

You realize that your dream car—the one you envisioned cruising down the coast with the wind in your hair—has approximately zero trunk space. You need groceries, but the thought of shoving a week's worth of frozen pizzas and kale into your luxury ride makes your eye twitch. So, you make multiple trips, wedging plastic bags awkwardly onto the passenger seat and praying the eggs survive the journey home.

By the third trip, the dream starts to feel... less dreamy. It's not that the car isn't amazing—it's just that it doesn't solve the deeper problem. You still have errands to run, bills to pay, and moments of wondering, *"Is this really it?"*

This is the paradox of financial success: it's shiny, enticing, and often celebrated as the ultimate prize. And yet, when it becomes the sole measure of achievement, it can leave you wondering why you're still not satisfied.

Success, as a Concept

Success, as a concept, is easy to chase but surprisingly hard to define. Most of us are handed a version of it early on—often in the form of societal checkboxes like "steady job," "nice house," and "retirement plan that doesn't involve lottery tickets." We pursue these goals with vigor, ticking each box like a dutiful contestant in the great game of life, only to pause years later and wonder, *"Why doesn't this feel as satisfying as I thought it would?"*

That's the thing about success: it's not inherently fulfilling. It's shiny, yes—impressive to neighbors and former classmates stalking your LinkedIn profile—but it doesn't automatically come with a sense of purpose or joy. Success is external—measurable, visible, easy to frame and hang on the wall.

Fulfillment, on the other hand, is deeply personal. The quiet satisfaction comes from aligning your actions with your values, passions, and purpose. And the truth is, no amount of external success can fill the gap if fulfillment is missing.

The Pitfall of Chasing "More"

Entrepreneurs are especially prone to the endless pursuit of "more." More clients. More revenue. More accolades. It's a bit like running a race where the finish line keeps moving every time you get close. You might hit a revenue goal, land a big client, or finally buy that dream car, but after the initial glow fades, you're left thinking, *"Is this it?"*

This cycle—always chasing, never arriving—can feel like progress, but it's often just a hamster wheel in disguise. The truth is, if "more" becomes the sole driver of your work, you'll never reach a point where it feels like enough.

Here's where the sports car story comes back: it's not that the car isn't wonderful—it's that external milestones don't address the deeper question of fulfillment. Because, while financial success is valuable, it's only part of the equation. The real reward comes when your achievements align with your values and bring genuine meaning to your life.

The Real Fulfillment Formula

So, what does fulfillment look like for you? Not what looks good on paper, or what impresses people at cocktail parties, but *what makes you feel alive*?

Fulfillment is personal. For some, it might look like building a legacy—creating something that outlives them and leaves a positive mark on the world. For others, it could be about relationships—spending quality time with family, mentoring others, or simply being present for the people who matter most.

And for some, let's be honest, fulfillment might be as straightforward as having the time to take a guilt-free nap on a Wednesday afternoon.

There's no universal definition of fulfillment. It's as unique as a fingerprint, shaped by your values, priorities, and dreams. To help you start defining yours, reflect on these questions:

- *What activities or moments bring me genuine joy?*

- *When do I feel most at peace or energized?*

- *What legacy do I want to leave behind?*

Write your answers down, even if they feel messy or incomplete. The goal isn't perfection—it's clarity. Over time, these reflections will help you build a life that feels fulfilling—not just successful.

Redefining the Game

Here's the liberating truth: you get to define success and fulfillment on your own terms. You're no longer playing by someone else's rules or chasing goals that don't resonate with you. Instead, you're creating a life where achievement and happiness coexist, where your work serves your purpose, and where your days feel meaningful—not just busy.

It won't happen overnight, and that's okay. Fulfillment isn't a destination; it's a journey, one small, intentional step at a time. And along the way, you'll discover that true success isn't about what you achieve—it's about how it feels when you get there.

So let's move beyond the hamster wheel of success and start building something richer, deeper, and infinitely more rewarding. Because life isn't just about ticking boxes; it's about living fully, freely, and in alignment with what matters most to you.

The Limits of Traditional Success: When the Shine Wears Off the Trophy

Traditional success often feels like a shiny trophy gleaming on the metaphorical shelf of life. It's the milestone we work toward, the symbol of having "made it." But here's the thing about trophies: while they look great under the right lighting, their allure tends to fade over time.

Think about it. Maybe you've hit a big revenue goal, landed a prestigious award, or finally bought that dream house with the walk-in closet that could double as a small guest room. At first, it's exhilarating. You bask in the glow of achievement, savoring the validation that comes with it. But then, after a while, that glow starts to dim.

One day, you glance at the trophy—literal or figurative—and it feels more like a paperweight than a pinnacle. You're still proud of it, sure, but it no longer fills that space you thought it would. The sense of "What now?" creeps in, and you realize that while the trophy is nice, it didn't bring the lasting satisfaction you'd hoped for.

This is the limit of traditional success: it's external, measurable, and undeniably shiny, but it rarely satisfies the internal longing for meaning and purpose.

The Illusion of Arrival

Part of the problem is that traditional success often comes with the illusion of arrival. We're told that if we just work hard enough, achieve enough, and climb high enough, we'll reach a point where everything clicks—where we'll finally feel content, complete, and unequivocally successful.

But real life doesn't work that way. Success, as it's traditionally defined, is fleeting. It's a momentary peak, not a permanent plateau. And once we reach one summit, another looms on the horizon, whispering, *"Just one more climb, and then you'll really feel accomplished."*

The Missing Piece

The truth is, traditional success often leaves out the most important piece of the puzzle: fulfillment. Success may put a trophy on your shelf, but fulfillment puts a sense of purpose in your heart. It's the difference between achieving for the sake of appearances and building a life that genuinely resonates with your values.

Fulfillment asks deeper questions:

- *Does this work align with who I am?*

- *Am I spending my time in ways that matter?*

- *Is this success bringing me joy, or is it just another box I've checked off?*

If you've ever achieved something you thought would bring happiness, only to feel an odd emptiness afterward, you're not alone. It's a universal experience—and a clear sign that traditional success, while valuable, is only part of the equation.

Recognizing the limits of traditional success isn't about dismissing its value. Financial stability, professional accomplishments, and recognition all matter—but they're not the endgame. The real prize is finding a way to integrate those achievements into a life that feels meaningful and fulfilling.

So, if the shine has worn off your trophy, don't panic. It's not a sign of failure; it's an invitation to go deeper. To explore what fulfillment looks like for you and to start building a life that prioritizes not just success, but significance.

Because, at the end of the day, it's not about how many trophies you have on the shelf. It's about whether your life feels like it's truly yours—aligned, purposeful, and deeply satisfying.

The Myth of "Making It"

Entrepreneurs often talk about *"making it"* as though it's a tangible destination. It's painted as the glorious finish line after years of hustle, grit, and occasionally Googling things like, *"How do taxes actually work?"* You're told that once you've "made it," everything will fall into place. Life will be smooth sailing, your business will practically run itself, and you'll finally have time for all those hobbies you've been putting off—like perfecting your sourdough starter or learning to play the ukulele.

But here's the thing: "making it" is a myth. A mirage in the entrepreneurial desert. You run toward it with all the determination of a marathoner sprinting to the finish, only to arrive and find... well, not much. The trophy you expected turns out to be a paper cup of lukewarm water, the promised oasis looks suspiciously like a barren parking lot, and the only thing waiting for you is another finish line, even farther off in the distance.

The problem is that "making it" is often tied to external markers of success: a specific income level, a big client win, or that magical day when you can finally afford to upgrade your office chair. These markers aren't bad—they're important milestones. But the trouble comes when we expect them to be the *end* of the race.

Instead, what happens is this: you reach the milestone, feel a brief rush of accomplishment, and then realize the goalposts have moved. That big client? They come with bigger demands. That new income level? Suddenly, it doesn't seem like quite enough. The parking lot mirage morphs into a highway, and off you go again, chasing the next goal with the same relentless pace.

This myth of "making it" can leave entrepreneurs feeling strangely unfulfilled. You've hit all the milestones you set out for, yet the scenery feels barren—like opening a beautifully wrapped gift box and finding it empty.

Why? Because the race itself doesn't leave much room for fulfillment. When you're constantly chasing the next thing, there's little time to enjoy the present or reflect on whether the finish line you're aiming for even aligns with your values.

It's not that financial success or growth goals are meaningless—they're crucial parts of the journey. But when they're seen as the ultimate prize, they often fall short. What really matters isn't just *getting there*; it's what "there" looks like when you arrive.

Redefining the Finish Line

The good news is that the finish line doesn't have to be a mirage. You can redefine it—design it to include fulfillment, joy, and a sense of purpose alongside measurable wins.

Ask yourself:

- *What does "making it" truly mean to me?*

- *What kind of life do I want to build while I grow my business?*

- *What goals feel meaningful, not just impressive?*

When you let go of the myth that "making it" is a singular destination, you free yourself to enjoy the journey. The path might still be challenging—it's entrepreneurship, after all—but it's far more rewarding when it's shaped by your vision of success, not someone else's.

Because at the end of the day, "making it" isn't about the finish line. It's about finding fulfillment along the way—and maybe, just maybe, stopping to enjoy the scenery.

The 'What Now?' Syndrome

Picture this: after years of relentless effort, late nights, and enough coffee to fuel a small power plant, you've finally done it. You've achieved the wealth, the accolades, the proverbial *"I've made it"* moment. Maybe you even bought yourself a shiny reward—a luxury car, a dream home, or that designer watch you've been eyeing for years. For a brief, glorious moment, it feels like all the struggle was worth it.

And then... it hits you.

It's subtle at first—a flicker of restlessness, a whisper of *"Is this all there is?"* You shrug it off, thinking maybe you just need another milestone to chase. But the whisper grows louder, and soon you find yourself staring into the unsettling void of *What Now?*

It's a bit like visiting one of those over-hyped vacation destinations you've dreamed about for years. You've seen the Instagram photos: crystal-clear beaches, majestic mountain views, and sunsets that look like they were painted by a celestial artist. You finally book the trip, imagining how magical it will be.

And then you arrive... to find the beaches overcrowded, the mountains shrouded in fog, and the sunsets mostly obscured by a large fast-food billboard. It's not terrible—it's just not what you expected. And that disappointment lingers, because you built it up in your mind to be so much more.

This is how *What Now?* Syndrome sneaks in. Wealth and success, like that over-hyped vacation, are wonderful in theory but can feel unexpectedly hollow if they're not tied to a deeper sense of purpose or fulfillment.

When the Achievement High Wears Off

Let's be clear: wealth and success aren't bad. They provide freedom, security, and undeniably valuable opportunities. But they're not an end-all-be-all. Too often, we treat them as the pinnacle of achievement, only to discover they don't automatically bring the happiness or meaning we thought they would.

Examples abound:

- The entrepreneur who sells their company for millions but wakes up the next day unsure of what to do with themselves.

- The executive who climbs the corporate ladder only to find the view from the top surprisingly lonely.

- The celebrity who seems to have everything but struggles with a sense of emptiness that no red carpet or award ceremony can fill.

The problem isn't the wealth or success itself—it's the lack of clarity about what comes next. Without a sense of purpose, the victory can feel like a hollow win, like reaching the peak of a mountain only to realize there's no view because you forgot to pack your binoculars.

Filling the Void

The key to avoiding *What Now?* Syndrome isn't to stop striving—it's to strive with intention. Achievements are wonderful, but they're far more satisfying when they're tied to something meaningful.

Start by asking yourself:

- *What do I want to build, not just achieve?*

- *How can my success create impact—on others, on my community, or even on my own sense of fulfillment?*

- *What legacy do I want to leave behind?*

When you align your goals with your values, the finish line becomes more than just a stopping point—it becomes a springboard for something greater.

Redefining the Destination

Think of it this way: the vacation isn't the problem—it's the lack of a thoughtful itinerary. Success is still a fantastic destination, but it's far more rewarding when you plan for what comes next. By tying your wealth and achievements to a purpose, you ensure that your journey doesn't end with *What Now?* but evolves into *What's Next?*

And maybe, just maybe, that means redefining the dream. Not as a single peak or trophy, but as a series of meaningful milestones, each one more fulfilling than the last.

Why Money Alone Isn't Enough

Let's get one thing straight: money is fantastic. It's the key that unlocks many of life's comforts, like a roof over your head, good food on the table, and the occasional splurge on something ridiculous yet delightful (hello, heated massage chair). But here's the thing: while money can solve a lot of problems, it's not a cure-all.

Sure, financial success can buy you plenty of things—a bigger house, a faster car, even a private jet if you're feeling particularly flashy. But it can't buy the things that truly sustain us: love, connection, purpose, or the ability to sleep soundly at night knowing your life aligns with your values. A pile of cash might look impressive, but it won't keep you warm at night—unless, of course, you light it on fire, and even then, it's more chaos than comfort.

The Misconception of "Enough"

It's easy to fall into the trap of thinking, *"If I just had a little more money, everything would be perfect."* We tell ourselves that the next milestone—the next raise, the next big client, the next successful quarter—will bring the contentment we're craving.

But here's the rub: money doesn't have the power to fill the deeper gaps in our lives. It can't fix a fractured relationship, reignite a lost passion, or create meaning where there's none. In fact, chasing financial success without addressing those gaps often magnifies them, leaving you with more stuff but the same lingering emptiness.

Now, this isn't a "money is bad" lecture. Money is a tool—a powerful one that can provide freedom, opportunities, and a sense of security. It can fund your dreams, support your loved ones, and give you the resources to make a positive impact on the world.

But that's the point: it's a *tool*, not the whole toolbox. Financial success is one component of a good life, not the entirety. It's like salt in a recipe—you need it, but if it's the only ingredient, you're not going to end up with much of a meal.

The Whole Picture

A truly fulfilling life balances financial success with other essential ingredients: meaningful relationships, a sense of purpose, and time to enjoy the fruits of your labor. Without these, even the biggest bank account can feel hollow.

Imagine someone with all the money in the world but no one to share it with, no passions to pursue, and no sense of why they're getting out of bed in the morning. They might have a house that's the size of a small castle, but if the rooms are empty, it's not much of a home.

Redefining Wealth

The good news is, you don't have to choose between financial success and personal fulfillment. The goal isn't to abandon ambition but to align it with what truly matters to you. When money becomes a means to support your values and goals, rather than an end in itself, it transforms from a source of stress to a source of freedom.

So, yes, strive for financial success. Build that business, grow your wealth, and enjoy the comforts it brings. But don't forget to invest in the things money can't buy: time with loved ones, the pursuit of passions, and a life that feels rich in every sense of the word.

Because at the end of the day, a pile of cash might make a great photo op, but it's the warmth of a life well-lived that truly keeps you cozy.

Understanding Fulfillment: What's Joy Got to Do with It?

When we talk about fulfillment, it's tempting to lump it together with achievement, as though they're two sides of the same coin. But here's the truth: while they're related, they couldn't be more different. Achievements are the external markers of success—the shiny trophies, framed certificates, and Instagram-worthy milestones. Fulfillment, on the other hand, is deeply personal. It's an internal experience that comes from living in alignment with your values and finding joy in the process.

To understand the distinction, let's look at a metaphor that's as familiar as it is foundational: a house versus a home.

Fulfillment vs. Achievement

Building a house is an achievement. It's a tangible, measurable goal that involves blueprints, permits, and more trips to the hardware store than you care to admit. When the last nail is hammered, and the structure stands complete, you have every reason to celebrate—it's an impressive feat.

But here's the thing: a house isn't automatically a home.

A home is where you feel at peace, where you find comfort, connection, and belonging. It's not just about the square footage or the fancy appliances; it's about how the space feels and how it supports the life you want to live. Turning a house into a home takes intention, care, and a focus on what truly matters—much like finding fulfillment.

Achievement gets you the house, but fulfillment makes it a home.

Why the Difference Matters

The distinction between achievement and fulfillment is more than just philosophical; it's practical. Achievements are important—they give us direction, purpose, and a sense of progress. But without fulfillment, they can feel oddly hollow, like an echo in an empty room.

Think of it this way: you can achieve great things—launch a successful business, win awards, or even build your dream house—but if those achievements aren't tied to something deeper, they won't bring the lasting joy you're searching for.

That's because achievements answer the question, *"What have I done?"* while fulfillment answers the question, *"How does it feel?"*

Bringing Fulfillment into Focus

To move beyond achievement and into fulfillment, you need to ask yourself:

- *What makes me feel truly alive?*

- *How do my goals align with my values?*

- *Am I chasing trophies or creating a life that feels meaningful?*

The answers won't come all at once, and that's okay. Fulfillment isn't a finish line you cross; it's a process of building, refining, and aligning. It's about turning your achievements into a foundation for a life that feels rich in every sense of the word.

So, yes, celebrate the house you've built—enjoy every nail, beam, and brick of your accomplishments. But don't stop there. Take the time to make it a home, a space where your joy, purpose, and passions can thrive. Because at the end of the day, fulfillment is what turns success into something that truly feels like yours.

The Joy Audit

If there's one thing we often overlook in the pursuit of success, it's joy. Not the fleeting, Instagram-filtered kind that comes with likes and compliments, but the deep, belly-laugh, "this is where I'm meant to be" kind of joy. It's the secret ingredient to fulfillment, and yet it's so easy to lose sight of it amid deadlines, meetings, and the ever-tempting lure of productivity apps.

So, let's take a moment for a joy audit. Think of it as an internal inventory—not of your achievements or to-do lists, but of the moments that make you feel genuinely happy. And no, we're not talking about the temporary relief that comes from checking something off your list or finally remembering to defrost the chicken for dinner. We're talking about the times that make your soul sit up and say, *"Yes, more of this, please."*

Finding Your Joy

Start by reflecting on this simple, lighthearted prompt: *What makes you feel alive—not just awake after coffee?*

For some, it's the rush of creativity when they're knee-deep in a project that excites them. For others, it's the quiet contentment of a Sunday afternoon spent reading a book, gardening, or sharing a meal with loved ones. Joy doesn't have to be big or extravagant—it can be as simple as laughing until your stomach hurts or watching the sunrise in peace.

If you're feeling stuck, think about the last time you lost track of time in the best possible way. What were you doing? Who were you with? Chances are, that's a clue to what brings you joy.

Why Joy Matters

Here's the thing about joy: it's not just a nice-to-have; it's essential to fulfillment. When you're in touch with what makes you happy, it's easier to align your life and work with your values. Joy becomes a compass, pointing you toward the things that matter most and away from the things that drain you.

And let's not underestimate the power of joy to recharge your batteries. Achievements might boost your confidence, but joy is what keeps you going. It's the fuel that makes the journey worth it, not just the destination.

Your Joy List

To take this audit one step further, grab a notebook—or the back of an envelope, whatever's handy—and start a Joy List. Jot down anything and everything that comes to mind:

- The little things that make your heart smile (puppy cuddles, a perfectly brewed cup of tea, that song you can't help but dance to).

- The big, unforgettable moments (watching your kid's first soccer goal, finally nailing that sourdough starter, or traveling to a place you've always dreamed of).

- The activities that make you lose yourself in the best way possible (writing, painting, hiking, or even assembling IKEA furniture—hey, no judgment).

There's no right or wrong answer here—your Joy List is yours. Once you've written it, take a look. How often do these things show up in your life? Are there ways to incorporate more of them into your routine?

Making Room for Joy

The purpose of a joy audit isn't just to reflect—it's to act. Life gets busy, but joy doesn't have to be reserved for vacations or special occasions. Start small: carve out 15 minutes for something on your Joy List today. Schedule time for it like you would a meeting, because joy is just as important as anything else on your calendar.

Because at the end of the day, fulfillment isn't about how much you've accomplished; it's about how much you've truly lived. And joy? That's the spark that lights the way.

Purpose as a Compass

Let's talk about purpose—the secret sauce of a fulfilling life and the thing that keeps us from feeling like we're wandering aimlessly through a maze. And speaking of mazes, have you ever been to IKEA without a map?

It starts innocently enough. You're here for one thing—say, a bookshelf—and you figure you'll be in and out in no time. But then you take a wrong turn at the lighting section, get distracted by some oddly-shaped cushions, and suddenly find yourself in a labyrinth of flat-packed furniture, completely unsure of where you are or how to escape. You might eventually stumble upon your bookshelf, but by then, you're exhausted, slightly irritated, and carrying at least three things you didn't intend to buy.

This is what life feels like without purpose. You might achieve things along the way, but without a clear sense of direction, the journey can leave you feeling lost and unsatisfied—like you've been chasing success for the sake of it, without really knowing *why*.

The Difference Between Purpose and Success

Success, as we've discussed, is external—it's about hitting milestones, achieving goals, and collecting accolades. Purpose, on the other hand, is internal. It's your "why"—the deeper reason behind what you do.

Purpose is what turns success into something meaningful. It's the difference between chasing trophies and building a legacy, between running in circles and walking a path that feels uniquely yours.

Think of purpose as a compass. It doesn't just point you toward your goals; it ensures those goals align with who you are and what you value. Success without purpose is like walking through life with no map—sure, you might end up somewhere, but it's anyone's guess whether it's where you actually wanted to go.

Why Purpose Matters

Here's the beauty of purpose: it simplifies things. When you know your purpose, decisions become clearer, priorities fall into place, and distractions lose their grip. You're no longer chasing every shiny opportunity or saying yes to every request because you have a guiding principle that keeps you focused on what truly matters.

Purpose isn't about making life easy—it's about making it meaningful. It's the anchor that keeps you steady when things get chaotic and the light that guides you through uncertainty.

Finding Your Compass

Discovering your purpose might sound daunting, but it doesn't have to be. Start by asking yourself:

- *What do I care about deeply?*

- *What kind of impact do I want to have on the world—or even just on the people around me?*

- *What gets me out of bed in the morning (besides coffee and an unrelenting alarm clock)?*

Your answers don't have to be grand or world-changing. Purpose isn't about solving global crises (though more power to you if that's your thing); it's about aligning your actions with what matters most to you.

Walking with Purpose

Once you've identified your purpose—or even just started to uncover it—you'll find that life feels less like wandering through IKEA and more like following a well-marked trail. Sure, there will still be twists and turns, but you'll know where you're headed and why you're on the journey.

Purpose isn't a destination; it's a direction. It's not about avoiding challenges but about facing them with clarity and confidence, knowing that each step is part of a bigger picture.

So, grab your metaphorical compass, take a deep breath, and start charting your course. Because when purpose guides you, every step—whether toward a bookshelf or a lifelong dream—feels a little more meaningful.

Aligning Business with Values: Putting Your Money Where Your Heart Is

For many entrepreneurs, the dream begins with a spark of passion—an idea, a skill, or a vision they can't ignore. But as businesses grow, it's easy to get swept up in the day-to-day grind and lose sight of what truly matters. That's where aligning your business with your values comes in.

Your values are the heart of your business, the principles that guide your decisions and define your legacy. When your business reflects your values, it feels authentic and fulfilling—not just successful on paper but meaningful in every way.

Let's start with a little exercise to uncover those values and make sure they're front and center in everything you do.

The Values Discovery Process

Imagine, if you will, that you're stranded on a desert island. Not just any island, mind you—this one comes with your business. Somehow, your office, laptop, and team have all miraculously washed ashore with you (we'll ignore the logistics for now).

Now ask yourself: What would you want to preserve?

Would it be the way your business supports your community? The innovative spirit that drives your ideas? The relationships you've built with your team or clients? Think about the essential aspects of your business—the parts you'd fight to protect, even if everything else had to go.

Write these down. They're your core values—the elements that define your business at its best.

Why Values Matter

When you identify and align with your values, they become a compass for every decision you make. Should you take on that new client? Expand into a different market? Say yes to that partnership opportunity? Instead of chasing opportunities for the sake of growth, you'll have a clear framework to ensure every step supports your bigger picture.

Your values aren't just good for you—they're good for your business, too. Clients and customers are drawn to authenticity, and nothing is more authentic than a business that operates in line with its values. It's not just about making money; it's about making an impact in a way that feels true to who you are.

Your Desert Island Blueprint

Now that you've identified your core values, let's make them actionable. Go back to your list from the desert island exercise and ask yourself:

- *How do these values show up in my business today?*

- *Where might I be drifting away from them?*

- *What changes could I make to better align my business with these values?*

For instance, if "building strong relationships" is one of your core values, are you investing enough time in connecting with your team or clients? If "innovation" is a priority, are you creating space for creativity and new ideas, or are you stuck in the routine of what's already working?

This isn't about perfection—it's about progress. The goal is to bring your business closer to its truest expression of your values, one intentional step at a time.

Putting Your Money Where Your Heart Is

When your business aligns with your values, every decision feels a little more purposeful. You're not just chasing profits; you're building something that reflects what you care about most. And in the end, isn't that what entrepreneurship is all about?

So, whether you're stranded on a desert island or navigating the everyday challenges of business, keep your values at the forefront. They're the foundation of a business that doesn't just succeed but also fulfills—and that's a goal worth striving for.

Purpose-Driven Business Models

What do a chocolatier, a tech founder, and the inventor of a coffee-and-cat café have in common? No, it's not the setup for a bad joke—it's the magic of purpose-driven business models. Each of these individuals took their personal passions and values and turned them into thriving ventures that don't just generate revenue but also align with who they are at their core.

This is the beauty of a purpose-driven business model: it's not just about what you sell or how much you earn—it's about the *why* behind it all.

Chocolate with a Purpose

Take, for example, a chocolatier who adores their craft but also dreams of giving back to their community. Instead of just churning out truffles, they create a business that uses locally-sourced ingredients, partners with local farmers, and even offers workshops to teach kids about sustainable farming. The result? A business that's as sweet in its impact as it is in its product.

This is what happens when passion meets purpose. The chocolatier isn't just selling chocolate; they're creating connections and making a difference.

Tech Meets Education

Then there's the tech founder who loves innovation but is equally passionate about education. Instead of diving into the next big app fad, they develop software that helps underfunded schools access quality teaching resources. It's not just another tech startup—it's a business with heart.

By aligning their technical skills with their values, this founder isn't just solving problems; they're changing lives. And as a bonus, their work feels deeply meaningful, even on the most stressful days.

Coffee, Cats, and Quirkiness

And of course, we can't forget the visionary entrepreneur who decided to combine coffee and cats—a business model that is, quite literally, purrfect for a specific audience.

Sure, it might sound quirky, but it's a brilliant example of a purpose-driven venture. This person took their love for caffeine and feline companionship and turned it into a café where customers can sip lattes while cuddling adoptable cats. The result? A business that's equal parts charming and impactful, creating joy for customers and homes for stray cats.

Why Purpose-Driven Models Work

What all these businesses have in common is that they're rooted in more than just profits. They reflect their founders' passions and values, making them authentic, inspiring, and deeply fulfilling.

Purpose-driven models don't just attract customers—they create communities. People are drawn to businesses that stand for something, that tell a story, and that make them feel like they're part of something bigger.

Your Turn: Building with Purpose

So, how do you create a purpose-driven business model? Start by asking yourself:

- *What am I passionate about?*

- *What values are most important to me?*

- *How can I integrate these into my business in an authentic way?*

You don't have to reinvent the wheel—just find ways to bring your unique perspective and passions into what you do. Whether it's creating a product that aligns with your values, offering services that reflect your passions, or building a company culture that prioritizes what matters most to you, the possibilities are endless.

And who knows? Maybe your purpose-driven business model will become the next big thing—like chocolate that changes the world, software that transforms classrooms, or, yes, even a coffee shop where cats rule the roost.

The Win-Win of Alignment

When a business aligns with its founder's values, something magical happens. It's like finding the perfect pair of shoes: they're comfortable enough to wear all day, stylish enough to make you feel good, and durable enough to last the distance. In the same way, a values-driven business supports the entrepreneur's sense of purpose, attracts loyal customers, and creates a lasting impact—all without pinching or falling apart at the seams.

Comfortable Fit: Authenticity in Action

A business built on values feels right—not just for you, but for everyone involved. As an entrepreneur, you're no longer forcing yourself to fit into a mold that doesn't suit you. Instead, you're designing something that feels authentic and natural, like slipping into a pair of shoes that were made just for you.

Authenticity has a ripple effect. When your business reflects your values, your team, customers, and partners can sense it. They see a business that's not just chasing profits but genuinely cares about its mission. And that kind of authenticity is magnetic—it attracts people who share your vision and want to be part of what you're building.

Much like the perfect shoes that make you stand out for all the right reasons, a business aligned with its values becomes more appealing to customers and stakeholders. People are drawn to brands that reflect their own values, and they're more likely to stick around when they see those values in action.

Think of it this way: you wouldn't wear clunky, uncomfortable shoes to an event where you wanted to make an impression. Similarly, a business that's aligned with its values presents a cohesive, confident image—one that resonates with customers and builds trust.

Durable for the Long Haul: Sustainable Success

Finally, alignment creates durability. When your business reflects what matters most to you, staying motivated and weathering the inevitable challenges is easier. You're not just working for a paycheck; you're building something that feels meaningful, which makes the hard days a little less hard.

On the flip side, a values-driven business creates long-term loyalty among customers and stakeholders. People want to support a business they believe in, and when they see your commitment to your values, they're more likely to stick around—even when competitors try to tempt them away.

The best part? Alignment isn't just a win for you—it's a win for everyone involved. Your team benefits from a clear sense of purpose, your customers feel good about supporting your business, and your community gains from the positive impact you create.

It's the ultimate win-win: a business that fits like a glove (or the perfect pair of shoes) and leaves everyone feeling a little better about the journey.

Walking the Talk

So, how do you ensure your business aligns with your values? Start by reflecting on what matters most to you and how those principles can guide your decisions. From the way you treat your team to the way you engage with customers, alignment should be at the core of everything you do.

Because, much like finding that perfect pair of shoes, a values-driven business supports you in all the right ways—helping you move forward confidently, comfortably, and stylishly, no matter where the road takes you.

Sustaining Fulfillment: The Daily Art of Not Losing Your Marbles

Fulfillment isn't a one-and-done deal. It's not like a certificate you hang on the wall or a trophy you dust off once a year. No, fulfillment is more like tending a garden: it requires daily attention, patience, and the occasional willingness to pull a few metaphorical weeds. The trick, of course, is to cultivate habits that keep your marbles securely in place—even when life feels like a bit of a juggling act.

Let's start with one of the most underrated tools in the fulfillment toolbox: gratitude.

The Gratitude Habit

Ah, gratitude. The word itself conjures images of serene people journaling with fountain pens in soft candlelight, listing profound and poetic things they're thankful for. And then there's the rest of us—staring at a blank page in the morning, groaning, *"Do I really have to do this?"*

Let's be honest: gratitude can feel like a chore, especially on tough days. You sit there, trying to muster up three things you're grateful for, and all you can think is, *"I guess I'm grateful the Wi-Fi is working? And that I didn't burn the toast? Is that lame?"* But here's the funny thing—it works.

Even on days when it feels like pulling teeth, the simple act of acknowledging what's going right has a way of shifting your perspective. It's like putting on glasses after wandering around blurry-eyed all morning. Suddenly, the world looks clearer, brighter, and a little less overwhelming.

Gratitude isn't just about being polite to the universe—it's a powerful tool for sustaining fulfillment. Research shows that cultivating gratitude improves mental health, reduces stress, and even strengthens relationships. It's like a cheat code for life, and best of all, it's free.

When you make gratitude a habit, you start to notice the small, wonderful things you'd otherwise overlook: the warmth of your first cup of coffee, the sound of rain on the roof, or the way your dog looks at you like you hung the moon. These moments might seem insignificant, but they add up, creating a foundation of joy and resilience.

Making Gratitude Fun (and Doable)

The trick to building a gratitude habit is to keep it light and manageable. Forget the pressure to write an essay about your blessings—start with the small stuff. Keep a notebook by your bed or open the notes app on your phone, and jot down three things you're grateful for each day.

And yes, it's okay if your list includes things like *"good Wi-Fi"* or *"that funny cat video I saw earlier."* Gratitude doesn't have to be grand or profound—it just has to be real.

You can also mix it up:

- Share something you're grateful for over dinner with your family or friends.

- Take a moment during a coffee break to mentally list a few things going right.

- Make it a game—challenge yourself to notice something new every day.

Gratitude, like any habit, gets easier with practice. And the more you do it, the more natural it becomes—a quiet but steady way to sustain fulfillment, even when life throws you curveballs.

The Takeaway

Gratitude might not solve all your problems or make your to-do list magically disappear, but it will make the journey a little sweeter. It's a small, daily act with big rewards, helping you hold onto your marbles—and maybe even find a few you thought you'd lost.

So, the next time you sit down to write your gratitude list and draw a blank, remember it's okay to start small. Because sometimes, noticing the little things is exactly what keeps life from feeling overwhelming. And who knows? You might just find yourself grateful for the habit itself.

Joyful Rituals

Life, as wonderful as it can be, has a habit of becoming a series of to-do lists and deadlines. Before you know it, your days start to blur together in a haze of emails, meetings, and reheated leftovers. But here's the secret to shaking things up: joyful rituals.

Think of them as small, intentional pockets of happiness that remind you that life is meant to be lived—not just managed. These rituals don't have to be complicated or time-consuming. In fact, the simpler, the better. The goal is to infuse your days with moments that make you smile, relax, or even laugh out loud.

Little Moments, Big Impact

A joyful ritual could be as simple as:

- Taking a quiet morning walk to soak in the sunrise before the day's chaos begins.

- Savoring a mindful coffee break where you actually sit down, breathe, and enjoy the coffee instead of gulping it while answering emails.

- Throwing an impromptu dance session in your office when no one's looking—or better yet, when they are.

And yes, about that dancing: it may not solve your client's woes, but it might just keep you from chucking your laptop out the window. There's something undeniably uplifting about cranking up your favorite song and moving like no one's watching (even if they are).

Why Rituals Matter

Rituals, even tiny ones, serve as anchors in a busy day. They're reminders to pause, breathe, and reconnect with yourself. In a world that often feels like it's spinning too fast, these moments of joy can ground you and give you a little boost of energy and perspective.

Plus, they're an easy way to create boundaries between work and life. That morning walk? It's your time, a quiet buffer before the emails start pouring in. That coffee break? It's a chance to reset and focus on something *just for you*.

Making It Your Own

The beauty of joyful rituals is that they're entirely customizable. Not a morning person? Try a bedtime ritual instead—reading a chapter of a book or journaling about your day. Hate coffee? Switch it out for tea or a fruit smoothie. The point isn't the specific activity; it's the intention behind it.

Here are a few ideas to get you started:

- **Morning Walks**: Leave your phone behind (or at least put it on silent) and focus on the sights, sounds, and smells around you.

- **Mindful Breaks**: Whether it's coffee, tea, or a midday snack, take five minutes to enjoy it fully—no multitasking allowed.

- **Creative Bursts**: Keep a doodle pad on your desk, or write down a funny thought or idea when inspiration strikes.

- **Dance It Out**: Create a playlist of your go-to feel-good songs, and commit to one quick jam session a day. Bonus points if it makes your coworkers laugh.

- **Gratitude Pause**: Before bed, think of one joyful moment from your day—it's a great way to end on a high note.

The Ripple Effect

Here's the thing about joyful rituals: they're contagious. When you start incorporating them into your life, you'll find they influence your mood and the people around you. A happy, centered you is a gift to everyone you interact with—whether it's your team, your clients, or the barista who's perfected your latte.

So go ahead: dance, walk, sip, or scribble your way to a little more joy. These rituals won't solve all your problems, but they'll make the journey a whole lot more fun—and maybe even keep you from yelling at your inbox.

Reflection as Maintenance

Let's face it: life has a way of pulling us in a million directions at once. Between deadlines, emails, and the occasional existential crisis, it's easy to lose sight of whether our business—and, by extension, our life—is heading where we want it to go. That's where reflection comes in. Think of it as the regular maintenance your life needs to avoid veering into the ditch of burnout or getting stuck in the mud of misalignment.

And yes, it's a bit like checking the alignment of your car wheels. Ignore it for too long, and you'll start to notice the telltale signs: the odd pull to the left, a bumpy ride, or the unnerving sensation that you're constantly overcorrecting to stay on course. The same thing happens in life and business. Without periodic reflection, you might find yourself working harder and harder just to keep things from spinning out of control.

Why Reflection Matters

Reflection is the unsung hero of fulfillment. It's what allows you to pause, assess, and ask the big questions:

- *Am I still heading in the right direction?*

- *Does my business align with my values and the life I want to build?*

- *What adjustments do I need to make to get back on track?*

Much like your car, your business and personal fulfillment need regular check-ins. The good news? This kind of maintenance doesn't involve grease or an overenthusiastic mechanic—it just takes a little time, intention, and honesty.

The Reflection Tune-Up

Here's a simple way to perform your reflection tune-up:

1. **Schedule It**: Just as you wouldn't wait for your car to break down before heading to the shop, don't wait for a crisis to reflect on your alignment. Set aside time every month, quarter, or year to check in with yourself.

2. **Ask the Key Questions**:

    - *What's working well?*

    - *What feels off or out of sync?*

    - *Am I spending my time and energy on what matters most?*

    - *Have my priorities shifted?*

3. **Make Small Adjustments**: If you notice areas of misalignment, start with small tweaks. Maybe it's delegating a task that's draining you or carving out time for a passion project you've been neglecting. These

minor shifts can have a major impact over time.

Avoiding the Veer

The beauty of reflection is that it keeps you proactive rather than reactive. When you regularly check your alignment, you're less likely to career wildly off-course and wonder how you ended up in a metaphorical ditch.

Plus, reflection doesn't just prevent problems—it fosters growth. Each check-in is an opportunity to celebrate progress, refine your goals, and deepen your sense of fulfillment. It's like upgrading your ride from a clunky station wagon to a sleek, well-tuned sports car.

Making It Fun

Reflection doesn't have to feel like a chore. Treat it as a moment of self-care—grab your favorite drink, find a cozy spot, and take a few minutes to reconnect with yourself and your vision. You might even turn it into a ritual, like a quarterly "alignment retreat" where you reflect, recharge, and recalibrate.

And if nothing else, just remember: regular reflection keeps your wheels straight, your ride smooth, and your journey toward fulfillment firmly on track. Because the road to a meaningful life is much more enjoyable when you're not constantly wrestling with the steering wheel.

Conclusion: Success Redefined

As we come to the end of this journey, let's take a moment to reimagine what success can look like. For so many of us, it's been painted as a skyscraper—tall, impressive, and towering over everything else in life. We've been told to climb, floor by floor, chasing that elusive penthouse view. But here's the thing about skyscrapers: the higher you go, the less space there is to stretch out and truly live.

Instead, let's think of success as a garden.

A garden isn't about towering heights or singular goals; it's about growth, balance, and care. It's a space where everything works together—different plants, each with their own needs, thriving side by side. It's not about reaching the top but nurturing what matters most, cultivating beauty, and finding joy in the process.

The Gentle Art of Fulfillment

Fulfillment, much like tending a garden, is a daily practice. It's about weeding out what no longer serves you, planting seeds of purpose and joy, and taking time to appreciate the blooms along the way.

The beauty of this approach is that it shifts the focus from achievement to experience. Success is no longer a finish line you must reach to feel validated; it becomes part of the ongoing journey—a result of living in alignment with your values and passions.

Here's the truth: success will always be there, waiting at the finish line. But fulfillment? That's what lets you enjoy the run. It's what turns the uphill climbs into adventures, the setbacks into learning moments, and the everyday into something extraordinary.

So, as you move forward, embrace fulfillment as a practice—not something to master overnight but something to nurture day by day. Remember that success is not a one-size-fits-all endeavor, and your version of it will be as unique as the life you're building.

An Invitation to Redefine

Now it's your turn. Take the time to reflect, dream, and redefine what success means to you. Tend your garden with care, celebrate the small blooms, and don't be afraid to prune what no longer serves you.

Because when success is redefined as a life well-lived—a garden brimming with vitality, purpose, and joy—it's no longer something you chase. It's something you create, nurture, and, most importantly, savor.

And isn't that the point? To live a life not just of success, but of meaning.

Chapter Three

Reassessing Your Why

The Curious Case of the Wandering Why

LET'S BEGIN WITH A confession: we've all lost track of something important. Maybe it was your keys, phone, or grocery list you swore you put in your pocket. You know the drill—you retrace your steps, check the same counter three times, and eventually find the missing item in the most ridiculous place possible (like the fridge).

Now, imagine that instead of a set of keys, it's your purpose that's gone missing. When you started your entrepreneurial journey, your "why" was as clear as day. You had big dreams, bold ideas, and enough enthusiasm to power a small city. But somewhere along the way—between quarterly reports, client meetings, and late-night brainstorming sessions—it wandered off, leaving you wondering, *"Wait, what was this all for again?"*

It's a bit like finding an old notebook buried under a pile of paperwork. You open it to discover pages of ambitious plans and motivational scribbles in your own handwriting. Except now, you're staring at it, thinking, *"Who wrote this, and why were they so optimistic?"*

The Wandering Why

Here's the thing about your "why": it's not a set-it-and-forget-it kind of deal. Much like a favorite jacket, it must be tried on every now and then to ensure it still fits. The business you started five years ago, or even five months ago, might look very different from the one you're running today. Your goals, priorities, and passions evolve—and your purpose needs to evolve with them.

But instead of mourning the fact that your original "why" has changed, consider this an opportunity. It's a chance to reassess, refine, and realign. To ask yourself whether your current path still reflects what matters most to you—or whether it's time for a few adjustments.

Reassessing your "why" isn't about scrapping everything and starting over. It's about reconnecting with the deeper meaning behind your work and ensuring that your business aligns with your values and goals.

Because, here's the truth: when you lose sight of your purpose, it's easy to get caught up in the hamster wheel of busyness—chasing every opportunity, saying yes to everything, and wondering why you feel stretched so thin. But when your "why" is clear, it acts as a compass, guiding your decisions and keeping you focused on what truly matters.

So, let's treat this chapter as a search-and-rescue mission for your purpose. Whether it's misplaced, outdated, or just a little dusty, we'll find it, try it on for size, and, if needed, give it a thoughtful update.

After all, your "why" isn't something you lose forever—it's something you rediscover, time and time again, with each new chapter of your journey.

Rediscovering Purpose: Dusting Off Your Why (Or Finding a New One)

Purpose, like a favorite book or an old recipe card, has a way of getting buried under the clutter of life. It's not that you meant to ignore it—it just got crowded out by everything else demanding your attention. But here's the good news: re-discovering your purpose isn't about returning to square one. It's about revisiting it with fresh eyes, understanding how it's evolved, and, if necessary, giving it a thoughtful upgrade.

Let's start with the simplest way to reconnect: reflection.

The Power of Reflection

Think of reflection as revisiting the manual for a gadget you swore you knew how to use. When you first opened that shiny new device—be it a blender, a camera, or your entrepreneurial dream—you were confident you'd figure it out on your own. Who needs instructions, right? But somewhere along the way, things stopped working as expected. The camera's settings don't produce the photos you want, the blender keeps jamming, or—gulp—your business starts to feel more like a chore than a passion.

So, you finally dig out the manual (or Google it, because who keeps those things?) and discover something enlightening: either there's been an update you didn't know about, or, perhaps more humbling, you've been pressing the wrong buttons all along.

This is what revisiting your "why" feels like. It's a chance to step back, reflect, and ensure you're still on the right track—or to course-correct if you've been spinning in circles.

For entrepreneurs, a clear "why" isn't just a nice-to-have; it's the foundation of everything they do. It drives their decisions, keeps them motivated during tough times, and ensures their business aligns with their values and goals. But just like that gadget manual, their "why" needs revisiting.

Why? Because businesses evolve, markets shift, and, most importantly, *you* change. The purpose that fueled you in the early days of your entrepreneurial journey might not fit the person you've become or the business you're running now. Reflection lets you acknowledge those changes and realign your purpose with your current reality.

A Simple Reflection Exercise

To dust off your "why," try this:

1. **Carve Out Time**: Find a quiet moment to think without distractions. A cozy coffee shop, a favorite chair, or even a long walk can work wonders.

2. **Ask the Big Questions**:

    ○ *What inspired me to start this business?*

    ○ *What part of my work brings me the most joy?*

    ○ *Have my values or goals shifted since I began?*

3. **Take Notes**: Write down your thoughts, even if they're messy. The goal isn't perfection—it's clarity.

As you reflect, you might find that your original "why" still resonates, albeit with a few tweaks. Or, you might discover that your purpose has evolved into something entirely new—and that's perfectly okay. The important thing is to reconnect with the deeper meaning behind your work.

Reflection is less about finding something lost and more about uncovering what's been there all along, just waiting for you to notice it again. Whether your "why" needs a little polishing or a complete overhaul, this process is your chance to ensure it's as vibrant and inspiring as the day you first dreamed it up.

Because, let's face it: no one wants to press the wrong buttons forever. By revisiting the manual—your purpose—you'll find yourself back on track and more excited than ever to keep building, growing, and thriving.

Guided Reflection Exercise: Explaining Your Business to an Eight-Year-Old

Sometimes, the complexities of running a business can cloud the clarity of your original purpose. To reconnect with your "why," try this playful exercise:

Imagine you're explaining your business to an inquisitive eight-year-old. How would you describe what you do and, more importantly, why you do it? The simplicity required to communicate with a child can strip away the jargon and reveal the core of your mission.

Steps to the Exercise:

1. **Find a Quiet Space:** Set aside a few minutes in a comfortable environment where you can think without interruptions.

2. **Visualize the Conversation:** Picture an eager eight-year-old asking, "What do you do for work?"

3. **Simplify Your Explanation:** Describe your business in straightforward terms, focusing on the essence of your work.

4. **Articulate Your 'Why':** Explain why you do what you do, emphasizing the purpose and passion behind your business.

Example:

"I help people find books they'll love because reading can make them happy and smart."

This exercise encourages you to distill your business's mission into its purest form, shedding light on your fundamental motivations. You may rediscover the passion that inspired you to start your entrepreneurial journey by articulating your purpose in simple terms.

Symptoms of a Lost Why

It's easy to lose sight of your "why" amid the hustle and bustle of running a business. At first, it's subtle—an extra sigh here, a missed spark of excitement there. But over time, the symptoms of a lost connection to purpose become impossible to ignore. If any of this sounds familiar, you might need to pause and reconnect with your "why."

Feeling Stuck or Uninspired? Tasks that once thrilled you now feel like a slog through molasses. That fire that used to get you out of bed in the morning? It's more of a flicker now, barely visible under the weight of endless to-dos. Creativity feels like an old friend who hasn't called in years, and you find yourself simply going through the motions.

The Cranky Entrepreneur Syndrome. Do you feel inexplicably annoyed during team meetings, even when nothing catastrophic is happening? Maybe the sound of someone's keyboard typing too loudly or a slightly off-topic discussion has you gripping your coffee mug a little too tightly. This irritability can often be traced back to a deeper frustration: the disconnect between your daily grind and your original purpose.

The Existential To-Do List. You glance at your never-ending task list and wonder, "What's the point of all this?" You might even hear that small, nagging voice whisper, *"Is this really what I wanted when I started this journey?"* This sense of futility can be a glaring sign that your work no longer aligns with your core values or aspirations.

Procrastination Nation. Tasks that used to energize you are now met with dread—or worse, avoidance. You find yourself scrolling social media, organizing your sock drawer, or deep-cleaning the fridge instead of tackling the things that actually need to be done.

A Decline in Joyful Engagement. Even successes feel a little hollow. You check off a major milestone, but instead of celebrating, you feel indifferent. The joy that used to accompany your achievements has been replaced with a "what's next?" mentality.

The Great Disconnect. Your team, clients, or community no longer feel like the partners they once were in your grand adventure. Instead of collaboration and excitement, you feel increasingly isolated, as though you're carrying the burden of your business alone.

Why These Symptoms Matter

Losing your "why" isn't just a personal issue—it affects your business, your relationships, and your overall well-being. These signs are like warning lights on the dashboard of your entrepreneurial vehicle, telling you it's time to pull over and reassess.

Reconnecting with your purpose can reignite your passion, clarify your priorities, and make the journey enjoyable again. Because while the road might be bumpy at times, driving with purpose makes the ride infinitely more meaningful—and way less cranky.

Evolving Goals: When Your Why Outgrows Its Shoes

The thing about your "why" is that it's not a fixed entity. It evolves, much like our tastes do. Remember that snack you couldn't get enough of as a kid? Maybe it was neon-orange cheese puffs or an ice cream sandwich with the consistency of foam rubber. At the time, it was culinary heaven. But if you've revisited it as an adult, chances are you've found it... well, disappointing. Turns out, some things just don't age well.

Your "why" is similar. The purpose that once propelled you out of bed with the energy of a caffeinated squirrel might now feel a bit stale. And that's okay. Life has a funny way of changing us—through new experiences, shifting priorities, or the sheer exhaustion that comes from answering one too many late-night emails.

The Dynamic Nature of Purpose

Purpose isn't static. It's not like a diploma you hang on the wall and forget about. Instead, it grows, shrinks, and occasionally transforms into something completely unrecognizable. Sometimes, it's because of positive changes—a new opportunity, a revelation about what truly matters to you. Other times, it's because life throws a curveball, and your priorities need to shift accordingly.

For example, when you first started your business, your "why" might have been financial freedom. But now, after years of grinding away, you might find that freedom means more than money—it's about time, relationships, or leaving a legacy that matters.

It's like a pair of shoes you've outgrown. They were perfect when you bought them—comfortable, stylish, and a reflection of who you were at the time. But as your journey continues, those shoes start to pinch. They no longer fit the person you've become. And let's be honest: hobbling around in ill-fitting footwear isn't a good look for anyone.

Signs It's Time to Reassess

How do you know if your "why" has outgrown its shoes? Start by asking yourself:

- *Does my work still excite me?*

- *Am I chasing goals that feel meaningful or just checking off boxes?*

- *Have my priorities shifted without my realizing it?*

If the answers leave you scratching your head—or worse, sighing—it's time for a closer look.

The Beauty of an Evolving Why

Here's the good news: an evolving purpose isn't a sign of failure. It's a sign of growth. It means you're paying attention to what matters to you now, not clinging to what mattered five or ten years ago.

Embracing this evolution allows you to realign your goals with your current self, making your journey not just successful but also fulfilling. It's about finding the new "shoes" that fit you perfectly—shoes that can carry you forward comfortably and confidently.

So, if your "why" feels a little off or outdated, don't panic. Instead, take a moment to reflect. What do you value most today? What excites you, inspires you, or makes you feel alive?

Reassessing your purpose is like upgrading that childhood snack. Sure, the cheese puffs were great at the time, but now you've discovered artisanal popcorn with just the right amount of sea salt. It's different, it's better, and it's perfectly suited to where you are now.

Because at the end of the day, purpose isn't about staying the same—it's about staying true to yourself as you grow.

Recognizing Shifts in Priorities

Life has a way of shuffling our priorities when we least expect it. One day, you're charging full speed ahead, driven by a single, clear goal—financial independence, perhaps, or building an empire from the ground up. Then, something happens. Maybe it's kids. Maybe it's turning 40 and realizing your knees make odd noises when you stand up too quickly. Whatever the catalyst, your perspective shifts. Suddenly, the goalposts you'd been sprinting toward seem a little less relevant, and new priorities sneak onto the field.

When Financial Independence Meets Flexibility

Take the entrepreneur who started their business with dreams of financial independence. Early on, they worked tirelessly to make it happen—late nights, long hours, the whole hustle culture package. But now? They've realized that all the money in the world isn't worth missing bedtime stories with their kids or skipping their weekly game of pickleball (a surprisingly addictive pastime for the over-40 crowd).

Their focus has shifted from earning more to living more—valuing flexibility, family time, and the ability to step away from the grind without everything falling apart.

The Great Parenting Epiphany

Nothing reshapes priorities quite like becoming a parent. One minute, you're laser-focused on business growth; the next, you're Googling "how to remove crayon from walls" while wondering how anyone gets anything done with toddlers around.

It's not just that kids are a handful (though they are); it's that they remind you of the things that matter most. Suddenly, your "why" might revolve less around hitting revenue goals and more around creating a life where you're present for the moments that matter—like first steps, soccer games, or even the simple joy of Sunday pancakes.

Of course, you don't need kids to experience a shift in priorities. Sometimes, it's as simple as reaching a milestone birthday and realizing that life is shorter than you thought—and maybe a little too short to spend it in back-to-back Zoom meetings.

At this stage, priorities often pivot from accumulation to appreciation. You might find yourself valuing time over money, purpose over productivity, or health over hustle. And yes, you might even start saying things like, "I'd rather be happy than busy," without a hint of irony.

Why Shifts in Priorities Are a Good Thing

Here's the beauty of shifting priorities: they're a sign of growth. They mean you're paying attention to what matters to you now, not clinging to a vision of success that no longer fits.

Acknowledging these changes isn't a betrayal of your original goals; it's an evolution of them. It's about ensuring that your "why" grows alongside you, supporting the life you want today—not the one you wanted a decade ago.

So, whether it's kids, knees, or a newfound love of pickleball, embrace the shifts. They're not a detour; they're the next step on your journey toward a life that truly aligns with who you are.

Here's a liberating truth: evolving goals aren't failures. They're signs of growth, like a tree sprouting new branches or a traveler deciding that the beach sounds better than the mountains. The thing about life—and business—is that destinations change. Sometimes, it's because your priorities shift; other times, it's because you've arrived somewhere and thought, *"Wait, this isn't quite what I had in mind."*

When the Map No Longer Fits

Think of your goals as a travel plan. Maybe, in the beginning, you set out with a clear map and a destination circled in red: financial independence, rapid growth, or maybe just the thrill of being your own boss. But somewhere along the way, you realized that the path you were on wasn't leading to the life you envisioned.

Perhaps the view along the route caught your eye, and suddenly, you're more interested in exploring a hidden village off the beaten path than reaching the bustling city you originally planned. Or maybe the destination itself has changed—a sandy beach with swaying palm trees now holds more appeal than the summit of a freezing, windswept mountain.

The beauty of a journey is that it's yours to shape. Changing your route isn't giving up; it's embracing the freedom to follow what feels right.

And then, there are times when you realize the map itself is the problem. It's outdated, limiting, or simply doesn't reflect who you are anymore. In these moments, the best thing you can do is toss it aside and trust yourself to navigate using your own instincts and evolving vision.

This isn't reckless—it's courageous. It's acknowledging that growth means letting go of what no longer serves you and creating space for new opportunities, dreams, and goals.

Why Pivoting is Powerful

Pivoting isn't about failure; it's about flexibility. It's recognizing that clinging to a plan that no longer aligns with your values is far more detrimental than recalibrating your course. It's giving yourself permission to adapt, explore, and redefine success on your own terms.

Every pivot is a chance to realign with what matters most. It's an opportunity to create a business—and a life—that reflects not just where you've been but where you want to go. So, if you find yourself at a crossroads, wondering whether to stick to the original plan or take a different route, remember this: you're not lost—you're evolving. The map was always just a guide, and the destination was never set in stone.

Whether you choose to tweak your goals, overhaul your business, or abandon the map entirely, trust that the journey is yours to shape. And who knows? You might just discover that the unexpected detours lead to the most fulfilling adventures of all.

Purpose as a Compass: Navigating Life and Business Without Hitting Icebergs

Life and business are full of unexpected twists, turns, and the occasional looming iceberg—those hidden obstacles that can sink even the most ambitious plans if you're not careful. That's where a clear sense of purpose comes in. Your "why" isn't just an abstract motivator; it's a practical tool, like a trusty compass, keeping you pointed in the right direction even when the path gets murky.

Your Why as a Decision-Making Tool

Imagine hiking through a dense forest. The trail forks in a dozen directions, each one equally promising—or equally confusing. Without a compass, you'd spend hours wandering in circles, debating which way to go, and probably end up somewhere entirely unintended (and far from where you left the car). But with a compass? Every decision becomes clearer.

The same is true for your "why." When you're faced with a choice—big or small—your purpose acts as a guiding star, helping you navigate the forest of options without getting lost.

Big Decisions Made Simple

Let's say you're considering expanding your business. Should you take on a new client, enter a new market, or invest in a flashy new product? Instead of weighing endless pros and cons, ask yourself:

- Does this align with my purpose?

- Will this move me closer to the life and business I want to build?

- Does this choice reflect what I value most?

If the answer is yes, you can move forward with confidence. If it's no—or even a hesitant maybe—it's time to reevaluate. Your "why" cuts through the noise and points you toward decisions that matter, like a compass steering you toward true north.

The Small Stuff Matters, Too

But it's not just the big decisions where your "why" shines. It's also in the everyday moments—deciding whether to accept another meeting request, delegate a task, or respond to that one email (you know, the one that's been sitting in your inbox for three days).

With your purpose in mind, these seemingly minor choices become opportunities to stay aligned with your goals. Instead of drowning in endless email threads or overloading your calendar, you can prioritize what truly matters and let the rest go.

Of course, even the best compass can't guarantee smooth sailing. There will still be challenges, setbacks, and those metaphorical icebergs waiting to test your resolve. But when you're clear on your purpose, you're better equipped to steer around them—or at least minimize the damage when you hit one.

Purpose doesn't eliminate uncertainty; it gives you the confidence to navigate it. It's the difference between drifting aimlessly and charting a course that reflects your values, goals, and vision. So, the next time you feel overwhelmed by decisions or stuck in a forest of options, take a moment to consult your compass—your "why." Let it guide you, clarify your path, and remind you of what's most important.

Because with a clear purpose, you're not just hiking through life and business—you're on a meaningful, intentional, and uniquely yours journey. And as long as you're holding that compass, you'll always know which way to go.

Avoiding the Siren Call of Shiny Objects

Ah, the siren call of shiny objects. They glimmer in the distance, whispering promises of success, innovation, and Instagram-worthy accolades. For entrepreneurs, these distractions can take many forms—a trendy new market, a too-good-to-be-true opportunity, or the sudden urge to start selling artisanal socks because, well, everyone else seems to be doing it.

Here's the thing: shiny objects aren't inherently bad. Sometimes, they lead to growth and excitement. But more often than not, they're detours that pull you away from your purpose and leave you wondering why you're knee-deep in wool blends instead of focusing on what really matters.

The Allure of Artisanal Socks

Let's unpack the sock scenario for a moment. You've built a solid business—maybe in web design or organic skincare—but then you notice a sudden explosion of artisanal sock sellers. Their Instagram feeds are a mosaic of colorful knits, happy feet, and hashtags like #SockGoals. You think, *"I could do that. It looks fun. And profitable! Who doesn't need socks?"*

Before you know it, you're researching knitting machines and pondering slogans like *"Socks That Rock."* The problem? Socks have absolutely nothing to do with your core business or your "why."

Why Shiny Objects Are So Tempting

Shiny objects are enticing because they promise novelty and excitement—two things that can feel scarce when you're in the trenches of your daily grind. They're also great at masking themselves as opportunities. After all, isn't entrepreneurship about seizing opportunities?

Well, yes. But it's also about discerning which opportunities align with your purpose and which are just distractions dressed up in pretty packaging.

How to Stay Focused on Your Compass

When you are tempted by a shiny object, pause and consult your "why." Ask yourself:

- Does this align with my core purpose and values?

- Will this contribute to my goals for myself and my business?

- Am I genuinely passionate about this or chasing it because it looks fun or trendy?

If the answers don't resonate with your purpose, it's best to let the shiny object pass. Sure, those sock sellers might be thriving, but they're running their race—not yours.

The Cost of Distraction

Pursuing shiny objects can pull valuable time, energy, and resources away from what really matters. Instead of deepening your impact or growing your business in meaningful ways, you're spreading yourself thin—and likely ending up with a closet full of unsold socks.

Staying True to Your Path

The key to avoiding the siren call of shiny objects is staying rooted in your "why." Your purpose acts as an anchor, keeping you steady even when the winds of distraction blow fiercely.

So, the next time you feel tempted to veer off course—whether it's for artisanal socks, gourmet pet treats, or the latest TikTok trend—take a moment to reflect. Is this a shiny object, or is it a genuine opportunity?

Because at the end of the day, success isn't about chasing trends—it's about staying true to the journey you've chosen. And while socks are lovely, they probably aren't the key to fulfilling your deepest purpose.

Staying Aligned in a Noisy World

In a world brimming with advice, trends, and opinions, staying true to your purpose can feel like trying to hear your favorite song in the middle of a family Thanksgiving—while Uncle Gary insists you'd make a fortune selling decorative soap on Etsy. The noise is constant, the distractions plentiful, and the unsolicited advice often just confusing enough to sound plausible.

But here's the thing: you don't have to take every suggestion or follow every trend. Staying aligned with your purpose means tuning out the noise and checking in with yourself before making decisions, big or small.

The Gut-Check Method

Think of your gut as your internal compass. When faced with a decision, pause and ask yourself: *"Does this feel right?"* Not in a "will it make me rich?" way, but in a "does this align with who I am and what I want to create?" way.

If the idea fills you with genuine excitement and resonates with your purpose, that's a green light. If it makes you hesitate, grimace, or picture Uncle Gary saying "I told you so," it's worth reconsidering.

Ask the Big Questions

When the gut check isn't enough, try these purpose-focused questions:

- *Does this align with my core values?*

- *Will this move me closer to my long-term goals?*

- *Does this reflect the kind of business or life I want to build?*

These questions act as a filter, sifting out the noise and highlighting what's truly worth pursuing.

Ignore the Thanksgiving Soap Sellers

Let's circle back to Thanksgiving, that annual showcase of well-meaning but utterly baffling advice. Your cousin insists you should pivot your business to cater exclusively to left-handed people. Aunt Doris thinks you'd make a killing selling gluten-free cupcakes shaped like dinosaurs. And Uncle Gary? He's still on about the soap.

Here's your strategy: smile, nod, and politely ignore them. Not every idea—even the well-intentioned ones—deserves your time or energy. Remember, *they're not steering your ship; you are.* Sometimes, the simplest approach is the most effective. Before making a decision, ask yourself: *Does this feel right?* Not "Does this seem popular?" or "Would this impress people?" but *"Does this resonate with my purpose and values?"*

If the answer is yes, proceed with confidence. If it's no—or if you feel a pang of doubt—give yourself permission to step back and reevaluate.

Tuning Out the Noise

Staying aligned in a noisy world isn't about building walls or ignoring feedback entirely. It's about knowing which voices to listen to—your own, above all—and which to let fade into the background.

Because at the end of the day, your purpose is the song you're meant to hear. And while Thanksgiving advice and shiny objects might try to drown it out, you have the tools to stay in tune: gut checks, big questions, and a healthy dose of humor about Uncle Gary's soap empire.

Rebuilding Passion: Reigniting the Spark Without Setting the House on Fire

Running a business can feel a lot like tending a garden. When you first start out, everything is fresh, exciting, and full of possibility. You plant seeds, water them diligently, and marvel at the first signs of growth. But then life happens. Weeds creep in. The weather doesn't cooperate. Before you know it, the joy you once felt is buried under a tangled mess of tasks, deadlines, and maybe a touch of burnout.

But here's the good news: just like with a garden, it's never too late to rediscover the joy.

Finding Fulfillment in the Day-to-Day

Reigniting your passion doesn't require grand gestures or sweeping changes. Often, it starts with reconnecting to the small, everyday things that first drew you to your business—the parts that made you smile, laugh, or feel a sense of pride.

Take gardening, for example. Let's say you used to love tending to your plants, but over time, the chore of pulling weeds and keeping everything alive began to overshadow the fun. One day, you decide to give it another go—this time with no pressure to achieve perfection. You dig your hands into the soil, rediscover the earthy smell of a freshly turned bed, and find quiet satisfaction in watching something you've nurtured come to life.

Your business works the same way. Somewhere in the weeds of invoices, meetings, and endless emails, there's still that spark—the reason you started in the first place. Finding it again requires stepping back, clearing some of the clutter, and remembering what you loved about the work.

Reconnecting with What You Love

Here are a few simple ways to rediscover fulfillment in the day-to-day:

1. **Reflect on Your "Why"**: Take a moment to think about what inspired you to start your business. Was it the joy of creating? The thrill of helping others? Revisit those feelings and ask yourself how you can bring them back into your daily work.

2. **Celebrate Small Wins**: When you're in the thick of things, it's easy to overlook progress. Take time to acknowledge even the tiniest victories—whether it's a satisfied client, a well-executed project, or simply making it through a tough week.

3. **Do What You Love (Again)**: Focus on the parts of your business that excite you most. If you love brainstorming new ideas but hate account-

ing, delegate the latter and spend more time on the former.

The Joy of Nurturing Passion

Rediscovering your passion isn't about avoiding the weeds altogether—it's about managing them so they don't choke the joy out of your work. When you reconnect with the parts of your business that light you up, you'll find that even the less glamorous tasks feel more manageable.

Passion isn't a one-time fix; it's something you nurture continuously. Just like a garden, it needs regular care and attention. But with a little effort—and maybe a few weeds pulled along the way—you can reignite that spark and enjoy the daily beauty of what you've built.

Because at the end of the day, it's not just about running a business—it's about loving the life it helps you create. Once you've rediscovered your "why," the real magic happens when you integrate it into your daily operations. Think of it like adding a secret ingredient to your favorite recipe—it doesn't change the structure, but it transforms the experience, making everything more enjoyable and fulfilling.

Work on What Excites You

Start by prioritizing projects that genuinely excite you. These are the tasks that make you feel alive—the ones that remind you why you started your business in the first place. Maybe it's brainstorming innovative ideas, working directly with clients, or developing new products. Whatever it is, carve out time for these activities.

And let's not forget the flip side: delegating the things that don't excite you. If spreadsheets make your head spin or you'd rather attend a mime convention than reconcile your books, it's time to let someone else handle the accounting. Trust me, there's a special breed of person who *loves* balancing columns and tracking expenses. Let them have their fun while you focus on what fuels your passion.

Align Your Team

Purpose isn't just for you—it's for your team, too. When everyone understands and embraces your "why," it creates a sense of alignment and motivation that makes the daily grind feel less, well, grind-y.

Start by sharing your rediscovered purpose with your team. Explain how it shapes the direction of your business and invite them to think about how their roles connect to the bigger picture. Encourage them to bring their own passions into their work, and watch as the energy and creativity multiply.

Purpose-Driven Projects

Another way to infuse purpose into your operations is to focus on projects that reflect your values. For example:

- If your "why" is about helping others, prioritize initiatives that directly impact your clients or community.

- If creativity is your spark, dedicate time to projects that allow for innovation and experimentation.

- If family time is a top priority, consider streamlining your operations to free up evenings and weekends.

Purpose-driven work not only feels more rewarding but also inspires everyone around you—clients, team members, and even the UPS guy dropping off your latest shipment.

The Joy of Letting Go

And let's circle back to delegation for a moment. Delegating isn't just about freeing up your schedule—it's about creating space for the things you love. So, go ahead: hand off those monotonous tasks that drain your energy. Whether it's hiring a virtual assistant for admin work, a bookkeeper for your finances, or a copywriter for your marketing, think of it as reclaiming your brainpower for the things that matter most.

Besides, do you really want to spend another Tuesday night staring at a spreadsheet, wondering why Excel hates you?

A Purposeful Daily Routine

Finally, consider how you can weave purpose into your everyday routine. Maybe you start each day by revisiting your goals, setting intentions, or working on something that excites you. Maybe you end each day by reflecting on how your work contributed to your purpose.

The point is to make purpose a living, breathing part of your work—not just an abstract idea but a tangible, energizing force that guides everything you do.

Small Wins, Big Impact

Passion doesn't always come roaring back like a fireworks display. Often, it sneaks in quietly, sparked by small, purposeful actions that remind you of what you love about your work. Think of it like pancakes. Sure, pancakes are fine on their own—perfectly serviceable. But add a handful of chocolate chips, and suddenly, they're not just pancakes; they're a revelation.

In the same way chocolate chips elevate breakfast, small wins can transform your day. These wins don't need to be grand or headline-worthy. They can be as simple as completing a task you've been avoiding, receiving a heartfelt thank-you from a client, or finally figuring out how to set up that email automation that's been mocking you for weeks.

Each small victory builds momentum, rekindling the spark that might have dimmed over time. It's not about overnight transformation; it's about making consistent, meaningful progress—one chocolate chip at a time.

Celebrating the Little Things

Here's the secret: Celebrate those wins. All of them.

- Sent an email you've been procrastinating on? Victory.

- Got through a meeting without checking your phone? Heroic.

- Took 15 minutes to focus on a task that actually excites you? Pure genius.

Acknowledging these moments, no matter how small, creates a ripple effect. The more you recognize what's going well, the more motivated you'll feel to keep building on that success.

Infusing Purpose into the Everyday

Small wins are especially powerful when they align with your rediscovered purpose.

- If helping others is your "way," celebrate the moments when you've made a tangible difference, no matter how small.

- If creativity lights your fire, cherish those bursts of inspiration that add a touch of magic to your work.

- If balance is your goal, recognize the significance of taking a guilt-free break in the middle of the day.

By tying these small actions to your larger purpose, you're not just rebuilding passion—you're making it a natural part of your daily life. The beauty of small wins is that they're cumulative. One tiny chocolate chip of success leads to another, and before you know it, you've created a stack of pancakes so delightful that you're practically giddy.

This momentum doesn't just reignite your passion; it also creates a sense of progress and fulfillment that carries you through the challenges. Because when you're focused on celebrating the little things, the big picture feels a lot less overwhelming.

Rediscovering Your North Star

Reassessing your "why" is a bit like cleaning out a closet. At first, it might feel overwhelming, even a little daunting. But as you sift through the mess, you start rediscovering treasures you forgot you had—like that perfect jacket you'd been searching for or the notebook filled with long-forgotten ideas. Sure, you'll find a few mismatched socks and items that have outlived their purpose, but that's part of the process too.

Your purpose is no different. It's not about throwing everything away and starting fresh. It's about uncovering what still fits, what still inspires you, and letting go of what no longer serves you. The beauty of purpose is that it's not static. Just as your closet evolves with the seasons, your "why" shifts and grows as you navigate life's changes. This isn't a one-and-done exercise. It's an ongoing process of reflection, adjustment, and renewal. And that's a good thing—it keeps you aligned, energized, and moving toward the life and business you've always envisioned.

No matter how far you feel from your original purpose, it's still there, waiting patiently like an old friend you haven't called in too long. The kind of friend who doesn't judge you for the time apart but greets you warmly when you reconnect.

So, take the time to rediscover your "why." Dust it off, nurture it, and let it guide your decisions, work, and life. Because when you're aligned with your purpose, the path forward becomes clearer and more fulfilling.

A Hopeful Note

You don't have to have everything figured out right away. Just start where you are. Reconnect with what matters most, celebrate the small wins, and trust that each step you take brings you closer to the business—and life—you've always dreamed of.

Because your "why" isn't just a goal: it's your North Star, guiding you through every twist and turn. And when you follow it, you're not just moving forward—you're moving forward with purpose, passion, and joy.

Chapter Four

The Power of Letting Go

A Practical Guide

The Art of Letting Go Without a Nervous Breakdown

LETTING GO IS HARD. Whether it's a childhood toy, you swore had magical powers, a petty grudge you've nurtured like a bonsai tree or an old sweater you haven't worn in years but *might* need for some future, highly specific occasion—it's human nature to cling to things long past their prime.

For entrepreneurs, this instinct often extends to their businesses. We grip our work with a white-knuckled intensity, convinced that if we don't do it all ourselves, the whole operation will collapse faster than a Jenga tower during an earthquake. It's as though we're trying to singlehandedly steer a cruise ship while also managing the buffet, entertaining passengers, and, for good measure, scrubbing the deck.

Spoiler alert: It doesn't work.

Letting go isn't just about delegating a few tasks or outsourcing the things you dread (though let's be honest, that's part of it). It's about rethinking how you approach your business entirely. It's about stepping back, trusting your team, and creating systems that allow your business to thrive without you hovering like a nervous parent watching their teenager take the wheel for the first time.

This chapter is your guide to letting go—not in a "throw your hands up and hope for the best" kind of way, but with practical strategies that ensure your business runs smoothly, efficiently, and, yes, joyfully, even when you're not in the driver's seat.

Because here's the truth: holding on too tightly isn't a badge of honor. It's a surefire way to burn out. And letting go? That's where the real magic happens. It's what allows you to create not just a successful business but one that supports the life you want to live.

Why Handing Over the Reins Feels Like Freefalling

Letting go isn't easy. For many entrepreneurs, the mere thought of loosening their grip on the business feels like stepping out of a perfectly good airplane and hoping the parachute works. It's thrilling, yes—but also terrifying, disorienting, and accompanied by a nagging voice in your head whispering, "Are you sure this is a good idea?"

Nowhere is this fear more palpable than in the entrepreneurial identity crisis.

The Entrepreneurial Identity Crisis

Running a business is personal. For most founders, it's not just what you do—it's who you are. You've poured your heart, soul, and probably more late nights than you'd care to admit into building this thing. Letting go can feel a bit like sending your kid off to college: you know they need independence to thrive, but you can't shake the image of them living on instant noodles and forgetting to do laundry.

Will the business survive without you meddling in every little detail? Will the team make the right decisions? And, perhaps most haunting of all: Who am I if I'm not the one running the show?

The Reluctance to Let Go: A Deeply Human Tale

As an entrepreneur, the idea of stepping back from your business can feel as unnatural as an actor exiting the stage before delivering their grand monologue. You've worn every hat—marketer, accountant, janitor, and therapist on more occasions than you'd like to admit. Whether calming a frazzled employee or consoling a high-strung client, you've been the glue holding everything together. Handing off those responsibilities feels like abandoning the play before the final act.

And then there's control. Oh, sweet, exhausting control. Micromanaging might leave you drained, but at least it feels predictable. You know the work is done "right" (by your standards, of course), even if it means checking every email draft or personally ensuring the coffee maker is descaled correctly. Trusting someone else to uphold your meticulously crafted standards? That feels a bit like freefalling without a safety net—thrilling in theory but nerve-wracking in practice.

Let's not forget the emotional attachment. Your business, after all, isn't just any old enterprise; it's your baby. It started as an idea, nurtured by sleepless nights and endless cups of coffee, and grew into something you're immensely proud of. Letting someone else take the reins can stir up emotions like leaving your toddler with a new babysitter for the first time. Will they care as much as you do? Will they pick up on all the quirks and nuances that make your business tick?

And then there's that nagging little voice in your mind: What if the business can function perfectly well without me? It's the ultimate existential crisis for a founder—this unsettling fear that your indispensability might be, well, dispensable. If the business thrives in your absence, does that mean you're not needed?

These feelings—complex, messy, and entirely human—are why stepping back often feels harder than the actual work itself. But here's the thing: recognizing these fears is the first step toward addressing them. Because while your business may always feel like your baby, it's also something designed to grow, evolve, and thrive. And just like a proud parent watching their child take their first steps, there's beauty in letting go—even if it initially feels a little terrifying.

Here's the good news: letting go doesn't mean losing your identity. It means redefining it. Just as sending a kid off to college isn't the end of parenting but the start of a new phase, stepping back from the day-to-day grind of your business allows you to focus on the bigger picture.

Letting go isn't about abandoning your work; it's about trusting it to grow and evolve under the care of others. And who knows? Your business might just surprise you, thriving in ways you never imagined—much like that college kid who somehow turns out okay, despite the ramen phase.

Common Fears

Let's get one thing straight: the fears that come with letting go are entirely normal. You're not the first entrepreneur to wake up in a cold sweat wondering, *"What if they mess up?"* Or to feel a twinge of existential dread thinking, *"What if they realize I'm just making this up as I go?"*

The truth is, these fears aren't a sign of failure—they're a natural part of transitioning from doing *all the things* to trusting others to help steer the ship. So, let's unpack a few of the most common ones.

"What if they mess up?"

This is the big one, isn't it? You've spent years building your business, and the thought of someone making a mistake on your watch feels about as pleasant as stepping on a Lego barefoot.

Here's the thing: they *will* mess up. At some point, someone will send an email with a typo, forget to CC the right person, or use Comic Sans in a presentation. (Yes, it still exists.) Mistakes are inevitable because humans are, well, human.

But here's the twist: mistakes are also how people learn. Just like you didn't get everything right the first time (remember your early attempts at invoicing?), your team needs the space to stumble and grow. Trust that they'll get it right more often than not—and when they don't, you'll all survive.

"What if I'm no longer needed?"

Ah, the classic entrepreneur's nightmare: your team gets so good at their jobs that they no longer need you. It's easy to conflate being "needed" with being valuable, but let's flip the script.

If your team can thrive without you micromanaging every detail, that's not a threat—it's a triumph. It means you've built something sustainable, something bigger than yourself. And it doesn't mean you're irrelevant; it means you've leveled up. Now, you get to focus on the vision, strategy, and growth of your business—the parts only you can do.

So, instead of asking, *"What if I'm not needed?"* try this: *"What incredible things can I do now that my team's got this?"*

"What if they realize I don't know everything?"

Just a heads-up: they already know.

Your team knows you're not an omniscient guru who holds all the answers—and guess what? That's okay. Leadership isn't about knowing everything; it's about empowering others, making informed decisions, and being humble enough to say, *"I don't know, but let's figure it out."*

In fact, admitting you don't have all the answers can make you more relatable and approachable as a leader. It shows your team that asking questions, making mistakes, and learning together is okay.

These fears aren't a sign that you're doing something wrong. They're a sign that you care—about your business, your team, and the legacy you're building. Letting go doesn't mean abandoning control; it means shifting your focus to where it matters most.

So the next time one of these fears pops up, take a deep breath, chuckle at the absurdity of Comic Sans, and remind yourself: letting go is hard, but it's also the gateway to freedom, growth, and a business that thrives.

The Myth of Perfection

Let's talk about perfectionism—that sneaky little saboteur that whispers, *"If it's not flawless, it's not good enough."* It's the voice that convinces you to redo a task three times to ensure it's "just right," even when "just right" is entirely subjective and possibly imaginary.

Perfectionism doesn't just slow you down; it amplifies every fear about letting go. After all, how can you trust someone else to handle something if you're convinced that only *you* can do it perfectly?

Picture this: you're creating a simple spreadsheet for tracking project deadlines. It starts innocently enough—a few columns, some basic data. But then perfectionism kicks in. Three hours later, you've color-coded the cells into a gradient that rivals a sunset, added custom fonts for each column heading, and meticulously aligned every single number.

You sit back, proud of your masterpiece, only to realize two things:

1. No one else will ever look at this spreadsheet.

2. You've just burned three hours on something that could've been done in fifteen minutes.

Perfectionism, my friends, is a time thief. And the worst part? It convinces you that you're being productive when, really, you're just polishing something no one else cares about.

Why Perfectionism Fuels Fear

When you hold yourself to impossible standards, you naturally assume others will fall short. It's easy to think, *"If I can't get it perfect, how can I trust anyone else to?"* But here's the kicker: perfection isn't required for success.

Sure, attention to detail is important, but perfectionism often leads to diminishing returns. Spending hours tweaking something already "good enough" doesn't improve your business—it just drains your energy and reinforces the idea that you have to do it all yourself.

Letting go means embracing imperfection—not in the sense of doing sloppy work, but in recognizing that *good enough* is often, well, good enough. Trusting your team to handle tasks their way (even if it's not your way) frees you to focus on the bigger picture.

After all, the goal isn't to create a perfectly formatted spreadsheet; it's to build a thriving, sustainable business. And that business doesn't need you to micromanage every detail—it needs you to lead, inspire, and let others step up.

The Cost of Holding On

Let's be honest: holding on too tightly feels safe. It gives you a sense of control, like gripping the reins of a runaway horse. But here's the rub—clutching those reins doesn't stop the horse from galloping at breakneck speed. It just leaves your hands raw, your arms aching, and your confidence shaken.

The same is true for entrepreneurs who refuse to let go. Over-control might seem like the responsible thing to do, but the hidden costs can quietly pile up until they're impossible to ignore.

Burnout: The Inevitable Crash

When you're answering every email, signing off on every project, and monitoring every decision, you're essentially running a marathon with no finish line. Sure, you can keep going for a while—powered by adrenaline and caffeine—but eventually, you'll hit a wall.

Burnout isn't just about feeling tired: it's about losing the passion and energy that brought you to your business in the first place. And ironically, the more you try to control everything, the more likely you are to burn out, leaving you unable to do the work you care about most.

Stagnation: The Business Bottleneck

By refusing to let go, you risk becoming the bottleneck in your own business. Every decision, task, and email has to go through you, slowing down progress and stifling innovation.

It's like insisting on driving the car while also navigating, checking the tire pressure, and making sandwiches for the road trip. Eventually, something's going to give—and it's probably going to be your sanity.

Exhaustion: The Endless Inbox

A special kind of fatigue comes from answering every email personally, especially when half of them start with "Just circling back..." or "Per my last message..." The mental load of managing every little thing is overwhelming, leaving you with no energy for the big-picture thinking that actually moves your business forward.

Why Letting Go Is Worth It

The cost of holding on is steep—burnout, stagnation, and exhaustion don't just affect you; they affect your team, your business, and even your personal life. But here's the silver lining: every time you let go of something, you reclaim a little piece of your time, energy, and sanity.

Delegating tasks, empowering your team, and trusting others isn't just good for your business—it's good for you. It allows you to step back, focus on what truly matters, and rediscover the joy that brought you to entrepreneurship in the first place.

Because the goal isn't to be the busiest person in the room; it's to build a business that works for you—not the other way around.

Empowerment vs. Delegation: The Difference Between Sharing the Load and Passing the Buck

Delegation is often hailed as the solution to entrepreneurial overload, and while it's undeniably helpful, it's not always enough. At least, it's not the way most people do it. Traditional delegation tends to look something like this: you assign tasks to others but keep the real control—the decision-making power—firmly in your grasp.

It's like letting a child "help" bake cookies. Sure, you let them sprinkle the chocolate chips or stir the batter, but only after you've measured every ingredient, cracked the eggs with surgical precision, and kept a hawk-like watch to ensure no rogue sprinkles end up on the floor. They might feel involved, but let's be honest—you're still doing all the heavy lifting.

This, dear reader, is the problem with delegation as most of us know it.

What Delegation Misses

When delegation stops at task-doling, you're still the bottleneck. Every decision, every tweak, every "final approval" comes back to you. Instead of freeing up your time, this approach keeps you at the center of every process, like a nervous baker who can't resist checking the oven every five minutes.

The problem? This isn't sharing the load—it's passing it around just long enough for it to land back in your lap. And while it might look like teamwork, it often leaves your team feeling more like assistants than trusted collaborators.

Enter Empowerment

Empowerment takes delegation to the next level. Instead of just handing off tasks, you're giving your team the autonomy to make decisions, solve problems, and take ownership of their work.

Think of it as stepping back and letting someone else take the lead on baking those cookies—not just stirring the batter but deciding how much chocolate to add, setting the oven temperature, and maybe even trying a new recipe altogether. Sure, they might make a mess (or use an alarming number of sprinkles), but they'll also learn, grow, and contribute in surprising ways.

Why Empowerment Matters

Empowerment isn't about relinquishing all control; it's about trusting others to handle meaningful responsibilities without micromanaging. When your team feels empowered, they're more engaged, more motivated, and—here's the kicker—better equipped to make decisions without your constant input.

This doesn't just lighten your load; it creates a ripple effect of creativity and innovation throughout your business. Suddenly, you're not the only one steering the ship—you've got a capable crew working alongside you, each one confident in their ability to navigate.

Empowering your team might feel risky at first. But as you watch them rise to the occasion, you'll realize it's not just good for your business—it's good for you. And as for those cookies? They might not be perfect, but they'll be filled with more collaboration, creativity, and—dare I say it—joy.

The Magic of Empowerment

Empowerment is where the real magic happens. It's not just about handing off tasks; it's about giving your team members ownership, responsibility, and trust. When done well, empowerment transforms your business from a one-person juggling act into a thriving ecosystem where everyone plays a vital role.

Think of it like teaching someone to fish. Sure, you could hand them a fillet every time they're hungry, but that's exhausting for you and limiting for them. Empowerment is teaching them to fish—and here's the kicker—they might end up catching better fish than you ever imagined.

When you empower someone, you're doing more than delegating. You're giving them the freedom to make decisions, solve problems, and take full ownership of their role. It's a shift from *"Here's what I need you to do"* to *"Here's the outcome we're aiming for—how do you think we can achieve it?"*

The result? Your team members feel trusted and valued, which boosts their confidence, creativity, and commitment. And for you, it means fewer decisions to make, fewer fires to put out, and more time to focus on the big-picture stuff that only you can tackle.

Now, empowerment doesn't guarantee perfection. Just like fishing, there will be times when your team misses the mark or reels in something unexpected. But that's part of the process—and often where the best growth happens.

And here's the best part: once they've got the hang of it, your team might start catching bigger, better fish than you ever could. They'll bring fresh ideas, new approaches, and insights you never considered, all because you gave them the space to step up and thrive.

Building a Culture of Empowerment

I've realized empowerment isn't just about stepping back and hoping for the best. It's not a matter of tossing tasks to your team like frisbees and expecting them to miraculously land in the right places. No, true empowerment is about setting your team up for success with the care and precision of someone orchestrating a dinner party—clear direction, subtle support, and a toast for every small victory.

First, there's the matter of providing clear goals. Imagine asking someone to bake you a cake but forgetting to mention that you're allergic to walnuts or that it's for a party celebrating your cat's birthday. Chaos, right? The same applies to your team. They need to know not just what they're doing but why it matters. When everyone understands the bigger picture, they're far more likely to create something meaningful—and less likely to add metaphorical walnuts where they shouldn't.

Then comes the delicate art of offering support without slipping into the role of a relentless backseat driver. Picture yourself on a road trip, guiding someone from the passenger seat. You're there to help with the map and point out the occasional landmark—not to grab the wheel every time you think they're taking a turn too wide. Being available for guidance while resisting the urge to hover is key. Your team doesn't need constant oversight; they need the confidence to know they've got this (and maybe a quick GPS check if they don't).

And finally, the most overlooked part of empowerment is celebrating wins and embracing lessons. Recognizing achievements—even the small ones—can do wonders for morale. It's like clinking glasses at the end of a dinner party to toast the host who made it all happen. And when things don't go as planned? Well, that's not a failure; it's a learning opportunity, a chance to figure out what went wrong and how to do better next time. After all, even the best chefs burn a soufflé now and then.

When you create a culture of empowerment, something magical happens. Your team doesn't just grow stronger—they thrive. They become more confident, capable, and invested in the business's success. And in the process, you get the ultimate reward: a thriving team that allows you to step back, breathe a little easier, and maybe even enjoy a soufflé of your own.

Empowering your team isn't about giving up control; it's about redefining what leadership looks like. It's about creating an environment where everyone feels capable and inspired to do their best work, knowing they have your trust and support.

And who knows? They might just teach *you* a few new fishing tricks along the way.

How to Empower Effectively

Empowerment isn't just about saying, *"Here, you handle this,"* and hoping for the best. It's a deliberate process that requires clear communication, mutual trust, and a willingness to let go of micromanagement (no matter how tempting it might be). Done well, it's like planting seeds in a well-tended garden: with the right care, your team will flourish, and your business will thrive.

Here's how to empower your team effectively:

1. Define the Destination, Not the Route

When assigning responsibilities, focus on the outcomes you're aiming for, not the exact steps to get there. Think of it as giving your team a map with the destination circled but letting them choose the best path.

For example, instead of saying, *"Use this template, follow these steps, and submit it by Friday,"* try, *"Here's the goal we need to achieve—how do you think we should approach it?"* This invites creativity, problem-solving, and ownership.

2. Trust Them to Do the Job

Here's the tricky part: once you've handed over a task, resist the urge to hover. Trusting your team doesn't mean abandoning them, but it does mean stepping back enough to let them find their way.

Remember, mistakes are part of the process. They're not a sign of failure; they're opportunities for growth. So when someone stumbles, offer guidance, not criticism, and watch as they come back stronger and more confident.

3. Provide Resources, Not Just Assignments

Empowerment doesn't mean throwing someone in the deep end and hoping they figure out how to swim. Set your team up for success by giving them the tools, information, and support they need to do the job well.

This might include:

- Sharing context or background information about the task.

- Providing access to training, tools, or mentors.

- Offering a clear point of contact for questions or guidance.

When your team feels equipped, they're more likely to take ownership—and less likely to panic.

4. Celebrate Wins and Learn from Missteps

Empowerment thrives in a culture of recognition and reflection. Celebrate your team's successes, no matter how small, and make it a point to acknowledge their contributions.

And when things don't go as planned, don't swoop in with an *"I told you so."* Instead, frame it as a learning moment. Ask questions like, *"What do you think we could do differently next time?"* to foster growth and continuous improvement.

5. Model Empowerment Yourself

Empowerment starts at the top. If you want your team to embrace responsibility and ownership, lead by example. Show them what it looks like to trust others, take calculated risks, and handle challenges with grace.

When your team sees you empowering others—whether it's delegating to them or collaborating with peers—they're more likely to follow suit.

Why Empowerment Matters

Effective empowerment isn't just a strategy; it's a mindset. It's about shifting from control to collaboration, from managing tasks to inspiring people. When you empower your team, you're not just lightening your workload—you're building a culture of trust, innovation, and shared success.

And best of all? You'll finally have time to focus on what you do best, while your team takes pride in what they're capable of achieving.

Define Clear Outcomes

One of the secrets to effective empowerment is learning to let go of the *how* and focus on the *what*. Instead of dictating every detail or micromanaging each step, set a clear vision for the result you want to achieve and give your team the freedom to figure out the best way to get there.

Think of it like handing someone a treasure map. You point to the X, marking the spot, explain why it's important, and then step back, trusting them to navigate the terrain in their own way. Sure, they might take a few unexpected paths or use a shortcut you hadn't considered, but the outcome remains the same—and sometimes even better than you envisioned.

Why Clear Outcomes Matter

There's a certain brilliance to focusing on results rather than getting lost in the weeds of how things are done. It's a bit like being an orchestra conductor: your job isn't to teach the violinists how to hold their bows or remind the trumpeters not to blow too hard. Your job is to guide the symphony, to ensure it sounds magnificent, and then step back and let the musicians do what they do best.

When you prioritize clear outcomes, something remarkable happens. First, you encourage creativity. Give your team a destination, but let them chart the route, and you'll often find they come up with ideas and solutions you never would have considered. It's like telling someone to bake a cake for a party but leaving the flavors up to them—what you get might just surprise you (in the best way possible).

Then there's the matter of fostering ownership. When you trust people to achieve a goal without micromanaging every step, they don't just do the work—they take pride in it. Suddenly, the project becomes theirs, not just something they're doing for you. It's a subtle but powerful shift, like letting someone borrow your car and finding they've not only returned it washed and fueled but also fixed that squeaky windshield wiper you've been ignoring for months.

And let's not forget the sheer joy of saving yourself time and energy. By focusing on outcomes, you're no longer bogged down in the minutiae of how every task gets done. You don't need to hover over spreadsheets, debate font choices for the company newsletter, or agonize over whether emails should end with "Best regards" or "Warm wishes." You get to step back, take a deep breath, and trust that the work will get done—and done well.

The best part? It's a win-win. Your team grows stronger, more capable, and more confident in their abilities. Meanwhile, you find yourself with a bit more mental space, a touch more freedom, and perhaps even the time to rediscover hobbies like gardening or finally finishing that half-read novel on your nightstand.

In the end, focusing on clear outcomes isn't just good for your team—it's good for you. And really, who wouldn't want to lead an orchestra where everyone plays beautifully while you sit back and enjoy the music?

How to Define Clear Outcomes

1. **Be Specific About the Result**: Instead of saying, *"I need this report done,"* clarify what you're looking for:

   - *"I need a summary of our monthly sales performance, highlighting trends and any areas for improvement."*

2. **Explain the Why**: People are more motivated when they understand

the purpose behind a task.

- ○ *"This report will help us refine our strategy for next quarter and identify growth opportunities."*

3. **Set Expectations for Quality and Timeline**:

- ○ *"I'd like a polished version ready by next Tuesday. Please include visuals where possible, but keep it concise."*

4. **Let Go of the Process**: Resist the urge to dictate every step. Trust your team to find their way to the result—even if their method looks a little different from yours.

Trusting the Journey

Yes, letting go of the "how" can feel unnerving at first—especially if you're used to being involved in every detail. But by focusing on outcomes, you create a space where your team can shine. They'll feel more invested, you'll feel less stressed, and together, you'll achieve results that make everyone proud.

And who knows? You might even learn a thing or two from the creative routes your team takes to get there.

Independent Thinking

Empowering your team to think independently is like handing them the instruction booklet for an IKEA dresser and saying, *"You've got this!"* At first, it might feel a bit like watching toddlers assemble it—there will be some confusion, a couple of missing screws, and probably a lot of sideways glances at those enigmatic little diagrams.

But here's the thing: they'll get better with practice (and a bit of trial and error). They'll learn to spot the patterns, figure out what works, and, most importantly, gain confidence in their problem-solving ability without constantly turning to you for guidance.

The Magic of Teaching Problem-Solving

Watching your team learn to handle problems independently is a peculiar kind of joy. It's the same satisfaction you might feel when a child learns to ride a bike without needing you to jog alongside, breathlessly shouting encouragement. Suddenly, they're off and pedaling, and you're left marveling at the freedom—for both of you.

When your team learns to tackle challenges independently, something wonderful happens: you get your time back. You no longer have to field endless interruptions with the dreaded question, "What should I do about this?" Instead, you can pour your energy into bigger-picture goals—or even indulge in a cup of coffee that doesn't require reheating three times.

But it's not just about freeing up your calendar; it's also about building confidence. As your team learns to trust their instincts, they start taking ownership of their decisions. The nervous "Am I doing this right?" morphs into a decisive "Here's what I recommend." It's like watching someone graduate from training wheels to full-on BMX tricks—they're not just getting by; they're thriving.

And then there's the unexpected bonus: innovation. When people feel empowered to solve problems without constantly checking in, they bring fresh perspectives and creative solutions you might never have considered. It's a bit like finding a surprise flavor in your favorite ice cream shop—unexpected, delightful, and a reminder that stepping back often leads to the best discoveries.

So, by giving your team the tools and confidence to navigate challenges, you're not just lightening your load. You're fostering a culture where ingenuity thrives, confidence blossoms, and you finally have time to breathe—and maybe even crack open that book you've been meaning to read. Because when everyone learns to pedal on their own, the whole team moves forward faster, and you're free to enjoy the ride.

The IKEA Method of Empowerment

Here's how to encourage independent thinking without letting things spiral into chaos:

1. **Provide Context, Not Solutions**: Instead of jumping in with the answer, give them the background they need to figure it out themselves.

    ○ Example: *"Here's what we're trying to achieve and why it's important. What options do you see?"*

2. **Normalize Mistakes as Part of the Process**: Let them know it's okay to try, fail, and learn along the way. Share a story about one of your own "learning experiences" to make it relatable.

3. **Offer Guidance Without Hovering**: Be available for questions, but resist the urge to take over. Encourage them to come to you with possible solutions rather than just problems.

    ○ Example: *"What's your recommendation?"* or *"What do you think would work best?"*

4. **Celebrate Progress, Not Perfection**: Acknowledge their efforts, even if the IKEA dresser has a drawer that doesn't quite slide right. The goal is growth, not perfection.

The Results of Independent Thinking

Over time, your team will surprise you. That dresser will be fully assembled—and with practice, they'll move on to tackling more complex furniture (or in this case, business challenges).

Encouraging independent thinking might feel slow at first, but it's an investment in their growth and your sanity. Because when your team learns to solve problems on their own, you're no longer the bottleneck—you're the leader, guiding them to success while keeping your hands blissfully free of those tiny IKEA wrenches.

Give Credit Where It's Due

Acknowledging success—whether it's a game-changing achievement or a small, everyday win—is one of the easiest and most effective ways to empower your team. When people feel appreciated, they're not just motivated to do their best—they're inspired to keep doing better.

Think of it like this: if someone handed you a trophy every time you successfully parallel parked, you'd probably become the world's most enthusiastic parker. Okay, maybe that's a stretch, but the point stands—celebrating wins, no matter how small, builds confidence and momentum.

Celebrate Like They've Discovered a Cure for Bad Coffee

The key is to make recognition fun, meaningful, and proportionate. Did someone knock a client presentation out of the park? Throw a mini celebration—maybe a round of applause at the next team meeting or a thoughtful email shoutout. Did someone save the day with a last-minute fix to the website? That's worth a coffee gift card or even just a hearty "You rock!"

Even small victories deserve acknowledgment. Did someone submit a report on time despite juggling five other tasks? Break out the metaphorical champagne (or at least the good snacks). Treat these moments like they've cracked the code on how to make office coffee taste like an artisanal latte—because, for your team, they're just as satisfying.

The Power of Recognition

There's something undeniably magical about giving credit where it's due. It's not just a kind gesture or an obligatory "thanks" tacked onto the end of a meeting;

it's a force that shapes the very culture of your business. Recognizing your team's contributions does more than make them feel good—it creates an environment where people feel seen, valued, and genuinely motivated to keep bringing their best to the table.

Start with confidence. When someone's efforts are acknowledged, it's like handing them a trophy labeled *"You Did That, and It Was Brilliant."* Suddenly, their sense of competence gets a boost. They're no longer second-guessing their work or worrying about whether anyone noticed—they know they've nailed it. And with each nod of appreciation, their self-assurance grows, making them all the more likely to excel in future endeavors.

Then there's initiative. Recognizing people's hard work has a curious way of inspiring them to take on even more challenges. It's as if your appreciation lights a spark, and they're suddenly fueled to go above and beyond. Knowing that their efforts won't vanish into the abyss but will be celebrated makes them eager to step up, try new things, and contribute meaningfully.

And let's not overlook loyalty, the unsung hero of team dynamics. A simple *"Great job on that project"* or *"Your idea really made a difference"* can have an outsized impact on building trust and commitment. It's the kind of gesture that says, *"I see you, I value you, and I'm grateful for what you bring to the table."* Over time, this consistent acknowledgment fosters a deep sense of loyalty, turning your team into a tightly-knit group that genuinely cares about the business—and each other.

Giving credit isn't about inflating egos or doling out empty compliments; it's about creating a culture where people feel empowered, appreciated, and ready to tackle whatever comes next. And the best part? The positive ripple effects extend far beyond the individual. A team that feels valued is a team that performs better, collaborates more seamlessly, and, dare I say it, actually enjoys coming to work.

So go ahead—dish out the recognition generously. Clap for their wins, big and small. Because when your team feels like rock stars, they'll bring the house down every single time. And as their leader, you get to bask in the glow of a thriving, motivated team that's ready to take on the world.

How to Make Recognition Meaningful

1. **Be Specific**: Instead of saying, *"Good job,"* highlight exactly what they did and why it mattered.

   ○ *"Your quick thinking during the client call really saved the day. Great work!"*

2. **Make It Timely**: Don't wait until the next quarterly review to give credit. Recognize achievements as they happen to keep the momentum going.

3. **Tailor It to the Individual**: Some people love public praise, while others prefer a quiet word of acknowledgment. Know your team and celebrate in ways that resonate with them.

Why It's Worth It

When you celebrate successes, you're not just handing out compliments—you're reinforcing the behaviors and attitudes that make your team thrive. And let's face it: a culture of appreciation is way more fun than one of constant criticism or endless grind.

So go ahead: cheer for the small wins, applaud the big ones, and treat every success like they've unlocked the secret to banishing bad coffee forever. Because, in their own way, they kind of have.

Systems of Independence: How to Set Your Business to "Autopilot" Without Crashing

There's a moment in every entrepreneur's journey when the dream of "autopilot" beckons. You envision your business humming along smoothly while you sip coffee on a sunny patio, blissfully unaware of the daily grind happening in your absence. The reality? If you don't have solid systems in place, "autopilot" can feel more like letting go of the wheel and hoping for the best.

This is where processes come in—a safety net that keeps your business running efficiently without requiring you to personally oversee every detail.

Building a Safety Net with Processes

Creating reliable systems is like assembling IKEA furniture with clear instructions. When you have a step-by-step guide, the assembly goes smoothly, and you end up with a functional piece of furniture (and maybe even your sanity intact). Without instructions? You're left staring at a pile of oddly shaped pieces and a single Allen wrench, wondering if the designers were secretly trying to test your patience.

In business, processes act as your instruction manual. They provide clarity, consistency, and direction, ensuring that tasks get done correctly—even when you're not there to oversee them.

The Unsung Glory of Processes

Processes might not be the most glamorous aspect of running a business, but let me assure you, they are the unsung heroes of order, efficiency, and sanity. Picture them as the sturdy scaffolding that holds up a skyscraper, the invisible thread that keeps a quilt from unraveling, or perhaps the trusty recipe card that ensures your grandmother's cookies taste the same every single time. Without them, chaos reigns, and no one—least of all you—has time for that.

First and foremost, clear processes reduce chaos. Imagine running a relay race where no one knows who's carrying the baton next, or worse, where the baton even is. That's what a business without processes looks like: frantic, inefficient, and full of unnecessary drama. With solid processes in place, your team knows exactly what to do and how to do it. They don't need constant hand-holding, last-minute interventions, or a miracle to keep things moving. Everyone's on the same page, and crises become the exception, not the rule.

Then there's the beauty of time saved. Processes are the ultimate antidote to reinventing the wheel every time a task comes up. Instead of spending hours figuring out "How did we do this last time?" or scrambling to cobble together a solution, workflows are streamlined, predictable, and gloriously efficient. It's like following a well-worn hiking trail instead of bushwhacking your way through an overgrown forest. The path is clear, and the journey is smoother—and faster.

And let's talk about scalability. As your business grows—and grow it will—processes become the key to maintaining quality and consistency. Whether you're doubling your staff or expanding to new markets, established workflows ensure that everything runs just as smoothly at twice the size. Think of it like running a bakery: with the right processes, you can scale from baking a dozen cookies to a thousand without sacrificing flavor or texture. It's the difference between organized expansion and an operational meltdown.

Processes might not steal the spotlight, but they are the bedrock of a thriving, sustainable business. They reduce chaos, save precious time, and provide the structure needed to grow without losing your mind—or your quality standards. So embrace them, refine them, and let them work their quiet magic. Because when your processes hum along like a well-oiled machine, you're free to focus on what really matters—like savoring the cookies your business baked at scale.

How to Build Effective Processes

1. **Document Everything**: Start by writing down the steps for key tasks—everything from onboarding new clients to handling customer complaints. Include as much detail as necessary to make the process repeatable.

   ○ Pro Tip: If it feels like you're over-explaining, you're doing it right. Remember, clarity trumps brevity when it comes to instructions.

2. **Involve Your Team**: Ask the people who are actually doing the work for input. They'll often have valuable insights about what works and what doesn't.

3. **Test and Tweak**: No process is perfect out of the gate. Let your team try it out, gather feedback, and make adjustments as needed.

4. **Use Tools to Streamline**: From project management software to automation tools, there's no shortage of resources to help implement and maintain your processes.

The IKEA Metaphor in Action

When your business has clear processes, it's like assembling furniture with a detailed guide and all the right tools. Your team can handle the task confidently, knowing exactly what goes where. Without processes, they're left fumbling through the chaos, guessing at the outcome and secretly wondering if that extra screw was supposed to go somewhere important.

Why Systems of Independence Work

With well-built processes, your business can operate efficiently without you hovering over every decision. It frees you to focus on growth, strategy, or simply taking a well-deserved break, knowing the safety net is there to catch any wobbling pieces.

So, take the time to assemble your processes with care—and don't forget to include clear instructions. After all, your business deserves more than a single Allen wrench and a wish for the best.

Automation as a Silent Partner

If processes are the instruction manual for your business, automation is the trusty robot assistant you never knew you needed. It quietly handles repetitive tasks, keeps workflows humming along, and frees you from the tyranny of having to remember every little detail—like which client needed a follow-up yesterday or when it's time to reorder printer paper.

Think of automation as the opposite of your overworked Post-It note system. You know the one: a rainbow of sticky reminders plastered on your desk, computer, and, occasionally, your coffee mug. It's colorful, chaotic, and somehow manages to lose the one note you actually need. With automation, you can finally retire those overburdened Post-Its and let technology do the heavy lifting.

The Delightful Efficiency of Automation

Let's take a moment to appreciate the quiet brilliance of automation. It's not flashy or loud, but it's the workhorse of the modern business world—the equivalent of having a reliable assistant who never takes a coffee break, forgets an instruction or misplaces a sticky note. Automation doesn't just streamline workflows; it transforms how you and your team spend your time, energy, and brainpower.

First, there's the marvel of reduced dependency. Automation sweeps in and takes care of the routine tasks that used to tug at your sleeve like a needy toddler. Whether it's scheduling emails, tracking invoices, or sorting data, these once-demanding chores no longer require your constant attention—or anyone else's, for that matter. This liberates your team to focus on higher-value work—the kind of creative, strategic tasks that humans excel at, like brainstorming the next big idea or solving complex problems.

Then there's the glorious reduction in errors. Humans are lovely creatures, but let's be honest, we're prone to the occasional blunder. We misplace files, miss deadlines, and sometimes write "teh" instead of "the." Automation, on the other hand, is unfailingly precise. It follows instructions flawlessly, whether it's processing orders or generating reports. No more sticky-note disasters, forgotten follow-ups, or moments of "Oh no, did I send that email to the wrong person?" With automation, those hiccups are a thing of the past.

And let's not forget the time-saving magic of it all. Automation streamlines workflows with the efficiency of a Swiss train schedule. The hours you once spent on repetitive tasks are suddenly freed up for more meaningful pursuits—whether that's strategic planning, team collaboration, or finally taking that lunch break you've been skipping. Imagine it: you, enjoying a sandwich while sitting down, instead of eating over your keyboard like a feral office creature.

The beauty of automation lies in its simplicity and its ability to quietly enhance every corner of your business. It reduces dependency, minimizes errors, and saves time, all while giving you the space to focus on what truly matters. So let automation take the reins on the mundane tasks, and enjoy the newfound freedom to tackle the exciting stuff—or relish that long-overdue lunch. Trust me, your keyboard will thank you for it.

Where to Start with Automation

1. **Communication**: Use tools like Slack or Microsoft Teams to keep everyone connected without endless email chains.

2. **Scheduling**: Automate meeting bookings with tools like Calendly, so you're not stuck in the back-and-forth of "Does Tuesday at 3 work for you?"

3. **Client Management**: CRM platforms like HubSpot or Zoho can track interactions, send automated follow-ups, and ensure nothing slips through the cracks.

4. **Financials**: Tools like QuickBooks or Xero can handle invoicing, expense tracking, and financial reporting faster than you can say, *"Wait, where did I put that receipt?"*

5. **Marketing**: Automate social media posts, email campaigns, and analytics with platforms like Buffer, Mailchimp, or Hootsuite.

The Silent Partner Effect

The beauty of automation is that it works quietly in the background, like a silent partner who doesn't demand equity or complain about the office coffee. It doesn't call in sick, doesn't need vacation days, and never misses a deadline. And while it won't replace the need for human creativity and decision-making, it does eliminate the need for you to spend three hours manually updating spreadsheets or sending reminders.

Imagine a world where you don't have to rely on a precariously balanced stack of sticky notes to keep your business running. Where workflows happen seamlessly, deadlines are met automatically, and you can finally see your desk again. That's the power of automation: it replaces chaos with calm, giving you the time and mental space to focus on what really matters.

So, go ahead—give those Post-Its a well-deserved break. They've served you valiantly, but it's time to bring in the robots.

Document Everything (Without Losing Your Sanity)

Documenting your business processes might not sound like the most thrilling activity, but it's a game-changer. Think of it as writing a recipe for your favorite dish—clear enough for others to replicate but flexible enough to allow for a sprinkle of their own creativity.

Without documentation, your team is left to guess at how things should be done, which leads to inconsistent results, frustration, and an alarming number of "quick questions" that land squarely in your inbox. But with a little effort upfront, you can create guides that not only save time but also empower your team to take ownership of their work.

The Understated Brilliance of Documentation

Documentation may not seem like the most thrilling part of running a business, but it's a quiet powerhouse that keeps everything humming along smoothly. Think of it as the unsung hero of consistency, efficiency, and scalability—a trusty manual ensuring everyone knows how the machine works, no matter who controls it.

First, let's talk about consistency. One of the great gifts of documentation is its ability to keep processes uniform, even when different people are handling them. It's like having a recipe for your business—follow the steps, and you'll always end up with the same delicious result, no matter who's in the kitchen. Without it, you risk a chaotic game of "telephone," where each person's interpretation of a task deviates slightly until the original intent is lost in translation. With documentation, there's no guesswork—just clarity and consistency.

Then there's the efficiency factor. When processes are clearly documented, your team spends less time asking for guidance and more time getting things done. There's no need for a scavenger hunt to determine who can complete a task or where that critical file is stored. Instead, everyone has access to the same playbook, which means fewer interruptions, faster workflows, and a lot less head-scratching. It's the difference between wandering aimlessly through an unfamiliar city and having a map that gets you exactly where you need to go.

Perhaps the most impressive benefit of documentation is scalability. As your business grows, documentation ensures that new hires can hit the ground running without requiring hours of one-on-one training. It's like handing them a guidebook that says, "Here's how we do things around here—welcome aboard." Processes become replicable, training becomes smoother, and you avoid the growing pains that often accompany expansion.

In short, documentation is the foundation of a business that thrives no matter who's in the driver's seat. It brings consistency to your operations, efficiency to your workflows, and scalability to your growth. And while it may not steal the spotlight, its impact is felt in every corner of your business—quietly, reliably, and without a single misplaced sticky note. So embrace the power of documentation, and watch as it transforms chaos into order, one well-documented process at a time.

How to Document Without Overcomplicating It

1. Keep It Simple

Start with the basics. Use plain language, bullet points, or checklists to break tasks into manageable steps. Think of it as writing a recipe for a beginner:

- *"Preheat oven to 350°F"* = *"Open the client CRM and select the 'New Lead' tab."*

- *"Mix ingredients until smooth."* = *"Enter client details and attach relevant documents."*

The goal isn't to create a masterpiece; it's to make the process easy to follow, even for someone new.

2. Use Visual Aids

Where possible, add screenshots, flowcharts, or short videos to clarify tricky steps. Imagine trying to bake a soufflé with only written instructions versus seeing a picture of what it's supposed to look like. Visual aids take the guesswork out of the process.

3. Invite Feedback

Once you've written the process, share it with your team and ask for input. They're the ones in the trenches, so they'll have valuable insights about what works and what needs tweaking. Plus, involving them fosters a sense of collaboration and buy-in.

4. Leave Room for Flexibility

No one likes rigid, step-by-step instructions that feel more like a chore than a guide. Leave room for team members to add their own flair, as long as they achieve the desired outcome. It's the difference between saying, *"Follow this exactly,"* and *"Here's the goal—feel free to adjust as needed."*

5. Store It Somewhere Accessible

Create a central repository for your documentation—a shared drive, a project management tool, or a digital notebook. Label things clearly so that team members don't have to play detective to find what they need.

The Recipe for Success

With good documentation in place, your team will be able to follow your "recipes" with confidence. They'll understand what's expected, feel empowered to take charge, and know where to turn if they need help. And the best part? You won't have to hover over their shoulder like a nervous sous-chef.

So, roll up your sleeves, start jotting down those processes, and get ready to hand off your secret sauce. Just don't forget to leave room for a little extra seasoning along the way.

Encouraging Problem-Solving

Empowering your team to solve problems independently is one of the most transformative steps you can take as a leader. It's about giving them the tools, authority, and confidence to tackle challenges head-on—without having to run every decision past you like you're the gatekeeper of the universe.

Here's the kicker: when you truly encourage problem-solving, you might just discover that your team's solutions are better than anything you'd have come up with. Yes, you read that right. Prepare yourself for the humbling—and oddly delightful—moment when someone wows you with an idea so good you have to wonder why *you* didn't think of it first.

The Tools for Independent Problem-Solving

To create a problem-solving powerhouse, you need to equip your team with three essentials:

1. **Clear Guidelines:** Define boundaries for decision-making. Let your team know which decisions they can handle solo and which ones require your input. Think of it as giving them the sandbox and saying, *"Build whatever you want in here, but stay out of the neighbor's flower bed."*

2. **Access to Resources:** Ensure they have the tools, information, and support to make informed decisions. This might mean sharing data, providing training, or even introducing them to that one elusive contact who knows *everything* about the billing system.

3. **Authority to Act:** Give them the green light to implement their solutions without constant approval. It's empowering, motivating, and saves everyone a lot of time.

When Problem-Solving Surprises You

Here's the fun part: the more you encourage independent problem-solving, the more likely your team is to surprise you—in the best way. They'll come up with creative, efficient, and sometimes downright brilliant solutions.

Case in point: you might find yourself marveling at a process improvement that eliminates hours of unnecessary work, all because someone on your team dared to think differently. Or they might develop a strategy so effective that you must sheepishly admit, *"I never would have thought of that."*

And if you're lucky, they'll do it with enough flair to make you genuinely excited to see what they tackle next. Encouraging problem-solving doesn't just lighten your load; it fosters a culture of trust and innovation. Your team becomes more confident, capable, and invested in the business's success.

And as for you? You get to step back, focus on the bigger picture, and occasionally bask in the glow of being the leader who made it all possible. Plus, there's the added bonus of learning from their solutions—and maybe even stealing a few ideas for yourself. (Don't worry; we won't tell.)

The Freedom of Trust: Trust Is the Glue (and Sometimes the Duct Tape)

Trust is often touted as the foundation of every successful team, and it's true—it holds everything together. But let's not sugarcoat it: trust can also feel a little scary.

It's not unlike lending your favorite book to a friend. You hand it over with a mix of hope and dread, wondering if they'll treat it with the same reverence you do—or if you'll get it back with a bent cover, coffee stains, and a suspiciously absent final chapter. Trust involves risk, vulnerability, and a leap of faith that things will turn out okay.

Why Trust Feels Scary

For entrepreneurs, the fear of trusting others often boils down to three big concerns.

Trusting others isn't always easy—especially when you've poured blood, sweat, and far too many late nights into building your business. It's like handing over the keys to a car you built with your bare hands. Suddenly, every fiber of your being screams, *"What if they crash it?!"* And yet, without trust, you're stuck driving every mile yourself.

Here are the three big fears that keep entrepreneurs clutching the steering wheel with white-knuckled determination:

1. Fear of Losing Control

This is the quintessential entrepreneur's fear—the moment of letting go of the reins and saying, *"This is yours now—don't break it."* It's like handing someone your prized collection of vintage vinyl records and hoping they won't scratch a single groove.

Control feels safe. It's predictable. But it's also exhausting, and trust means stepping back to let others take the lead. Yes, it's terrifying, but it's also liberating. The sooner you loosen your grip, the sooner you'll realize that your team is more than capable of holding the reins—and they might even steer better than you in certain situations.

2. Fear of Mistakes

Here's a hard truth: when you trust others, they *will* mess up occasionally. It's inevitable. But here's the thing—so will you. Think back to your own journey. How many times did you stumble, learn, and come back stronger?

Trust isn't about creating a mistake-free zone but a safe space where mistakes become lessons. Allow your team the same grace to learn and grow. After all, if every stumble were a disaster, humanity would still be living in caves, trying to figure out fire.

3. Fear of Being Disappointed

Let's be honest: trust doesn't always pay off immediately. Sometimes, you'll hand over a project, a task, or that metaphorical book you love, and it'll come back... well, less than pristine. But here's the twist: more often than not, people rise to the occasion.

When you trust your team, you allow them to surprise you—in the best way. Yes, there might be a bent cover or a misplaced chapter along the way, but the magic happens when they exceed your expectations. And when they do, it's not just rewarding for you—it's transformational for them.

Trust is a leap of faith, but it's one worth taking. Sure, there will be moments when you cringe, you're tempted to snatch back the reins, and maybe even when you mutter, *"I knew this would happen."* But those moments pale in comparison to the freedom, growth, and creativity that trust unlocks—for your team and for you.

Because when you trust, you're not just building a business—you're building something far more powerful: a team that thrives, innovates, and carries the torch forward. Even when you're not there to hover nervously over every detail.

The Leap of Faith

Trust isn't about being naive or blindly optimistic. It's about recognizing that, yes, there's risk involved—but the rewards far outweigh it. When you trust your team, you're not just delegating tasks; you're empowering them to contribute, innovate, and take ownership.

And when trust works, it's nothing short of transformative. Your team becomes more confident, your workload lightens, and your business starts to feel less like a constant juggling act and more like a well-oiled machine.

Here's the other thing about trust: it's not just glue that holds everything together—it's also duct tape for when things inevitably go awry. Trust doesn't eliminate problems, but it does create an environment where mistakes are addressed with collaboration rather than blame. It keeps your team resilient, adaptable, and ready to tackle challenges head-on.

Trust: The Ultimate Freedom

Yes, trust feels scary because it requires letting go of control. But when you lean into it, you discover something incredible: freedom. Freedom to focus on the bigger picture, freedom to innovate and dream, freedom to know your business is in good hands, even when you're not there.

So, lend out that metaphorical book. Sure, it might come back with a few creases, but often, it'll come back with notes in the margins that make it even better than before.

Building a Culture of Accountability

Trust and accountability go hand in hand. Without accountability, trust becomes shaky at best and disastrous at worst. But when you create a culture where both thrive, your team feels supported, empowered, and inspired to do their best work—even when things don't go perfectly (which they won't, because, you know, *humans*).

Let's start with a universal truth: mistakes are inevitable. They're as much a part of life as taxes, spilled coffee, and that one sock that vanishes in the wash. The key is fostering an environment where mistakes are treated as learning opportunities, not catastrophes. After all, the goal is to avoid Titanic-level disasters—not to turn every small bump into an iceberg moment.

Tips for Fostering Trust and Accountability

1. Set Clear Expectations

Ambiguity is the enemy of accountability. Make sure your team knows exactly what's expected of them, from deadlines to deliverables to the level of quality you're aiming for.

- Think of it like giving someone a treasure map: clear instructions get them to the X. Vague ones? They're wandering around the woods looking for buried gold that doesn't exist.

2. Offer Constructive Feedback

When mistakes happen (and they will), use them as opportunities to guide and grow. Constructive feedback isn't about pointing fingers; it's about offering insights that help your team improve.

- Example: *"Great effort on the presentation! Let's tighten up the messaging next time to wow the client."*

- Bonus Tip: Sandwich criticism between positive comments. It softens the blow and keeps morale intact.

3. Allow for Mistakes (But Learn from Them)

Mistakes aren't the enemy—repeating them without reflection is. Encourage your team to own their missteps, analyze what went wrong, and brainstorm how to do better next time.

- *"Mistakes are fine. Just try not to sink the ship—or at least let's patch the holes quickly if you do."*

4. Celebrate Accountability

Acknowledge when someone takes ownership of their work or goes above and beyond. Whether it's a shoutout in a meeting or a quick thank-you email, recognition reinforces accountability and builds trust.

- Example: *"Great job taking the lead on that project! Your initiative really made a difference."*

5. Lead by Example

Accountability starts at the top. When you admit your own mistakes, follow through on commitments, and remain transparent about your decisions, your team will be more likely to do the same.

- Bonus Humor: *"If I can admit I once spent three hours formatting a spreadsheet no one asked for, you can admit that typo in the client email."*

Why Accountability Matters

A culture of accountability isn't about avoiding mistakes—it's about creating a team dynamic where trust and responsibility flourish. When everyone understands their role, feels supported, and knows they can learn from failure, your business runs smoother, your team feels stronger, and you're not stuck micromanaging like a nervous captain navigating icy waters.

So, set the course, hand over the wheel, and let your team steer with confidence. After all, even the Titanic could have avoided disaster with better communication and a bit more accountability.

The Rewards of Trust

Ah, the sweet, sweet rewards of trust. Picture this: you, lounging on a sun-soaked beach, a frosty drink in hand, toes buried in warm sand as the waves lazily lap the shore. Your phone? It's not buzzing incessantly with urgent messages because your team has everything under control. In fact, they're running the show so smoothly that you're not even tempted to "just check in real quick."

This isn't a fantasy—it's the very real freedom that comes from trusting your team. When you let go of micromanaging and empower your people to take ownership, you gain something invaluable: time. Time to focus on strategic thinking, time to indulge in personal hobbies, or—brace yourself—even time for a genuine, work-free vacation.

The Freedom of Time: Rediscovering Your Life Beyond the Grind

Ah, the elusive freedom of time—the entrepreneurial Holy Grail. It's the dream that likely inspired you to start your business in the first place: the ability to focus on the big picture, rekindle old passions, and, dare I say it, take a vacation where your laptop stays blissfully untouched. Trusting your team and letting them handle the day-to-day tasks doesn't just give you time—it gives you back yourself.

First comes the luxury of strategic thinking. With your team handling the operational minutiae, you finally have the bandwidth to zoom out and focus on the bigger picture. Suddenly, those ambitious plans for growth, the exploration of new opportunities, or even that passion project you've been pushing aside don't feel so out of reach. It's like stepping out of a forest to realize you can finally see the entire landscape. You're not just putting out fires anymore; you're building something lasting, something extraordinary.

Then there's the sheer joy of reconnecting with personal hobbies—the ones you loved before your business started eating your waking hours like a particularly greedy Pac-Man. Maybe it's gardening, painting, or finally nailing that elusive sourdough starter you've been dreaming about. Whatever it is, trust gives you the mental and physical space to do it without guilt or distraction. Imagine yourself getting lost in an afternoon of creativity, your phone silenced and the weight of a thousand tasks temporarily lifted from your shoulders. It's not just leisure—it's therapy.

And let's not forget the pièce de résistance: vacations that don't involve your laptop. Trust means you can step away from your business without worrying that everything will collapse in your absence. Picture yourself lounging on a beach, the most pressing decision of the day being whether to order the piña colada or the mojito. No frantic phone calls, emergency emails, or scrambling to resolve client issues from a hotel room. Just you, the ocean breeze, and the sweet relief of knowing your team has everything under control.

Freedom of time isn't just about having more hours in the day—it's about reclaiming those hours for what truly matters. Strategic thinking, personal hobbies, guilt-free vacations—all of it becomes possible when you build a team you can trust. And as you rediscover this freedom, you'll find that life outside of work isn't just possible—it's wonderfully, gloriously worth it. So go ahead, dream a little bigger, pick up that paintbrush, or book that tropical getaway. Your business—and your sanity—will thank you for it.

The Beach Scene

Let's return to that whimsical vision of the entrepreneur on the beach. While you're sipping a mango mojito and debating whether to nap or read a book, your team is back at the office (or working remotely, if that's how you roll), expertly handling everything from client calls to invoicing.

Your business hums along like a well-oiled machine, thanks to the trust and systems you've put in place. You're not just surviving the entrepreneurial grind—you're thriving, living the life you imagined when you first started this journey.

And the best part? Your team feels just as empowered as you do. They're confident, capable, and thriving under the trust you've shown them. It's a win-win for everyone—and isn't that the dream?

The rewards of trust aren't just about making your life easier (though that's a big part of it). They're about creating a sustainable, balanced, and enjoyable business for everyone involved. Trust frees you to be the leader, the visionary, and the human you were meant to be.

So go ahead: pour yourself that mojito, let your team shine, and enjoy the freedom you've worked so hard to build.

Trust as a Two-Way Street

Trust isn't a one-sided affair. It's a dynamic exchange, like a good dance—both parties must be in sync, and at least one of you must resist the urge to step on toes. When leaders extend trust to their team, they often find trust reciprocated with enthusiasm, commitment, and innovation.

At first, though, it might feel a bit awkward. Imagine two people learning to tango: one hesitates, the other oversteps, and before you know it, someone's apologizing profusely while trying not to trip over their own feet. But with time, practice, and a little rhythm, the dance becomes seamless—a natural partnership where both parties move together effortlessly.

How Trust Flows Both Ways

Trust, as it turns out, is a bit like a sourdough starter. You have to nurture it, feed it regularly, and resist the urge to peek too often or over-fiddle. But when you get it right, it produces something magical. The good news? Unlike sourdough, it doesn't involve quite as much flour all over your kitchen counter.

Let's start with the leader—you. Trust begins with you showing faith in your team's abilities. And I don't just mean the casual "Oh, they'll figure it out" kind of faith. I mean the tangible, unmistakable kind that says, *"I believe in you."* It's like handing someone the keys to your beloved vintage car and saying, "Take her for a spin." Scary? A little. Necessary? Absolutely.

When you do this, you're doing more than assigning tasks. You're empowering your team to take ownership. You're saying, *"This isn't just a job; this is your chance to shine."* And here's the surprising part—they often do. They step up, they take charge, and they put in their best effort because they know you trust them to succeed.

Now, let's talk about the team. When people feel trusted, something remarkable happens. They start to care. Not just about clocking in and out or avoiding mistakes, but about genuinely contributing to the business's success. It's as if you've handed them not just the keys to the car, but the map and a playlist for the road trip. Suddenly, they're going the extra mile (sometimes literally), taking creative risks, and delivering results that make you wonder why you didn't trust them sooner.

Here's where it gets exciting: trust doesn't just result in hard work—it breeds innovation. In a supportive, trusting environment, your team feels safe to experiment. They're not paralyzed by the fear of failure or worrying that a minor misstep will send them hurtling off the career ladder. Instead, they're brainstorming, problem-solving, and trying out ideas that may be wildly unexpected—and wildly successful.

And often, those ideas lead to breakthroughs you wouldn't have achieved on your own. It's a humbling moment when your team's solution outshines anything you'd envisioned, but it's also exhilarating. It's the entrepreneurial equivalent of watching someone use your sourdough starter to bake the perfect loaf while you're still fussing over uneven crusts.

The takeaway? Trust isn't just something you give—it's something that grows, reciprocates, and creates extraordinary results when nurtured. And unlike sourdough, it doesn't require you to leave it in a warm cupboard overnight. Though, come to think of it, a little warmth never hurt anyone.

The Dance of Trust in Action

Picture this: you hand over a key project to a team member, giving them the autonomy to manage it from start to finish. At first, it's a bit wobbly—like trying to salsa after years of doing the robot. They might ask a few questions, take a tentative step, or even stumble. But as they gain confidence, their movements become smoother, more assured.

Soon, they're not just executing tasks; they're leading with creativity and flair, spinning ideas you never would have imagined. And you? You're no longer hovering awkwardly at the sidelines. You're dancing alongside them, enjoying the rhythm of a well-functioning team.

Why Trust as a Two-Way Street Matters

Trust is, at its heart, a reciprocal arrangement. It's not something you just dole out like candy at Halloween, nor is it something you demand with the stern authority of a bouncer guarding an exclusive club. It's a two-way street, a mutual exchange that, when done right, leads to some pretty extraordinary things—for your team, for you, and for your business.

Let's start with **mutual growth**. When you trust your team, they grow. It's that simple. By handing over real responsibilities and saying, *"I believe you can handle this,"* you give them the space to step up, learn, and thrive. And here's the beautiful symmetry: as they grow, so does your business. Their growth fuels innovation, strengthens operations, and even frees you to focus on bigger-picture goals. It's like planting seeds in a garden—what you nurture in them blossoms across the whole business.

Next up: **stronger relationships**. Trust is the glue that holds your team together (and, on bad days, it's the duct tape that keeps things from falling apart). When people feel trusted, they also feel valued. They know they're not just cogs in the machine but essential contributors whose skills and opinions matter. This sense of value fosters loyalty, respect, and camaraderie—making your workplace culture one where people actually enjoy coming to work. Shocking, I know.

And then there's the holy grail of teamwork: **shared success**. The best outcomes happen when everyone contributes their unique talents and perspectives. Trust creates an environment where collaboration thrives, where ideas bounce around like popcorn kernels in hot oil until something wonderful emerges. When you let people bring their best selves to the table, the resulting success feels sweeter because it's genuinely collective.

So, why does trust as a two-way street matter? Because it's the thing that transforms your team from a group of people doing tasks into a unified force driving your business forward. It's growth. It's connection. It's a success. And, perhaps most importantly, it's the key to ensuring that you—and everyone else—actually enjoy the journey.

Like any good dance, trust takes practice. There will be missteps along the way—awkward pauses, a few clumsy moves—but the more you practice, the smoother it gets. Over time, trust becomes second nature, creating a partnership that's as rewarding as it is effective.

So, take that first step, extend your hand, and start the dance. You might just be surprised by how gracefully your team moves when given the chance.

Letting Go Without Losing It

Letting go. For entrepreneurs, two little words can feel like the weight of the world. You've built this business, poured your soul into it, and now someone's asking you to trust other people with it? It sounds risky, reckless even—like handing over your baby and hoping it doesn't come back with crayons in its mouth.

But here's the thing about letting go: it's not about losing control. It's about gaining freedom. When you empower your team, you're not abandoning your business to chaos; you're giving it room to grow and thrive in ways you couldn't achieve alone.

Picture your team as a group of skilled kite-flyers. If only you let them, they're capable, creative, and perfectly positioned to catch the wind. By empowering them, you're handing over the string and watching them take your business to new heights. They'll stumble occasionally—every kite does—but when they catch the breeze, it's a marvel to behold.

Letting go also means you're no longer the bottleneck. You no longer have to review every email, approve every decision, or sign off on every minor detail. Instead, you've built systems, empowered your people, and created a business that can scale beyond what your own two hands can manage. It's no longer just *your* business; it's a collaborative enterprise, one that grows not just because of you, but because of everyone involved.

The Gift of Headspace

And then there's the most underrated benefit of all: headspace. When you're not mired in the minutiae of daily operations, you finally have the time and clarity to focus on the big picture. Maybe you'll tackle that next big opportunity, explore a passion project, or—dare we say it—take a proper vacation. Imagine sitting on a beach somewhere, drink in hand, while your team runs the show back home. The business is thriving, and so are you.

Letting go is a bit like flying a kite. At first, it feels counterintuitive to release the string. Your instinct is to hold on tightly, keeping it close, where you can monitor every little twitch. But as you loosen your grip and let the string out, something magical happens: the kite soars higher, catching the wind and dancing in the sky.

The connection is still there—you haven't cut the string—but you've given it the freedom to rise. And in doing so, you've unlocked its potential. Your business, like that kite, doesn't just float—it soars.

An Encouraging Note

Letting go isn't easy, but it's transformative. It's not about stepping back; it's about stepping up—into a role where you lead with vision, trust, and confidence in your team. And who knows? You might just find that your team surprises you, rising to the occasion in ways you never imagined.

So go ahead, loosen the string. Your business is ready to catch the wind, and you're ready to enjoy the view. After all, isn't that why you started this journey in the first place? For the freedom to dream, to create, and, yes, to let it all soar?

Chapter Five

Streamlining Your Business

The Beautiful Simplicity of a Well-Oiled Machine

LET ME TELL YOU about when I tried assembling a bookshelf that came with *very* optimistic instructions. The box promised a "quick and easy assembly," which, in hindsight, was the first red flag. Three hours, two stripped screws, and one completely backwards shelf later, I found myself on the floor, staring at an inexplicably leftover wooden dowel, and wondering if furniture companies were just trolling us for sport.

Navigating that assembly process felt less like building a piece of furniture and more like competing in an Olympic-level endurance event. The final result was... well, let's call it "functional," though it definitely leans a bit to the left, both literally and politically. And the worst part? The whole ordeal could have been avoided if the instructions had been clearer—or if I'd resisted the urge to "figure it out as I go."

Now, if that sounds like your business—complicated, frustrating, and prone to leaning precariously—it's not your fault. Businesses, no matter how brilliant their potential, have a sneaky way of transforming into tangled balls of yarn. Processes overlap, priorities multiply, and before you know it, you're spending more time sorting through the mess than actually running the show.

Here's the thing: streamlining a business isn't about stripping it down to the point of sterility. It's about creating simplicity amidst the chaos—untangling those metaphorical fairy lights without giving in to the very real temptation to toss them out the window.

In this chapter, we'll explore how to simplify, refine, and streamline your business so it runs like the well-oiled machine it was always meant to be. Whether it's automating repetitive tasks, trimming unnecessary steps, or just figuring out which parts of the process are absolutely essential, you'll find that elegance often hides behind a good declutter.

So, let's roll up our sleeves, put that extra wooden dowel to good use, and start building something truly functional—no leaning required. After all, the simpler your business, the freer you'll be to enjoy the entrepreneurial ride. And isn't that why you started in the first place?

Identifying Bottlenecks: Finding the Kinks in Your Hose

Bottlenecks are the great mysteries of life and business. They're those pesky chokepoints where time, resources, or your remaining slivers of sanity seem to vanish into the void, leaving you standing there, arms crossed, wondering how on earth things got so stuck.

Imagine this: you're at an airport, exhausted and ready to go home. You've survived the flight, escaped the labyrinth of duty-free shops, and now you're standing at the luggage carousel. It begins to churn, bags appear, and you think, *"Any second now, mine will arrive!"* Ten minutes pass. Then twenty. Suitcases for every other passenger roll by, including one with a hideous pattern you're sure was last seen in the '80s. But your bag? Still missing. That, dear reader, is a bottleneck.

In the world of business, bottlenecks are just as frustrating—though they usually involve fewer misplaced socks. They're the points in your processes where everything slows to a crawl, or worse, grinds to a halt. They can be as small as a single inefficient step or as sprawling as a system that hasn't worked properly since the Reagan administration.

What Are Bottlenecks?

At their core, bottlenecks are the parts of your business where progress jams up. They're like kinks in a garden hose: water (or productivity) trickles out at an excruciatingly slow pace, leaving you annoyed, parched, and tempted to throw the whole thing away.

These chokepoints can take many forms:

- A task that depends entirely on one overburdened person (often you).

- A process so convoluted it makes tax forms look breezy.

- Or a perfectly adequate system—if this were 1998.

The trick is spotting these bottlenecks before they drive you to the brink. While they might seem like minor inconveniences, left unchecked, they can clog up your entire operation.

Why Bottlenecks Happen

Bottlenecks don't just appear out of thin air; they usually sneak in thanks to three culprits:

1. **Over-reliance on a Single Step**: When one task becomes the linchpin for everything else, the entire process is at its mercy. Think of it as a traffic light stuck on red while cars pile up for miles.

2. **Outdated Systems**: Sometimes, the tools you're using are less "well-oiled machine" and more "rusty bicycle." That spreadsheet you started using five years ago? It's not handling your current volume very well, is it?

3. **Lack of Clarity**: If no one's entirely sure what the process *should* look like, it's bound to get messy. Imagine a relay race where the runners don't

know when to pass the baton—it's chaos.

Hunting Down the Hidden Bottlenecks

Identifying bottlenecks in your business is a bit like trying to solve the mystery of the missing sock. You know something's off—you feel it in the sluggish pace of progress or the mounting frustration in the air—but pinning down the exact culprit takes a bit of sleuthing. Bottlenecks have a knack for hiding in plain sight, quietly jamming up the works while everyone scrambles to notice.

Start by asking yourself, *Where are things slowing down?* These are the areas where deadlines seem to stretch endlessly, like a piece of overcooked taffy. Maybe it's a particular department that always lags behind or a recurring task that feels like wading through quicksand. Wherever the pace feels painfully slow, there's a good chance a bottleneck is lurking.

Next, tune in to the grumbles. If a process consistently makes people groan—or worse, mutter choice words under their breath—it's probably worth investigating. Frustration is a fantastic barometer for inefficiency, and let's be honest, nobody grumbles over things that run smoothly.

Then, take a closer look at your team. Is there one person who always seems buried under an avalanche of work? Someone who routinely looks like they've aged five years between Monday and Friday? If so, chances are they're at the center of a bottleneck. Overloaded team members are often stuck at the crossroads where tasks pile up faster than they can be tackled, and the whole business feels the strain.

For a more structured approach, consider mapping out your workflows step by step. Think of it as creating a treasure map to uncover the spots where productivity has been buried alive. Draw out each task, handoff, and decision point, and then look for the places where things get stuck or where steps seem unnecessarily convoluted. It might feel like a tedious exercise at first, but the "aha!" moments it reveals are well worth the effort.

Bottlenecks may be sneaky, but they're not invincible. With a bit of detective work and a willingness to dig into the details, you can pinpoint the trouble spots and clear the way for smoother, faster workflows. And who knows? In the process, you might even solve the case of the missing sock—or at least feel a little less tangled in the day-to-day chaos.

The beauty of bottlenecks is that once you've identified them, they're fixable. Yes, it might take some effort (and perhaps a bit of patience), but the payoff is enormous. Smoothing out these kinks not only makes your business more efficient—it also makes your life a whole lot easier.

So grab your metaphorical hose, unkink the trouble spots, and let the water (or workflow) flow freely again. Because when your business runs smoothly, everything feels just a little more beautiful.

Now, let's roll up our sleeves and find those kinks, shall we? Just don't blame me if your luggage is still late.

The Scavenger Hunt for Inefficiencies

Finding bottlenecks in your business can feel like a peculiar kind of treasure hunt, except instead of unearthing gold doubloons, you're uncovering things like unnecessarily complex approval chains and that one process that inexplicably requires three different logins. But fear not, dear reader, because I've assembled a handy, checklist to make this scavenger hunt as painless as possible.

Signs You've Found a Bottleneck:

1. **Tasks That Take Longer Than Cooking a Thanksgiving Turkey:** If something in your business takes hours, days, or (heaven forbid) weeks to complete, you've likely stumbled across a bottleneck. Bonus points if the process also involves as much coordination as hosting Thanksgiving dinner for your extended family.

   - *Example*: Approving expense reports that require not one, but four signatures, three of which belong to people perpetually "out of office."

2. **Processes That Involve More Back-and-Forth Than a Tennis Match:** Does a single task bounce between departments, inboxes, or, worse, Slack channels so many times you lose track of who had it last? Congratulations, you've found another bottleneck.

   ○ *Example*: Drafting a proposal that pings from marketing to sales to legal and back again, only to end up looking remarkably similar to the first draft.

3. **The Groan Factor:** Any time you mention a particular task or process and your employees respond with audible groans, eye rolls, or a palpable sense of dread, you're onto something.

   ○ *Example*: The monthly meeting that everyone seems to attend out of obligation but no one quite knows why—or what they're supposed to accomplish.

4. **The Panicked Employee Look:** If certain tasks routinely cause staff to break out in a cold sweat or mutter, "This is going to take forever," while frantically rummaging through papers, you've likely unearthed a bottleneck.

   ○ *Example*: Onboarding new clients using a system so clunky it feels like navigating with a compass and a map from 1862.

5. **"That's How We've Always Done It" Syndrome:** If a process has been in place since the dawn of your business and no one can quite explain why it works that way, you've likely got a legacy bottleneck on your hands.

   ○ *Example*: Still using a manual filing system because it "worked fine in the early 2000s."

What to Do Once You've Found a Bottleneck

Once you've identified these inefficiencies, resist the urge to weep or throw your hands up in despair. Instead, channel your inner detective and ask:

- *"Is this step necessary?"*

- *"Could this be done faster, simpler, or by someone else?"*

- *"Does this require three logins, or is one really enough?"*

Addressing bottlenecks is like tackling that cluttered drawer in your kitchen—you won't believe how much smoother life becomes when you finally clear it out. And while the process might involve a few groans of your own, the payoff will be well worth it.

So grab your metaphorical magnifying glass, put on your Sherlock Holmes hat, and start hunting down those inefficiencies. Just be prepared for the groans—they're part of the fun.

The Human Bottleneck Dilemma

Now, let's address the elephant in the room—or, more accurately, the person in the mirror. Yes, it's entirely possible that the biggest bottleneck in your business is ... you. I know, it stings a little, but bear with me.

Picture this: You're hosting a dinner party. In a burst of culinary ambition, you decide to handle everything yourself. You're chopping vegetables with the speed of a tortoise, stirring three pots at once, and simultaneously trying to plate the appetizers while also greeting guests at the door. Meanwhile, your oven timer is beeping, the soufflé is sinking, and your friends sit awkwardly in the living room wondering if they should call for pizza.

That's you, the overly ambitious cook of your business. By insisting on doing everything personally, you've inadvertently become the bottleneck, slowing down the entire operation. And just like at that dinner party, your well-meaning efforts are creating more chaos than you realize.

The Three Faces of a Bottleneck (Yes, They're Yours)

If there's one uncomfortable truth about bottlenecks, it's this: sometimes, the bottleneck is you. Yes, you, the well-meaning captain of the ship, who may unknowingly be anchoring it in shallow waters. Don't worry—you're not alone. Bottlenecking your own business is practically a rite of passage for entrepreneurs. Let's take a closer look at the usual suspects.

First up is the classic "Only I Can Do This" mentality. The inner voice whispers, "I'll just do it myself—it's faster that way." While this mindset might save a few minutes in the short term, it often causes delays in the long run. Why? Because no matter how talented, efficient, or borderline superhuman you are, you're still just one person. Trying to personally handle every decision, every task, and every email is like being the lone chef in a busy restaurant kitchen. Eventually, something's going to burn—or you will.

Next, we have the dreaded Micromanagement Madness. This one's tricky because it often comes from a place of good intentions. You want everything to be just right, so you hover over every detail, flipping metaphorical pancakes while hungry patrons wait for breakfast. But here's the rub: by micromanaging, you're not just slowing down the process—you're also sending a less-than-encouraging message to your team. When you hover, you essentially say, "I don't trust you to get this right without me." And nothing deflates morale (or creativity) quite like that.

Finally, there's Unclear Delegation, the sneakiest bottleneck of them all. Tasks pile up on your desk, not because you're a control freak, but because no one else knows they're supposed to handle them. It's the organizational equivalent of being the only person who thought to bring food at a potluck. Suddenly, you're not just cooking the meal; you're also washing the dishes, setting the table, and whipping up dessert. The result? Exhaustion, chaos, and probably some very underwhelming pie.

The good news? These bottlenecks are fixable. Recognizing them is the first step toward unclogging the works and letting your business flow more smoothly. So, take a deep breath, hand off that spatula, and let someone else flip the pancakes. You might just find that breakfast—like your business—runs a whole lot better when it's not all on your plate.

Recognizing the Signs

The human bottleneck is easy to spot if you know where to look. Ask yourself:

- Are there tasks no one else is allowed to touch?

- Does your team spend more time waiting for your approval than actually getting work done?

- Do you often work late into the night while everyone else is blissfully asleep?

If any of these sound familiar, it might be time to hang up the apron—or at least share the kitchen.

Why Letting Go Matters

Here's the thing: you don't have to be the hero of every story in your business. When you let go of the need to control every detail, you empower your team to step up, take ownership, and, dare I say, do things better than you might have done them yourself.

Yes, it's hard to trust someone else with your soufflé (or your quarterly budget), but the rewards are enormous. A business that doesn't revolve around you is a business that can grow, thrive, and yes, even survive while you're on vacation.

The Dinner Party Redemption

Now, imagine a different dinner party. This time, you've delegated tasks to trusted friends. One handles appetizers, another pours drinks, and someone else sets the table. You? You're calmly chatting with guests, enjoying the evening, and basking in the glory of a well-run event. That's what your business can feel like when you stop being the bottleneck and start being the host who trusts their team.

So, step away from the stove. Let others flip a few pancakes, stir a few pots, and handle the soufflé. You'll be amazed at how much smoother—and more enjoyable—things become when you're not trying to do it all yourself.

Process Simplification: Turning Gordian Knots Into Neat Bow Ties

Simplifying your business processes is a bit like decluttering a closet. At first glance, the mess is overwhelming—piles of mismatched shoes, sweaters you haven't worn since the Clinton administration, and at least one rogue sock you've been meaning to pair up for years. But with a little determination and a willingness to part with things that no longer serve you, you can unearth treasures you forgot you had, like those perfectly comfortable yet stylish shoes that somehow got buried under an avalanche of old gym clothes.

Business processes, much like closets, have a way of accumulating clutter. Over time, what started as a straightforward procedure turns into a convoluted mess of unnecessary steps, redundant approvals, and baffling detours. It's as if every time you solved one small problem, you tacked on another layer of duct tape and string until your once-elegant system resembled a Gordian knot of inefficiency.

But here's the thing: processes, much like closets, function best when they're streamlined, organized, and purposeful. Simplification isn't about throwing everything out and starting over; it's about identifying what's essential, what's useful, and what's just taking up space.

Take, for example, the approval process in many businesses. What should be a simple "yes" or "no" often turns into a labyrinthine ordeal involving half a dozen people, three different software platforms, and a series of emails that could rival the length of *War and Peace*. By the time the decision was made, the urgency had passed, and everyone involved had aged approximately five years.

Simplifying that process might mean consolidating decision-making authority, cutting unnecessary steps, or adopting a tool that streamlines communication. It's the business equivalent of tossing out the moth-eaten scarves and neatly folding your favorite sweaters. The result? More efficiency, less frustration, and the sudden realization that you actually enjoy opening the closet—or, in this case, tackling your workflows.

The beauty of simplification is that it doesn't just make life easier; it also uncovers hidden value. That overly complex onboarding process that drove new hires to despair? Simplify it, and suddenly you've got a team that hits the ground running. That outdated expense reporting system that required three separate spreadsheets? Streamline it, and voilà, you've freed up hours for more meaningful work (or at least for coffee breaks).

Simplification is about creating clarity and focus. It's about turning chaos into order, knots into bow ties, and frustration into something resembling joy. And while the process might involve a bit of effort—sorting through the clutter always does—the payoff is worth it. Because in the end, a simplified business is a beautiful thing: elegant, efficient, and remarkably satisfying, like finally finding those perfect shoes exactly where they're supposed to be.

Steps to Simplify Workflows: Following the Pirate Map to Buried Treasure

Simplifying workflows starts with a task that feels a bit like following one of those old, spaghetti-like pirate maps. You know the kind—the ones with wiggly lines leading in every direction, strange symbols scribbled in the corners, and an ominous "Here Be Dragons" warning somewhere along the way. Mapping out your business processes isn't far off. You're tracing the journey of a task as it weaves through your organization, dodging bottlenecks, encountering redundancies, and occasionally vanishing into the dreaded abyss of "Pending Approval."

Start by sketching out your key processes. Whether it's how invoices are handled, how projects move through your team, or even how decisions get made, lay it all out in plain view. At first, it might look like a chaotic tangle of steps that would make even the most seasoned pirate throw up their hands in frustration. But that's part of the charm—you can't simplify what you can't see.

Trimming the Fat

Once you've mapped it all out, it's time to trim the fat. This is where you take a long, hard look at each step and ask, *"Is this really necessary?"* If the answer is anything less than a resounding "Yes!" it's probably time to let it go.

Take, for example, the story of a business owner who spent two hours buying stamps. Not because stamps are particularly complicated, mind you, but because the process had somehow grown to involve an outdated approval form, a trip to three different offices, and a baffling requirement for a manager's signature. By the time the stamps were finally purchased, the value of everyone's time had far outweighed the cost of the actual stamps. Simplifying workflows means finding those absurdities and politely but firmly sending them on their way.

Streamlining Communication

Then there's communication—the lifeblood of any organization, but also, let's be honest, the source of endless inefficiency. If you've ever sat through a meeting that could have been an email (or read an email that should have been a tweet), you know what I'm talking about.

One of the easiest ways to streamline workflows is to reduce unnecessary meetings and curtail those CC-all emails that clutter inboxes with messages as informative as a fortune cookie but five times as long. Instead, focus on clear, concise communication. Use tools that centralize information, set clear agendas for meetings, and encourage brevity in written exchanges.

Imagine, for instance, a project update that says: "Deadline extended to Friday, please review section 2." Now compare that to the email equivalent of a Russian novel that meanders through every irrelevant detail before casually mentioning the new deadline somewhere in paragraph six. Streamlined communication isn't just faster; it's kinder—to your team, to their sanity, and to the planet (fewer emails, fewer headaches).

The Joy of Simplification

As you map, trim, and streamline, you'll start to notice something extraordinary: workflows that actually work. Processes that once felt like navigating a hedge maze in the dark suddenly become clear paths to productivity. Tasks that used to drain your energy now feel manageable, even enjoyable.

The beauty of simplifying workflows isn't just the time you save—it's the mental clarity you gain. It's like discovering that the pirate map wasn't leading you to a dragon's lair after all, but to a treasure chest of free time, better communication, and a business that hums along like the well-oiled machine it was always meant to be.

So grab your metaphorical compass, trace those spaghetti lines, and start digging. There's treasure buried in your workflows, just waiting to be uncovered.

The Beauty of Efficiency

Now, let's pause for a moment and imagine what your life could look like once your workflows are untangled, streamlined, and simplified. Picture this: the clock strikes noon, and instead of frantically juggling emails, approvals, and tasks that seem to regenerate like weeds in a neglected garden, you find yourself with time. Actual, glorious, unclaimed time.

Efficiency isn't just about shaving minutes off your to-do list—it's about reclaiming whole hours of your day that were previously swallowed by the administrative abyss. It's about rediscovering energy you didn't even realize you were spending, like finding loose change in the couch cushions—only this time, it's enough to buy back your sanity.

Imagine finishing your day without that nagging sense of "I still have 12 things to do," or wrapping up a project without questioning why three different departments needed to weigh in on the font choice. Efficiency isn't just practical; it's beautiful. It's the feeling of clear skies after weeks of drizzle, of walking through a door that was always open but somehow blocked by an inexplicable stack of laundry.

When your business runs efficiently, you're not just saving time—you're creating room for what really matters. Whether that's focusing on growth, nurturing creativity, or even sneaking in an afternoon nap (a rare luxury that suddenly feels possible), the beauty of efficiency is that it gives you the freedom to breathe.

So take a deep breath, look at those newly streamlined workflows, and savor the simplicity. Because when everything works as it should, you're no longer managing chaos—you're building something elegant, purposeful, and entirely your own. And isn't that what this whole entrepreneurial adventure is really about?

Leveraging Technology: Let the Robots Do the Boring Bits

Let's take a moment to appreciate how far we've come as a species. Once upon a time, people wrote letters with quill pens, dipping them carefully into ink pots, smudging their fingers, and painstakingly scrawling one word at a time. A simple thank-you note probably took half an afternoon to complete. Fast-forward to today, and we have laser printers that can churn out an entire manuscript faster than you can say, "Chapter One."

The same leap forward is possible for your business—if you let technology do the boring bits. Automation is like swapping your quill pen for a laser printer:

it frees you from the tedium of repetitive tasks so you can focus on things that actually require your brain. And frankly, isn't that what technology is for?

Think about it. How many hours have you wasted manually updating spreadsheets, sending follow-up emails, or scheduling appointments? These are the business equivalent of peeling potatoes—not difficult, but mind-numbingly time-consuming. The beauty of automation is that it swoops in like a culinary robot chef, peeling those potatoes in seconds while you focus on perfecting the recipe.

The Joy of Automation

Automation doesn't just save time; it transforms the way you work. Imagine a world where invoices are sent automatically, emails are answered with pre-set responses, and inventory is tracked by software instead of someone squinting at a clipboard.

Let's take scheduling, for instance. In the old days (read: last year for some of us), scheduling a single meeting involved a dozen emails, a phone call, and, occasionally, divine intervention. Automation tools, by contrast, let clients book directly into your calendar, no back-and-forth required. It's like having a virtual assistant who never takes coffee breaks and always remembers time zones.

Or consider customer support. Instead of spending your evenings responding to basic inquiries like "What time do you open?" or "Where can I find the refund policy?" a chatbot can handle those questions with cheerful efficiency. Meanwhile, you can focus on the complex issues—or, better yet, not be interrupted at all.

Why Automation Matters

The beauty of leveraging technology is that it's not about replacing humans—it's about freeing them. When repetitive tasks are handled by software, you and your team can focus on the work that actually matters: brainstorming ideas, solving creative challenges, and building relationships with clients.

Automation doesn't just save time; it saves energy. It prevents burnout, reduces errors, and gives you the satisfaction of knowing your business is running smoothly—even while you're out grabbing a coffee or binge-watching your favorite show.

So, let the robots do the boring bits. Swap your quill for a laser printer, your manual spreadsheets for automated workflows, and your endless scheduling emails for a sleek online tool. The result? A business that runs faster, smoother, and with far less ink-stained frustration. And maybe, just maybe, you'll have the time to write that novel after all.

Top Tools to Know: Modern Solutions to Ancient Business Problems

Let's start with a simple truth: the right tools can make even the most tedious tasks feel manageable—or at the very least, less like a medieval accounting ritual. If automation is the way forward, then these tools are your trusty companions on the journey, ready to transform your business from a clunky contraption into a seamless operation.

First up is **customer communication**, a realm that has historically devoured countless hours of entrepreneurial life. Gone are the days of manually sending email campaigns or answering the same five questions over and over. Email marketing platforms like Mailchimp or Constant Contact allow you to send beautifully designed emails en masse, without ever hitting "send" more than once. And chatbots, those cheerful digital assistants, can handle basic inquiries on your website with the kind of patience most humans can only dream of. Imagine someone asking, "What are your store hours?" for the 47th time today. Now imagine a chatbot answering it for you, while you sip coffee in blissful peace.

Then there's **task management**, the unsung hero of the organized business. Tools like Trello or Asana are like digital corkboards where you can stick tasks, deadlines, and reminders without fear of them falling into a black hole of forgetfulness. These platforms not only keep everyone on the same page but also prevent that horrifying moment when someone says, "Wasn't that due yesterday?" and you realize you've lost track of time entirely.

And, of course, we can't forget **financial tracking**, a task so historically fraught with frustration that it once required entire rooms of people hunched over ledgers by candlelight. Modern invoicing tools like QuickBooks or Fresh-Books take the pain out of tracking income and expenses. No more chasing down late payments by carrier pigeon or performing mental gymnastics to balance the books. Instead, invoices are sent automatically, payments are tracked digitally, and your financial reports are neatly organized without a single ink-stained finger.

The beauty of these tools is their simplicity. They don't just make your life easier—they make your business smarter. With automation on your side, those tedious, repetitive tasks become a thing of the past, leaving you free to focus on what you do best: building, creating, and occasionally marveling at how you ever managed without them.

So, embrace the tools of the modern age. Bid farewell to the black holes of forgotten tasks, the endless emails, and the chaos of untracked invoices. The robots are here to help, and for once, they come with no strings attached—just an internet connection and a knack for making your life infinitely easier.

Balancing Automation and Human Touch

Ah, automation. It's tempting to embrace it with open arms and let it handle everything—until you find yourself in a slightly dystopian scenario where your customers are wondering if they're talking to an actual human or a robot named Gerald. And while Gerald is probably delightful in his own way, there's a fine line between streamlining and alienating the very people your business exists to serve.

Automation works best when it enhances your business, not when it takes over like a well-meaning but tone-deaf intern. Sure, chatbots can answer basic inquiries, but when someone has a more nuanced question, a friendly human touch can make all the difference. You want your customers to feel supported, not stuck in an endless loop of, *"I didn't quite catch that. Can you repeat your question?"*

Finding the right balance means letting technology handle repetitive, mundane tasks while ensuring that real people step in for moments that require empathy, creativity, or a genuine conversation. Think of it as your automation being the sous-chef, chopping onions and prepping ingredients, while you, the head chef, handle the final flourish that makes the dish memorable.

The Result: Newfound Freedom

When you strike that balance—when automation hums along efficiently in the background while the human touch shines where it matters—you unlock something extraordinary: freedom.

Picture this: Instead of spending your days hunting for missing emails, chasing down overdue invoices, or manually following up on project deadlines, you're focusing on the meaningful, rewarding parts of your business. Perhaps you're brainstorming your next big idea, connecting with clients in a way that deepens relationships, or even taking a well-earned afternoon off to enjoy a long lunch without your phone buzzing incessantly.

Your business becomes less of a juggling act and more of a symphony, with each automated process playing its part in perfect harmony. And you? You're the conductor, calmly guiding the whole thing without breaking a sweat—or accidentally dropping an email into the void.

In this new reality, automation doesn't replace humanity; it amplifies it. Your customers feel supported, your team feels empowered, and you feel like you finally have room to breathe. Because at the end of the day, the goal isn't just to run a business—it's to enjoy running it. And maybe even to send Gerald on a little holiday. He's earned it.

Focusing on Impact: Doing Less, Better (and With a Smile)

There's a moment in life when you look at your closet and realize the truth: most of it never sees the light of day. Sure, you have your favorites—the comfortable jeans, the go-to jacket, the shoes that somehow go with everything. But then there's the fluorescent tracksuit glaring at you from the hanger like a neon reminder of a questionable phase.

The same principle applies to your business. Enter the Pareto Principle, also known as the 80/20 rule, which elegantly suggests that 80% of your results come from just 20% of your efforts. Think about that for a moment. Most of what you're doing is the equivalent of that tracksuit: loud, time-consuming, and less productive than you'd hoped.

The beauty of the Pareto Principle is its simplicity. By focusing your energy on the 20% of activities that drive 80% of the outcomes, you can achieve more by doing less. It's not about working harder; it's about working smarter, with a dash of self-awareness and maybe a moment of introspection in front of your metaphorical closet.

The Pareto Principle at Work

Start by asking yourself: What are the key business success drivers? Maybe it's your top clients, the projects that bring the most profit, or the marketing strategies that consistently deliver results. Once you identify these golden 20%, the next step is to double down on them.

Meanwhile, take a hard look at the activities that eat up time without delivering much in return. Do you really need to attend that weekly meeting where nothing ever gets decided? Is it necessary to offer 15 different services when three of them generate almost all your revenue? And let's not forget the emails—oh, the emails. If 80% of your inbox consists of irrelevant updates and endless threads about who's bringing snacks to the next team meeting, it might be time to tidy that up too.

The goal is to streamline, prioritize, and let go of the things that don't move the needle. It's liberating, like donating the tracksuit to charity and reclaiming precious closet space for things you actually wear.

When you embrace the Pareto Principle, something magical happens. Your work feels less scattered and more intentional. You're no longer spinning your wheels on activities that don't matter—you're focusing on the ones that do, with clarity, purpose, and maybe even a little smile.

And the best part? You'll have more time and energy to invest in the things that truly make an impact. Whether that's nurturing client relationships, refining your craft, or simply taking a moment to breathe, the result is a business that feels lighter, sharper, and infinitely more effective.

So, channel your inner Marie Kondo and ask yourself: Does this task bring results? If the answer is no, thank it for its service, let it go, and focus on the 20% that truly matters. Because doing less, better, is the secret to doing it all—with a smile and without the tracksuit.

The ROI of Your Time

There's something profoundly satisfying about calculating the return on investment (ROI) for your time. It's like putting on a pair of glasses and suddenly realizing the world is much clearer than you thought. Except, in this case, the world isn't blurry—it's just full of activities that don't deserve as much of your precious time as you've been giving them.

Start by taking an honest look at where your time goes and, more importantly, what you're getting back in return. Is that daily two-hour deep dive into your inbox really moving the needle? Does the weekly brainstorming session that ends with nothing but a whiteboard full of arrows and question marks feel like progress? And, let's be honest, do the three hours you spent perfecting your color-coded sticky note system really qualify as time well spent?

Spoiler alert: probably not.

Measuring the Value

The ROI of your time isn't just about dollars and cents, though those are important. It's also about the other currencies that matter: customer satisfaction, team morale, and yes, your own personal sanity. Start by identifying the tasks that deliver the biggest wins in these areas.

For instance, if a 30-minute call with a top client leads to a long-term contract, that's a great ROI. If an afternoon spent mentoring your team improves their performance and frees you up in the long run, that's an investment worth making. On the flip side, if you're spending hours tweaking the font on your presentation slides (again), it might be time to rethink your priorities.

The thing about time is that it's the one resource you can't make more of, no matter how cleverly you optimize your schedule. That's why it's so important to spend it wisely, focusing on the activities that deliver real value—not just the ones that make you feel busy.

Imagine your time as a portfolio. Would you put all your investments into activities that barely break even? Of course not. You'd diversify, double down on the winners, and cut your losses on the ones that don't perform. The same principle applies to your daily work.

The Revelation

When you start thinking about the ROI of your time, you'll likely have a few revelations. Maybe you'll realize that those hours spent tinkering with spreadsheets or crafting the perfect email signature aren't as impactful as you thought. Or that the tasks you've been avoiding—like following up with a key client or delegating that monster of a project—are actually where the magic happens.

The beauty of this approach is that it brings clarity to how you spend your days. You'll stop chasing the illusion of productivity and start focusing on the things that truly matter. And with that clarity comes freedom—the freedom to say no to the time-wasters, yes to the game-changers, and maybe even take an afternoon off without a shred of guilt.

Because in the end, the ROI of your time isn't just about working smarter; it's about living better. Even if that means your sticky notes will never be perfectly color-coded.

Letting Go of the Rest

Letting go of tasks that don't add significant impact is one of the most liberating decisions an entrepreneur can make. But, oh, how hard it is. It feels a bit like pruning a tree. At first, you're filled with hesitation, second-guessing whether that branch really needs to go. What if it turns out to be vital? What if it's the secret to making your tree—er, business—flourish? But here's the thing: if you try to keep every single branch, you end up with a tangled, chaotic mess, not a masterpiece.

The art of pruning lies in knowing what to keep and what to cut. That scraggly branch growing sideways, threatening to poke you in the eye every time you walk past? Gone. The awkward cluster of twigs that's doing nothing but blocking the light? Snip. When you clear away the unnecessary, you make room for the essential parts of the tree to grow stronger, taller, and more beautiful.

The Cluttered Business

In a business, the branches are all those tasks you've been holding onto because, well, you always have. There's the newsletter you dutifully write every week, even though no one seems to read past the first paragraph. Or the endless data entry that could easily be automated. Or the insistence on being cc'd on every single email, just in case something happens that absolutely must have your input (it rarely does).

Holding onto these tasks might make you feel busy, but busy isn't the same as productive. In fact, clinging to them often prevents you from focusing on the work that truly matters—the big, impactful things that only you can do.

The Courage to Prune

Letting go takes courage. It means trusting your team to handle things without you, relying on technology to pick up the slack, and accepting that not everything requires your personal touch. But once you start pruning, you'll find it gets easier.

You'll discover the beauty of simplicity: fewer distractions, more focus, and a business that feels light, nimble, and full of potential. Like a tree that's been carefully tended, your business will have room to grow in all the right ways, instead of expending energy on things that don't serve its purpose.

The Masterpiece in Progress

As you step back and admire your work, you'll see that letting go isn't about losing control; it's about creating clarity. Each remaining branch is strong and intentional, contributing to the overall health and beauty of the tree. And those branches you cut? They were never going to bear fruit anyway.

In business, as in gardening, it's not about how much you keep—it's about what you nurture. So pick up those pruning shears, trim away the excess, and watch as your business transforms from a cluttered tangle into a masterpiece. And if anyone asks why you're walking around with a pair of metaphorical shears, just tell them you're making room for growth. Because that's what this is all about: creating space for the things that truly matter.

Savoring the Payoff

There's a quiet, almost profound joy in focusing only on what truly matters. It's the difference between mindlessly munching your way through a bargain-sized bag of mediocre candy and savoring a single, exquisite piece of dark chocolate. One leaves you feeling slightly regretful and vaguely unwell, while the other is a revelation—a perfect balance of indulgence and satisfaction.

When you let go of the tasks that don't add value and concentrate on the ones that do, your business starts to feel like that perfect piece of chocolate. Each win is meaningful, each step forward intentional, and your effort feels rewarding rather than exhausting.

Instead of rushing through your days, ticking off endless to-do lists filled with tasks that no one will remember by next week, you're free to invest your energy in the things that truly move the needle. That game-changing client meeting, the innovative idea that's been simmering in the back of your mind, or even just the luxury of stepping back and appreciating how far you've come—these are the moments that make all the difference.

Focusing on what matters doesn't just transform your business; it transforms how you feel about running it. It shifts your perspective from "How will I ever get through all this?" to "Look at what I've accomplished." You trade in the constant grind for fewer but far more satisfying wins, and suddenly, work doesn't feel quite so heavy.

So, as you prune the unnecessary, streamline your processes, and focus on the tasks that truly matter, take a moment to savor the results. Feel the weight lifting off your shoulders, the clarity returning to your vision, and the renewed excitement for what lies ahead.

Because when you focus on what matters, you're not just running a business—you're crafting a life. And much like that piece of chocolate, the experience becomes something to be cherished, savored, and remembered. After all, isn't that the point of this whole entrepreneurial adventure?

Streamlining Toward Sanity

Picture this: you, sitting at a cozy café, savoring a quiet cup of coffee. The world isn't spinning out of control, your phone isn't buzzing incessantly with crises disguised as questions, and your laptop remains firmly closed. Meanwhile, somewhere in the background, your business hums along beautifully, each process clicking into place like the gears of a well-crafted timepiece.

This is the joy of a streamlined business. It's not just about saving time, though that's certainly a delightful side effect. It's about creating space—space to breathe, to think, to focus on what truly matters. It's about reclaiming your days from the clutches of endless to-do lists and tasks that seemed important but, in retrospect, really weren't.

When your business operates with simplicity and elegance, it doesn't just run—it thrives. You're no longer the harried ringleader of a three-ring circus; you're the conductor of a symphony, guiding your team with calm assurance while the music unfolds beautifully around you.

So, as you look ahead, remember this: a streamlined business isn't just a goal—it's a gift. It's a chance to reclaim your time, rediscover your purpose, and maybe, just maybe, enjoy that coffee while it's still hot.

And let's keep things simple, shall we? Simplify your business, reclaim your time, and for heaven's sake, stop trying to reinvent the wheel—it's already round. Now, go forth and enjoy the ride.

Chapter Six

Designing a Life-First Business Blueprint

The Business Blueprint That Doesn't Forget About You

LET ME TAKE YOU on a little journey into one of humanity's universal experiences: assembling a piece of IKEA furniture without instructions. It begins with optimism—a confident glance at the parts and a cavalier attitude toward the incomprehensible diagrams. "How hard can it be?" you think as you align what you assume are table legs to what looks vaguely like a tabletop. Fast forward an hour, and you're staring at a wobbling, three-legged monstrosity, wondering why you have four screws left over and a deep, nagging sense of existential despair.

Now, if you've ever built—or tried to build—a business without a clear plan, this probably feels familiar. It's the same principle, really: a hopeful beginning, a flurry of activity, and then a dawning realization that something fundamental isn't quite working. Maybe the business is running, but it's teetering precariously, held together with late nights and sheer willpower. And much like that ill-fated table, it doesn't seem to be supporting the weight it's supposed to.

The problem is simple: too often, we build businesses without considering the life of the person running them. The focus is all on growth, revenue, and hustle, while the needs of the human at the center of it all are quietly pushed aside. The result? A business that runs you ragged, leaves you feeling out of control, and doesn't quite look like the dream you had when you started.

The Life-First Business Blueprint

Here's the good news: it doesn't have to be that way. A life-first business blueprint flips the script. It's not about working less for the sake of it—though fewer late nights and more leisurely mornings are certainly a perk. It's about designing a business that works for you, one that aligns with your values, priorities, and the life you actually want to live.

Think of it as designing a home. Would you ever build a house without considering the needs of the people living in it? Of course not. You'd think about how many bedrooms you need, where the light switches go, and whether the kitchen is big enough for your infamous chili nights. A life-first business is no different. It's about creating something that fits your lifestyle instead of forcing you to live in a way that doesn't make sense.

A life-first business doesn't just run efficiently—it runs meaningfully. It prioritizes your well-being, goals, and what makes you feel alive. It ensures that your work supports your life, rather than the other way around. And much like that properly designed home, it feels right—functional, fulfilling, and a joy to wake up to every day.

So, as we dive into this chapter, let's toss aside the chaotic approach of the building as we go and embrace the elegance of a plan that works. Because whether you're building a table, a house, or a business, the right blueprint makes all the difference. And I promise, this time, there won't be any leftover screws.

Clarifying Lifestyle Goals: Dreaming Big (But With Coffee Breaks Built In)

Let's begin with a little exercise. Close your eyes—or at least squint thoughtfully at the wall—and imagine your perfect day. Not the kind of day where you've ticked off everything on your to-do list and collapsed into bed feeling vaguely victorious, but a truly ideal day. The sort of day that makes you think, *This is exactly how life should feel.*

Picture it: You wake up at leisure, not because an alarm jolted you into consciousness, but because your body decided it was ready. The sun is peeking through the curtains, and the smell of freshly brewed coffee is wafting from the kitchen. There's no mad scramble to answer emails or deal with a sudden crisis; instead, you have time—glorious, unhurried time—to enjoy your morning.

Maybe there's a midday surf session, a brisk walk in the park, or an hour spent painting—purely for the joy of it. Lunch isn't a hastily gobbled sandwich over your laptop, but an actual meal, perhaps shared with someone whose company you genuinely enjoy. And somewhere in this dream day, there's a nap. Because, let's be honest, naps are the unsung heroes of productivity and happiness.

The work you do during this perfect day feels purposeful. It's not busywork or a treadmill of endless demands; it's meaningful, satisfying, and fits neatly into the rhythm of your life. By the time evening rolls around, you're not dreading the next day or lying awake cataloging unfinished tasks. Instead, you feel content—like you've struck the elusive balance between work and life, ambition and rest.

This whimsical thought exercise isn't just about daydreaming—it's about clarity. Because before you can design a life-first business, you need to know what kind of life you're designing it for. Your ideal day is the blueprint for everything else: your work schedule, your business goals, even the way you approach success.

And here's the secret: your perfect day doesn't have to involve winning awards or conquering mountains (though if that's your thing, go for it). It might be as simple as carving out time for a hobby, being home for dinner every night, or finally permitting yourself to take a guilt-free nap. The specifics don't matter—what matters is that it feels right for you.

So grab a notebook, pour yourself a cup of coffee (because everything is better with coffee), and start sketching out your dream day. Don't hold back, and don't worry about how practical it seems just yet. This is about vision, not logistics.

Because when you know what your perfect day looks like, you're one step closer to building a business—and a life—that makes it possible. And really, isn't that the whole point of this adventure?

Defining Work-Life Balance: The Snowflake That Won't Melt (Hopefully)

Work-life balance is one of those elusive concepts that everyone seems to talk about but few can actually define. It's a bit like a snowflake: utterly unique to each person, intricate in its design, and yet, when the pressure's on, it has an alarming tendency to disappear. But unlike actual snowflakes, balance doesn't have to melt. With the right mindset and a little planning, it's entirely achievable—though not without a few wobbly moments along the way.

Let's consider the challenge of balance through a relatable scenario: you're trying to carry a week's worth of groceries and a wriggling toddler at the same time. One arm is precariously cradling a carton of eggs, a loaf of bread, and something squishy you're trying not to think about, while the other is holding a child who has decided this is the moment to impersonate an octopus. It's tricky, yes. It's chaotic, absolutely. But with a bit of effort and the right approach, you manage. You get the groceries to the counter, the toddler calms down (eventually), and you walk out with your dignity mostly intact.

Work-life balance feels a lot like that. It's not about achieving perfection or keeping everything perfectly still—it's about finding a rhythm that works for you, even if it involves a bit of juggling.

What Balance Looks Like for You

Here's the thing: balance is deeply personal. For some, it might mean clocking out at 5 p.m. every day to spend uninterrupted time with family. For others, it could be having the flexibility to work late on a passion project but still take a morning off to recharge. Balance doesn't mean splitting your time 50/50 between work and life—it means aligning your priorities so that both feel fulfilling.

The key is figuring out what balance means for *you*. Maybe it's having the freedom to go for a run in the middle of the day. Maybe it's attending your child's school play without frantically checking emails under your seat. Or maybe it's simply carving out an hour each week to do something just for you, whether that's reading, gardening, or watching a guilty-pleasure TV show.

The Art of Achieving It

Achieving balance doesn't require a complete overhaul of your life. It's about small adjustments—setting boundaries, delegating tasks, and learning to say no (politely but firmly) to things that don't serve your priorities. It's about recognizing that you don't have to do it all or do it perfectly.

And, like balancing groceries and a toddler, it gets easier with practice. You'll find your rhythm, your arms will get stronger, and eventually, you'll figure out how to navigate the chaos without dropping the eggs—or losing your mind.

So, as you think about your version of work-life balance, remember this: it's not about comparison or keeping up with anyone else's definition of success. It's about designing a life that feels right for you—one that lets you carry what matters most, with both hands free for what you love.

Reflection Exercise: Mapping Your Priorities

Let's take a moment to pause, grab a pen (or your phone, if that's more your style), and map out the things that truly matter in your life. This isn't meant to be a long, soul-searching endeavor—more of a quick inventory of what makes your days meaningful. Think of it as creating a priority playlist, except this one doesn't require a Spotify subscription.

Start by listing your personal priorities and passions. What lights you up? What gives your life purpose? Maybe it's spending quality time with family, traveling, gardening, or diving into a creative hobby you've been neglecting. Write it all down. Don't overthink it—this isn't a final draft; it's a brainstorming session.

Now, add your non-negotiables. These are the things that keep you functioning and (mostly) sane. Coffee, for instance, should probably get a prominent spot on the list. Sleep, too—let's not underestimate its importance, even if it occasionally feels like a luxury. And let's be honest, a little Netflix binge here and there isn't just acceptable; it's practically a public service for your mental health.

Once you've jotted everything down, take a step back and look at your list. These are the elements that define your ideal work-life balance. These are the things your business should make room for—not crowd out.

What's Next?

The beauty of this exercise is that it's as practical as it is personal. It gives you a clear snapshot of what matters most, helping you align your business goals with your life goals. And it's a gentle reminder that balance isn't about cramming more into your day—it's about making space for what truly counts.

So go ahead, sketch out your priorities, leave plenty of room for coffee breaks and naps, and give yourself permission to design a life that's as fulfilling as it is productive. Because if there's one thing this exercise proves, it's that there's always time for the things that matter. You just have to make it

Life-Centric Business Models: Finding the Business That Lets You Breathe

Have you ever worn a pair of shoes that looked fantastic in the store but, after a few hours, felt like you were walking on hot coals? That's what running a business that doesn't align with your lifestyle feels like—great in theory, but utterly painful in practice. On the other hand, a business designed to fit your life, much like a well-made pair of shoes, feels supportive, flexible, and, most importantly, lets you move freely.

The secret to creating a life-centric business lies in choosing a model that complements your priorities. Whether you value location independence, a manageable workload, or predictable income, there's a business model out there that will fit like a glove—or, perhaps more aptly, a perfectly cushioned sneaker.

Business Models Built for Flexibility

Take, for instance, **remote-friendly businesses**, which offer the freedom to work from anywhere. Whether you're perched at your kitchen table, lounging at a café, or soaking in the view from a beachside bungalow, these setups let you run the show without being tied to a single location. For entrepreneurs who value flexibility and a change of scenery, this is the ultimate way to have your cake and eat it too (preferably somewhere scenic).

Then there are **subscription-based models**, which are like the gift that keeps on giving. Once you've set them up, they provide recurring revenue without requiring you to constantly chase new clients or projects. Think of it as creating a steady stream of income while freeing up your time for other pursuits—like finally learning how to bake sourdough or catching up on that book you've been meaning to read.

Project-based work is another option, ideal for those who thrive on variety. You can dive into a project, give it your all, and then enjoy a well-earned break before taking on the next challenge. It's the business equivalent of sprinting and resting, rather than running a never-ending marathon.

These models aren't just about making money; they're about creating space—space to breathe, think, and live the kind of life you've been envisioning.

Finding Your Fit

For example, finding the perfect pair of shoes and choosing a business model is all about what feels right for you. Are you someone who needs the freedom to travel? Look into remote or digital-friendly businesses. Do you crave stability and predictability? A subscription model might be your perfect match. Do you prefer bursts of intense work followed by downtime? Project-based setups could be the answer.

The beauty of life-centric business models is that they're as unique as the people running them. There's no one-size-fits-all solution, and that's the point. It's about finding what works for you—not for your neighbor, your favorite business guru, or the person with the flashy LinkedIn profile.

So, take a moment to step back, assess your priorities, and imagine your ideal business. Then, like slipping into the perfect pair of shoes, settle into the model that fits seamlessly with your life. No pinching, no blisters—just the freedom to walk, run, or even dance your way through the entrepreneurial journey.

Passive Income Without the Hype: Planting the Garden of Effort and Reward

Ah, passive income—the mythical creature of the business world. If you believe the hype, it's like discovering a magical money tree in your backyard, effortlessly dropping crisp dollar bills into your lap while you sip cocktails and nap in a hammock. But let's take a step back, shall we? Because while passive income is indeed possible—and wonderful—it's less of a magic trick and more like planting a garden.

Picture this: you start with a patch of fertile ground (your skills or business assets). You plant seeds (your passive income streams), water them diligently (initial effort), and pull the occasional weed (ongoing maintenance). Eventually, with patience and care, you end up with a flourishing garden that requires far less work to sustain than it did to create. But—and here's the crucial bit—it's not effortless. You still have to roll up your sleeves and get your hands dirty, at least in the beginning.

The Reality of Passive Income

Creating passive income streams isn't about flipping a switch and watching the money roll in. It's about investing time and effort up front to build something that generates value over time. Think rental properties, digital products, online courses, or dividend-generating investments. These are the seeds you plant, each requiring proper planning and setup before they begin to yield results.

Take an online course, for instance. You'll spend weeks—or months—developing the content, designing the platform, and marketing it to your audience. But once it's live, it can bring in steady income with only occasional updates and tweaks. It's like planting a row of tomatoes: a bit of labor at the start, but with the potential for a steady harvest later on.

Or consider rental properties. They're a classic passive income option, but they require research, investment, and management (or at least hiring someone to manage them for you). It's rewarding, yes, but there's no escaping the occasional metaphorical weed—like a leaky roof or a tenant with a passion for impromptu drum circles.

Stripping Away the Hype

The phrase "make money while you sleep" gets thrown around a lot, but let's be real: most passive income streams require you to be awake, at least some of the time. That doesn't make them any less worthwhile. It simply means you should approach them with realistic expectations.

Passive income isn't about avoiding work; it's about creating systems that work for you. It's not about instant gratification but rather building something sustainable that pays off over time. And while it might not make you an overnight millionaire, it can absolutely create more freedom, stability, and peace of mind in the long run.

The Reward of a Well-Planned Garden

When done right, passive income is like a well-tended garden: it grows steadily, bringing you rewards without constant effort. You can sit back and enjoy the fruits of your labor, knowing that your initial work has paid off. And while there will always be the occasional weed to pull, the joy of seeing your garden thrive makes it all worthwhile.

So, if you're considering adding passive income to your business blueprint, approach it like a gardener. Be thoughtful, be patient, and don't fall for the hype of instant riches. Because, much like a garden, the best things in life take time to grow—but they're well worth the wait.

Scaling Without Sinking: Growing Without Turning Into a Wonky Sunflower

Scaling a business is a bit like growing a plant. Do it right, and you end up with a thriving, vibrant creation that stands tall and proud. Rush the process, and you might end up with a wonky sunflower—too tall for its own good, leaning precariously to one side, and in desperate need of support stakes to keep it from toppling over.

For entrepreneurs, the temptation to scale quickly can be irresistible. The allure of doubling revenue, expanding into new markets, or adding shiny new products is hard to resist. But here's the thing: scaling isn't just about growing; it's about growing sustainably. If you don't align your expansion with your resources and lifestyle, you could end up with a business that looks impressive but feels completely unmanageable—much like our dear, overgrown sunflower.

The Art of Thoughtful Scaling

Scaling thoughtfully means asking the right questions before you start. What's driving the need to grow? Is it demand, a desire for more flexibility, or simply FOMO because your competitors seem to be doing it? Understanding the "why" behind your scaling ambitions helps you make smarter decisions about the "how."

Start with strategies that complement your lifestyle rather than overwhelm it. For instance, instead of opening a new location or taking on twice as many clients, consider automating parts of your business to handle increased demand without adding extra work. Or, instead of launching a dozen new products at once, focus on refining your current offerings to increase their value and profitability.

Avoiding the Sunflower Syndrome

Much like our metaphorical sunflower, scaling too quickly can leave you scrambling to keep up. Suddenly, you're spending more time fixing problems caused by rapid growth—hiring too fast, overpromising to clients, or dealing with quality control issues—than actually enjoying the benefits of your success.

The trick is to scale at a pace that feels manageable. Think gradual and steady, like watering a plant just enough to keep it healthy, rather than dumping a bucket of water on it and hoping for the best. Give your business room to grow, but also time to stabilize at each stage before taking the next leap.

The Beauty of Sustainable Growth

When you scale thoughtfully, your business grows in a way that enhances your life instead of consuming it. You can expand your reach, serve more clients, or increase your income without sacrificing your sanity—or your Saturday mornings.

Scaling doesn't have to mean chaos or exhaustion. Done right, it's an opportunity to build something bigger and better while still keeping your lifestyle front and center. And unlike the wonky sunflower, your business will grow tall, steady, and—most importantly—strong enough to thrive on its own.

Because at the end of the day, the goal isn't just to grow for the sake of growth. It's to grow in a way that lets you enjoy the view—preferably from the comfort of your well-tended garden.

Protecting Non-Negotiables: Boundaries – Not Just for Picket Fences

Let's talk about non-negotiables—those sacred elements of your life that deserve a protective barrier stronger than any picket fence. These are the things that keep you grounded, sane, and, dare I say it, happy. Whether it's family dinners, Saturday mornings reserved for lounging in pajamas, or the rare but cherished pleasure of reading an actual book (the kind with real pages, not just pixels), these are the moments that should remain untouched by the chaos of work.

But here's the catch: protecting your non-negotiables requires clarity. You can't defend what you haven't defined. Without that clarity, it's all too easy for work to creep into every corner of your life, like an invasive vine taking over a garden.

Defining What Matters Most

To start, ask yourself: What are the non-negotiables in your life? What are the activities, moments, or rituals that you can't imagine living without? Maybe it's sitting down for dinner with your family every evening, sharing stories about your day while the phone stays blissfully out of reach. Perhaps it's a Saturday morning routine of coffee, quiet, and a crossword puzzle that sets the tone for your weekend. Or maybe it's the freedom to take a long walk, listen to your favorite podcast, or simply sit in silence without feeling like you should be doing something else.

Whatever they are, write them down. Think of this as drafting your personal constitution—a set of guiding principles that ensure your life doesn't become entirely consumed by your business.

The Importance of Sacred Space

Protecting non-negotiables isn't just about preserving your sanity (though that's a major perk). It's also about setting an example—for your team, your clients, and even your family—that boundaries matter. When you carve out space for the things that are truly important, you're not just honoring your own needs; you're creating a ripple effect that encourages others to do the same.

And let's not forget the irony of running a business designed to support your life, only to let it trample all over the very things that make your life meaningful. Your non-negotiables are there to remind you why you're doing all this in the first place.

Keeping the Fence Sturdy

Of course, boundaries require upkeep. It's not enough to declare that Saturday mornings are off-limits—you have to actively protect that time. That might mean saying no to a "quick" meeting, ignoring emails that can wait until Monday, or training your team to respect your downtime.

Yes, it can feel uncomfortable at first, especially if you're used to being available 24/7. But here's the thing: your non-negotiables are non-negotiable for a reason. They're the foundation of a balanced life, and without them, everything else starts to wobble.

So go ahead—build your boundaries, protect your priorities, and keep that picket fence as sturdy as it needs to be. Because when you honor what matters most, you're not just creating space for yourself—you're creating a life that's worth every moment of the effort.

Setting Boundaries Without Guilt: Saying No Without Feeling Like You've Kicked a Puppy

For many entrepreneurs, setting boundaries can feel suspiciously like committing a crime against humanity—or at least against your inbox. Declining a late-night email frenzy or gently refusing a last-minute request can leave you feeling like you've just let someone down, kicked a puppy, and maybe stolen its chew toy for good measure. But here's the truth: setting boundaries isn't an act of cruelty; it's an act of self-preservation—and a smart one at that.

Let's consider the late-night email scenario. You're winding down after a long day, maybe with a cup of tea and an episode of your favorite series, when suddenly your phone lights up. A client has sent an email marked "urgent," and the subject line practically screams, "Drop everything!" Now, you have a choice: dive into the email frenzy or politely let it wait until morning.

Choosing the latter doesn't mean you're neglecting your responsibilities. It means you're honoring the boundaries that protect your time, energy, and mental well-being. And the beauty of this approach is that it actually teaches others to respect those boundaries, too.

How to Set Guilt-Free Boundaries

First, let's tackle the guilt, that sneaky little voice that insists you're somehow failing by saying no. The best way to quiet it? Reframe your perspective. Boundaries aren't walls—they're guideposts. They don't shut people out; they simply show them where the line is, ensuring both parties can navigate the relationship more effectively.

Start by clearly defining your boundaries. For example, decide that work ends at 6 p.m., emails can wait until morning, and weekends are sacred. Communicate these boundaries kindly but firmly. A simple "I'll take a look at this first thing tomorrow" goes a long way, conveying professionalism without sacrificing your personal time.

The Power of Polite Declines

If declining feels daunting, try pairing your no with an alternative solution. Instead of saying, "I'm not available," say, "I can't tonight, but let's revisit this in the morning." It's a way of maintaining control over your time without shutting the door entirely.

And when someone pushes back (because someone inevitably will), remind yourself that honoring your boundaries is what allows you to show up as your best self—focused, energized, and ready to tackle the real emergencies when they arise.

A Lighthearted Example

Imagine you're a lifeguard at a pool. Someone's frantically waving, claiming their towel fell into the water. It's an inconvenience, sure, but it's not life-threatening. If you jump in every time someone drops a towel, you'll be too exhausted to save the kid doing cannonballs in the deep end. The same principle applies to your business. Not every request is an emergency, and it's okay—necessary, even—to prioritize.

Boundaries That Build Respect

The beauty of boundaries is that they don't just protect your time; they also set expectations. Clients, team members, and even friends learn to respect your availability, making interactions smoother and more productive. And here's the kicker: you'll likely find that the world doesn't end because you didn't respond to an email at 10 p.m.

So, the next time guilt tries to nudge you into overextending yourself, re-member this: setting boundaries isn't selfish—it's smart. It's what allows you to be present for the things that matter most, from work to family to that elusive creature known as "me time." And if all else fails, just think of the lifeguard and the towel. It's not your job to dive in for every splash—save your energy for the cannonballs.

Communicating Boundaries to Others: Taming the Overzealous Colleague and Other Boundary-Testers

Ah, the art of communicating boundaries—a delicate dance of asserting yourself without stepping on toes. It's not enough to set boundaries; you also have to let others know they exist. Otherwise, you'll find yourself endlessly fielding late-night requests from that one overzealous colleague who seems to think sleep is optional and boundaries are a suggestion.

Here's the secret: communicating boundaries is less about drawing a hard line in the sand and more about planting a friendly signpost. Something like, "This is my lane; feel free to join me, but please don't honk the horn after hours." It's about clarity, kindness, and consistency, delivered with just enough charm to make people respect your limits without taking offense.

How to Say It

Start with clients. They're the backbone of your business, but that doesn't mean they get to dictate your schedule. When discussing boundaries, keep it professional but clear. For example, "I typically respond to emails within 24 hours, Monday through Friday. If there's an urgent issue, please mark it as such, and I'll get back to you as soon as I can." This sets expectations without coming across as unapproachable, and it reassures them that their needs will still be met.

For employees, the approach can be more collaborative. Frame your boundaries as a way to foster balance for everyone. "I'm setting some guidelines to ensure we all have time to recharge. I'm unplugging after 6 p.m., and I encourage you to do the same. If something urgent comes up, let's address it during work hours so we can keep after-hours stress to a minimum." This not only communicates your limits but also sets a healthy example for the team.

And then there's that overzealous colleague, the one who sends emails at midnight with subject lines like "Quick thought!" but whose "thoughts" always involve you doing more work. A light yet firm response works wonders here. "I saw your email—let's tackle this tomorrow during business hours so we can give it the attention it deserves." It's polite, professional, and subtly says, "I'm not working at midnight, and you shouldn't be either."

Consistency Is Key

The trick to communicating boundaries is sticking to them. If you tell people you don't work weekends but respond to every Saturday email, you're sending mixed signals. Consistency not only reinforces your boundaries but also builds respect over time. People will learn that when you're on, you're fully engaged, and when you're off, you're genuinely off.

Expect a Few Pushbacks

Not everyone will immediately accept your boundaries, especially if they've been used to you being constantly available. That's okay. Pushbacks aren't a sign you're doing something wrong; they're just part of the process. When they happen, stay calm, restate your boundaries, and remember why you set them in the first place.

The Upside of Clear Boundaries

When you communicate your boundaries effectively, you create an environment of mutual respect. Clients know when and how to reach you, employees feel empowered to respect their own time, and even that overzealous colleague might start rethinking their midnight emails.

And the best part? You're no longer playing defense. You've set the rules of engagement, ensuring that your time, energy, and sanity remain intact. So go ahead—plant those signposts, keep them friendly, and don't forget to celebrate your newfound freedom with a well-earned coffee break. Because boundaries, after all, are the cornerstone of a life-first business—and a well-balanced life.

Mending Boundaries When They Get Trampled

Let's face it: even the sturdiest fences sometimes need a little maintenance. Maybe a storm knocked a panel loose, or a particularly ambitious neighbor decided to hop over uninvited. Whatever the reason, when boundaries get tested—or outright trampled—it's time to grab your metaphorical fence repair kit and get to work.

Boundaries, much like actual fences, aren't meant to be unyielding walls. They're there to mark a respectful divide, to let people know where your space begins and ends. But when someone tests those limits, it's not a sign to tear the whole thing down in frustration. It's simply a cue to reinforce, mend, and strengthen what you've built.

The first step is recognizing when a boundary has been crossed. It might be a client who insists on calling during your off-hours, a colleague who keeps piling on last-minute tasks, or even your own habit of breaking your own rules (we've all been there). Before you can fix the issue, you need to understand what's broken and why.

Ask yourself: Was the boundary unclear? Did someone misunderstand its purpose? Or is this simply a case of someone seeing how far they can push? Identifying the root cause helps you address the problem effectively, rather than just slapping on a Band-Aid and hoping for the best.

Once you've identified the issue, it's time to reinforce the boundary—firmly but kindly. Think of it as rebuilding the fence with stronger, clearer materials.

If it's a client who's overstepped, a gentle reminder works wonders: "I understand this feels urgent, but I've committed to keeping evenings for family time.

I'll get back to you first thing tomorrow." For colleagues or employees, frame it as a mutual benefit: "To keep things running smoothly, let's revisit our workflow to avoid last-minute requests that cut into personal time."

And if you're the one breaking your own rules (hello, midnight email responder), take a moment to reassess and recommit. Sometimes, the hardest fence to maintain is the one we set for ourselves.

If someone continues to test your boundaries, it's okay to address it more directly. Think of it as politely but firmly saying, "This fence is here for a reason." Stay calm, keep the tone professional, and explain why the boundary is important. Most people aren't deliberately trying to trample your metaphorical garden—they just need a little nudge to stay on their side of the line.

Fences Make Good Business

The beauty of mending fences, literal or metaphorical, is that it strengthens relationships in the long run. Clear, well-communicated boundaries don't just protect you; they also create a framework of respect and trust. People know what to expect from you, and you know your needs are being honored.

Like any good repair kit, your boundary toolbox should include a few essentials: clarity, consistency, and a willingness to reset when necessary. Whether it's reinforcing your availability hours, revisiting team expectations, or simply learning to say no without guilt, each step strengthens the fence and ensures it stands firm against future storms.

So, the next time your boundaries feel a little wobbly, don't despair. Roll up your sleeves, grab your repair kit, and get to work. Because a well-maintained fence doesn't just protect your time and energy—it makes your life and business thrive. And let's be honest: who doesn't want a sturdy, beautiful fence that says, "I value myself, and you should too"?

Adapting Over Time: When Life Changes, So Should Your Blueprint

Life has a funny way of shifting under our feet, doesn't it? One moment, you're completely devoted to building a business that lets you travel the world, and the next, you find yourself daydreaming about a slower pace and a garden full of tomatoes. Priorities evolve, circumstances change, and what once seemed like the ultimate goal might start to feel about as appealing as reheated leftovers.

Think of your life goals as a favorite playlist. When you first put it together, it was a perfect blend of hits—uplifting, energizing, and totally reflective of where you were at the time. But as the years roll on, some tracks start to lose their luster, while new ones beg to be added. A life-first business blueprint works much the same way. It's not carved in stone; it's a living document that should grow and adapt with you.

The Evolving Nature of Priorities

As life shifts, so do the things that matter most. Maybe you started your business to achieve financial independence, but now you're craving more time to focus on family or personal passions. Or perhaps you once thrived on the hustle of constant growth, but lately, the idea of scaling back and simplifying feels far more appealing.

These changes aren't failures or signs that you've lost your way—they're natural progressions. What fulfills you at one stage of life may not fulfill you in the next, and that's perfectly okay. Just as a playlist needs updating to reflect new tastes, your business goals need revisiting to align with your current priorities.

The key to adapting your blueprint is taking time to check in with yourself. Ask the big questions: Are my current goals still serving me? Do they align with what I value most right now? What's changed since I first set these intentions?

And don't be afraid to admit when something no longer fits. Holding onto outdated goals out of sheer stubbornness is like keeping a pair of jeans that haven't fit in years—it's not helping anyone, least of all you.

Embracing the Update

Updating your blueprint doesn't mean starting from scratch. It's about making adjustments, adding what's needed, and letting go of what no longer serves you. Maybe it's revising your schedule to make room for a new hobby or pivoting your business to reflect a growing passion. Or perhaps it's scaling back entirely to focus on the life you've worked so hard to build.

The beauty of a life-first business is that it's yours to shape. You're not bound by anyone else's definition of success or fulfillment. If your priorities change, your blueprint should too—it's not a sign of indecision but a mark of growth.

So, as you move forward, think of your business and your life as an ever-evolving playlist. Keep the tracks that resonate, add new ones that inspire you, and don't be afraid to skip the ones that no longer hit the right notes. Because when your blueprint reflects who you are and what you value, it's not just a plan—it's a symphony, uniquely yours.

Recognizing the Need for Adjustments: When the Blueprint Stops Fitting

Sometimes, the realization that your business model no longer aligns with your priorities hits you like a bolt of lightning. Other times, it's more of a slow, creeping suspicion—like discovering that your favorite pair of shoes now give you blisters, or that you can't remember the last time you laughed at a truly awful pun (and you *used* to love a good groaner).

The truth is, life sends subtle—and occasionally not-so-subtle—signals when it's time to make adjustments. Ignoring them only leads to more stress, burnout, and a nagging sense that something is off. Spotting these signs early, however, can save you from the perpetual frazzled state of someone juggling flaming torches while trying to answer emails.

The Telltale Signs

First, let's talk about the feeling of being perpetually overwhelmed. If you're constantly rushing, multitasking to the point of exhaustion, or wondering if cloning yourself might be a viable solution, it's time to pause. Your business should challenge you, yes—but it shouldn't leave you feeling like a contestant in a never-ending game show where the buzzer keeps going off.

Next, take note of your emotional state. Have you become more irritable, less patient, or prone to snapping at innocent bystanders (like your dog, your coffee machine, or, heaven forbid, your family)? Do you find yourself dreading the tasks you once loved or avoiding decisions because everything feels like too much?

And then there's the laughter test. If you can't remember the last time you genuinely laughed—whether at a bad pun, a clever joke, or even just the ridiculousness of a minor mishap—it's a sign that joy has taken a backseat to stress.

The good news is, these signs aren't failures; they're indicators. They're your brain and body waving tiny red flags, saying, "Hey, something's not working here." Recognizing them is the first step toward making meaningful changes.

Take a moment to reflect on your current reality. Is your business supporting your life, or has it started to feel like a ball and chain? Are your goals still in line with what you truly want, or have they become obligations you're trudging through out of habit?

Recognizing the need for adjustments doesn't mean you've failed—it means you're paying attention. Life evolves, priorities shift, and your business blueprint should, too. It's not about tearing everything down and starting over; it's about realigning your work with your current values and goals.

So if you've been feeling frazzled, uninspired, or humorless, don't brush it off. Take it as an opportunity to revisit your blueprint and make the changes that will bring balance, fulfillment, and—most importantly—a good, hearty laugh back into your life. After all, even the best blueprints need revisions every now and then.

Strategies for Realignment: Swapping Flip-Flops for Proper Running Shoes

Let's face it—if life is a marathon, some of us have been attempting to run it in flip-flops. And while that's certainly a choice (and possibly a bold fashion statement), it's not exactly the most practical approach. At some point, you have to stop, assess the situation, and decide it's time to invest in proper running shoes. Realigning your business blueprint is much the same. It's about taking a step back, figuring out what's not working, and making adjustments that set you up for a smoother, more comfortable run.

Shifting Business Hours

One of the simplest tweaks you can make is rethinking your work hours. If your current schedule has you burning the candle at both ends, it's time to blow one of those flames out. Maybe you decide that evenings are strictly for family, hobbies, or Netflix marathons that require no emotional investment. Or perhaps you shift your start time to better align with your natural rhythm—whether you're an early bird or someone who believes mornings are a cruel joke.

The key is to create a schedule that serves you, not the other way around. Because let's be honest: there's no medal for answering emails at midnight, and the world will keep spinning even if you don't attend every meeting marked "urgent."

Pivoting Services

Another strategy is to take a hard look at what you're offering and ask yourself, *Does this still align with what I enjoy and excel at?* If certain services feel like a slog or cater to clients who drain your energy faster than a faulty phone charger, it might be time to pivot.

Maybe you narrow your focus to the projects you're most passionate about. Maybe you expand into new areas that excite you. Or maybe you finally let go of that one service that's been more trouble than it's worth, like trying to sell ice to penguins. Pivoting isn't about abandoning ship; it's about steering it in a direction that feels more fulfilling.

Hiring Support

If you've been doing everything yourself, congratulations—you're officially the flip-flop marathoner of entrepreneurship. It's time to acknowledge that you can't (and shouldn't) do it all. Hiring support, whether it's a virtual assistant, a project manager, or a team member with skills that complement yours, can be a game-changer.

Think of it as upgrading your toolkit. Suddenly, tasks that once felt like hauling boulders up a hill become manageable, even enjoyable. And while delegating might feel like handing over the reins of your prized horse, it's actually an investment in your sanity and your business's growth.

The Joy of Realignment

Realigning your blueprint isn't about throwing everything out and starting fresh. It's about fine-tuning, like adjusting the straps on those metaphorical running shoes so they fit just right. With each tweak—whether it's setting better hours, pivoting services, or bringing in support—you create a business that feels more aligned with your values, goals, and ideal lifestyle.

And here's the best part: once you've swapped those flip-flops for proper running shoes, you'll wonder why you didn't do it sooner. Suddenly, the marathon doesn't feel like a relentless struggle. It feels like a journey you can enjoy, one step at a time, with fewer blisters and a lot more joy.

Future-Proofing Your Blueprint: Building a Business as Flexible as a Lego Set (Dragons Optional)

When it comes to designing a life-first business, the trick isn't just to build something functional—it's to build something flexible. Think of it as assembling a Lego set. At first, you might create a modest little house with a charming roof and a door that kind of sticks. But then, as your needs and imagination evolve, you might decide to add a castle tower, a secret passage, or even a dragon perched on the roof for dramatic flair.

The beauty of Legos is that they're endlessly reconfigurable, and your business blueprint should be, too. By designing with flexibility in mind, you allow your business to grow, adapt, and shift alongside you, no matter what life throws your way.

The Case for Flexibility

Life is unpredictable. One day, you might be focused on growth and expansion; the next, you're craving simplicity and a slower pace. A rigid business model can feel like being trapped in a structure that no longer fits—like trying to live in a house where the walls won't move, even when you need an extra room.

A flexible blueprint, on the other hand, gives you the freedom to adapt. It allows you to pivot when priorities shift, scale up when opportunities arise, or scale down when life demands a little more breathing room.

Start by keeping things modular. Just like a Lego set, your business should have pieces that can be easily added, removed, or rearranged. Maybe it's a service that can be paused during slower seasons, or a revenue stream that can expand as your capacity grows. The goal is to create a structure that serves your needs now while leaving room for future evolution.

Next, embrace the idea of upgrades. As new tools, technologies, or strategies become available, don't be afraid to swap out old pieces for newer, better ones.

Think of it as replacing the Lego castle's drawbridge with a sleek motorized version—because who doesn't love a little innovation?

And don't forget the dragon. By which I mean: leave room for creativity, experimentation, and fun. A flexible business blueprint isn't just practical; it's also a canvas for your imagination. Whether it's launching a new project, exploring a passion, or simply adding a playful twist to your work, these "dragons" keep things exciting and uniquely yours.

Reconfiguring as Needed

The beauty of future-proofing is that it's not about locking yourself into a single vision. It's about giving yourself the tools and freedom to reconfigure whenever you need to. As your goals evolve, your business can, too—transforming from a simple house to a sprawling castle, a futuristic spaceship, or even a cozy hobbit hole, depending on where life takes you.

Why It Matters

A flexible blueprint isn't just a safeguard against change; it's an invitation to embrace it. It ensures that your business remains a source of joy and fulfillment, not a source of frustration or stagnation. And, perhaps most importantly, it lets you approach the future with confidence, knowing that no matter what happens, you've built something that can grow, adapt, and thrive.

So, grab your metaphorical Lego bricks, leave space for a dragon or two, and start designing. Because the best business blueprints aren't rigid—they're as dynamic, creative, and full of potential as the people building them.

The Blueprint for a Business That Fits Your Life:

From Hamster Wheel to Hammock—A Business That Works for You

Let's take a moment to step back and admire the work you've done. You've laid the foundation for something remarkable—a business that doesn't run you ragged on an endless hamster wheel but instead cradles you like a cozy hammock on a sunny afternoon. This is the essence of a life-first business blueprint: it supports you, fits your lifestyle, and gives you the freedom to enjoy the ride.

Think of your blueprint as a treehouse with the perfect view. It's sturdy enough to weather storms but flexible enough to add a new ladder, a rope swing, or even a telescope as your needs and dreams evolve. It's not just a structure—it's a sanctuary, designed to reflect who you are and what matters most to you.

Revisiting the Joys of a Life-First Business

When your business aligns with your life, something magical happens. Work becomes less about grinding and more about purpose. You find space for creativity, connection, and those little moments of joy that make it all worthwhile. You're no longer trapped by your own ambitions but empowered by them, free to grow your business without sacrificing your well-being.

It's not about perfection—because let's face it, even the most idyllic treehouses occasionally need repairs. It's about creating something that evolves with you, offering both stability and flexibility as life's seasons change.

Your Next Steps

As you move forward, remember that this blueprint is yours to design and redesign. Tweak it, test it, and build on it as your priorities shift. Whether you're adding new branches, streamlining old processes, or simply adjusting the view, know that you have the tools to make it work for you—not the other way around.

And if the metaphorical hammock feels wobbly at times, that's okay. It's all part of the process. The important thing is that you're creating something intentional—something that supports your goals, nurtures your passions, and leaves room for the moments that matter most.

A Hopeful Nudge

Your life-first business blueprint is more than just a plan; it's a chance to design something beautiful, functional, and uniquely yours. Like a treehouse with the perfect view, it's built for you and by you, reflecting the life you want to live.

So go ahead—dream big, start small, and don't be afraid to tweak and build as you go. Because the best businesses aren't just about success; they're about creating a life that feels deeply, unapologetically yours. And that, my friend, is the ultimate view.

Chapter Seven

Delegation and Outsourcing

The Fine Art of Letting Someone Else Do It

LET ME SET THE scene for you. Picture a parking lot on a breezy Saturday afternoon. There I am, valiantly attempting to juggle a full shopping cart packed with precariously balanced groceries, a coffee cup teetering dangerously close to disaster, and a very excitable dog on a leash who seems to think squirrels are a divine calling. It was a moment of pure, unfiltered chaos—a symphony of bags tearing, coffee splashing, and the dog lunging with unbridled enthusiasm.

Why didn't I ask for help, you ask? Excellent question. Perhaps I wanted to prove I could handle it all. Or perhaps I foolishly thought, *How hard could it be?* Spoiler: it was very hard, and I ended up chasing an onion across the parking lot while my coffee soaked into the pavement.

This, dear reader, is precisely the entrepreneurial dilemma. We charge headfirst into our businesses with the confidence of a superhero, determined to do it all ourselves. Every task, every decision, every email—it all rests squarely on our shoulders. And before we know it, we've become a one-person circus act, juggling flaming torches while riding a unicycle and wondering why we're so exhausted.

The entrepreneurial spirit is a curious thing. It whispers sweet nothings about independence and self-sufficiency, convincing us that no one else could possibly do the job as well as we can. It's why we find ourselves formatting spreadsheets at midnight, fixing website glitches we barely understand, or answering client emails while cooking dinner.

But here's the thing: doing it all isn't just inefficient—it's unsustainable. The more we insist on clinging to every task, the more we dilute our energy, creativity, and sanity. It's like trying to hold onto a pile of marbles while someone keeps tossing in more. Sooner or later, they're going to scatter.

The Secret Sauce of Success

This is where delegation and outsourcing come in. Contrary to popular belief, handing off tasks isn't an admission of weakness. It's the secret sauce that allows you to focus on what you're best at while letting others handle the rest. It's the difference between being the ringleader of a circus and being the star performer—you get to do what you love without having to clean up after the elephants.

When you delegate effectively, you create space for growth, creativity, and, dare I say it, even relaxation. Outsourcing isn't about giving up control; it's about taking control of your time and energy. It's a strategic move that says, "I value my work—and myself—enough to let others help."

In this chapter, we'll explore the fine art of letting someone else do it. We'll talk about identifying the tasks that belong on someone else's plate, finding the right people to trust, and mastering the delicate balance of delegation without micromanaging.

Because, let's face it, no one starts a business to become a harried juggler of endless responsibilities. You started this journey to create something meaningful, to build a life you love, and maybe—just maybe—to enjoy the occasional quiet coffee without worrying about the hundred things waiting for you.

So, let's put down the shopping cart, leash, and coffee (metaphorically, of course) and embrace the liberating power of letting go. Because the only thing better than doing it all yourself is realizing you don't have to.

Recognizing Opportunities for Delegation:

What to Offload and Why You'll Thank Yourself Later

Let's begin with a confession: entrepreneurs have a peculiar knack for thinking they can do it all. It's a mindset that starts innocently enough—how hard could it be to handle a little bookkeeping, whip up a logo, or unclog the office coffee maker? But before you know it, you're knee-deep in tasks that range from "mildly annoying" to "entirely out of your depth," and your to-do list reads like the credits of a one-person indie film.

This is what I like to call the DIY Trap. It's the entrepreneurial equivalent of trying to pilot an airplane while simultaneously serving drinks in coach. Sure, you *can* do it, but should you? Probably not—unless you enjoy turbulence and unhappy passengers (both literal and metaphorical).

The DIY mindset often stems from a well-meaning but misguided belief that no one else can do the job quite like you. It whispers in your ear, "You know what you're doing—why trust this to someone else?" It convinces you that hiring help is an unnecessary expense, a sign of weakness, or, worst of all, a risk to your precious control.

But here's the kicker: doing everything yourself doesn't just burn you out—it holds your business back. When you're bogged down in minutiae, you have less time and energy for the things that truly matter, like strategy, growth, and even the occasional afternoon off.

Identifying What to Offload

The first step in escaping the DIY Trap is figuring out what, exactly, belongs on someone else's plate. Start by asking yourself a few key questions:

- Does this task require my unique expertise?

- Is this something I dread, avoid, or feel woefully unqualified to handle?

- Would outsourcing this free up time for higher-impact activities?

If the answer to the last two questions is "yes," congratulations—you've just found a prime candidate for delegation. Think bookkeeping, graphic design, IT troubleshooting, or any of the countless administrative tasks that sap your energy without adding much value.

When you start offloading tasks, something magical happens. You free yourself from the endless churn of low-value work, giving you the bandwidth to focus on what you're truly good at. It's like upgrading from a pedal boat to a speedboat—you're still steering, but now you've got the horsepower to move forward at a pace that feels exhilarating rather than exhausting.

The Power of Prioritization

Delegation isn't about throwing every task at the nearest willing person. It's about strategically choosing what to hand off so you can spend your time on the things that make the biggest difference. By recognizing opportunities for delegation, you're not just lightening your workload—you're setting the stage for a business that runs more smoothly, grows more efficiently, and allows you to be the kind of leader you always imagined.

So, let's leave the DIY Trap behind and embrace the art of letting go. Because piloting the plane is hard enough without trying to pour coffee at the same time—and trust me, the passengers will thank you for it.

The 3 Ds - Delegate, Defer, or Delete: A Framework for Finally Letting Go

When it comes to recognizing what to offload, entrepreneurs often need a little nudge—or perhaps a full-blown shove—out of their "I'll just do it myself" mindset. That's where the 3 Ds come in: Delegate, Defer, or Delete. It's a simple framework that cuts through the noise and helps you decide what stays on your plate and what can be gracefully handed off to someone else (or kicked to the curb entirely).

Think of it as triaging your to-do list, separating the things you *must* handle personally from the things you absolutely shouldn't touch, like tax forms or a client's website design (unless you happen to be a CPA or a web designer, in which case, carry on).

Dreaded Tasks

First up: the tasks you dread. You know the ones—they sit on your to-do list for days, taunting you with their sheer unpleasantness. Maybe it's cold-calling potential clients, wrangling expense reports, or attempting to fix that printer jam for the umpteenth time.

The rule here is simple: if the mere thought of a task makes you sigh audibly or suddenly remember five other things you'd rather do (like reorganize your sock drawer), it's probably time to delegate. Not only will you save yourself the agony, but you'll also get the job done faster by entrusting it to someone who doesn't actively despise it.

Tasks You're Terrible At

Next, let's talk about the tasks you're absolutely terrible at. It's okay to admit this—we all have our strengths, and graphic design or number crunching doesn't have to be one of them.

If you've ever spent hours formatting a spreadsheet only to have it look like a ransom note, or designed a logo that could be mistaken for a third grader's art project, it's time to hand those tasks over. Someone out there can do it faster, better, and with far less colorful language involved.

Tasks Someone Else Could Do Better

Finally, we have the tasks that someone else could do faster, better, or with significantly less grumbling. Just because you *can* do something doesn't mean you *should*. If a task is eating up hours of your day and adding little value, it's a prime candidate for delegation.

Picture this: you're painstakingly managing social media posts, spending hours crafting hashtags that may or may not land. Meanwhile, a marketing pro could whip up a month's worth of engaging content in half the time. Why not let them handle it while you focus on what you do best?

Defer or Delete

Of course, not every task needs to be delegated—some can simply be deferred or deleted altogether. Ask yourself: *Does this really need to be done right now? Or at all?* You'd be amazed at how many items on a typical to-do list turn out to be non-essential fluff. Deleting them doesn't just save time; it clears mental space, too.

Why the 3 Ds Matter

By applying the Delegate, Defer, or Delete framework, you'll not only lighten your workload but also rediscover the joy of focusing on the tasks that truly matter. It's like cleaning out a cluttered closet—once you get rid of the things you don't need, you're left with a streamlined, functional, and downright satisfying system.

So, grab your to-do list, take a deep breath, and start sorting. Because life's too short to spend it wrestling with tasks you dread, bungle, or could easily hand off to someone else—and no one wants to be remembered as the person who spent their best years battling spreadsheets and printers.

How to Spot a Delegate-Worthy Task

Not all tasks are created equal. Some are straightforward, manageable, possibly even enjoyable. Others? They're the stuff of entrepreneurial nightmares—time-draining, soul-sucking, and so convoluted they make you question your life choices. These are the tasks that practically beg to be handed off to someone else. But how do you spot them? Let's break it down with a few telltale signs.

The Overly Complicated Spreadsheet

If you've ever created a spreadsheet so intricate it looks like it was pulled straight from a conspiracy theory documentary—complete with color-coded tabs, pivot tables, and cryptic abbreviations even you don't remember—congratulations, you've found a delegate-worthy task. There's someone out there who genuinely enjoys wrangling data into submission, and it's time to let them have at it.

The Eternal Email Chain

Then there are the email chains that seem to stretch into infinity. You know the ones—emails that bounce back and forth so many times they start to resemble a digital tennis match, complete with subject lines like "Re: Re: Re: Just Circling Back." If you find yourself typing the words *"Per my last email"* for the third time, it's a clear sign this task needs to be handed off to someone who thrives on follow-ups.

The Pinterest-Worthy Presentation

Let's talk about tasks that require an artistic touch. If you're spending hours designing a PowerPoint presentation and the result looks less like a sleek corporate pitch and more like a middle school science project, it's time to delegate. Graphic designers exist for a reason, and they can turn your vision into a masterpiece while you focus on things that don't involve font selection.

The Tedious Admin Task

Anything that involves repetitive clicking, copying, or formatting is a prime candidate for delegation. This includes inputting data, scheduling meetings, and processing invoices. If it makes you feel like a robot, there's probably a tool—or better yet, a person—who can handle it for you with far less frustration.

The Task You Keep Avoiding

Finally, there's the task that sits on your to-do list like a dark cloud, lingering for days, weeks, or even months. Maybe it's reconciling receipts, responding to that difficult client, or updating your website's "About" page. Whatever it is, if you keep finding reasons to do literally anything else, it's time to let someone else tackle it.

Hand It Off and Move On

The beauty of spotting delegate-worthy tasks is that it frees you to focus on what you're truly good at—whether that's strategic planning, creative work, or finally having time for that second cup of coffee. Delegation isn't just about saving time; it's about preserving your sanity and ensuring your business runs smoothly without you shouldering every burden.

So, the next time you're knee-deep in a task that feels more like a conspiracy theory than a necessity, ask yourself: *Do I really need to do this myself?* Chances are, the answer is no—and you'll thank yourself later for letting it go. After all, no one ever regretted delegating the creation of a color-coded, borderline-unreadable spreadsheet.

The ROI of Delegation: Clearing the Garage of Your To-Do List

Delegation is one of those magical tools that feels daunting at first but, once embraced, can completely transform your workday—and your sanity. Think of it as tackling the metaphorical garage of your to-do list. You know the one: packed to the brim with half-finished projects, things you swore you'd get to, and a few mysteries you don't even remember adding in the first place.

When you delegate effectively, it's like clearing out that cluttered space. Suddenly, the cobwebs are gone, the chaos is replaced with order, and you can actually see the floor—or, in this case, the bigger picture of your business.

Time: Your Most Precious Resource

Let's talk about time, the one thing you can't make more of (unless you've cracked the code for time travel, in which case, I'd love to hear about it). Delegating frees up hours that you've been wasting on tasks that could easily be handled by someone else.

Instead of spending two hours reconciling receipts or scheduling social media posts, imagine using that time to focus on strategy, innovation, or simply having lunch without also juggling emails. Delegation gives you the gift of time—time to work smarter, grow your business, and maybe even take a breather.

Mental Energy: The Invisible ROI

But it's not just about hours saved; it's also about the mental energy you get back. Every task you delegate is one less thing cluttering your mind. It's like clearing out the mental equivalent of those boxes in the garage labeled *"Miscellaneous"* that you've been avoiding for years.

With fewer low-level tasks weighing you down, you'll find it easier to concentrate on the things that truly matter. Decisions come more easily, creativity flows more freely, and you're not constantly distracted by the nagging feeling that you forgot to update the company calendar.

The Bigger Payoff

Delegation doesn't just make your to-do list shorter; it makes your business stronger. By entrusting tasks to capable hands, you're building a team that's empowered, efficient, and invested in the success of the business. Meanwhile, you're free to focus on the high-impact work that only you can do—whether that's crafting the next big idea, forging partnerships, or just enjoying the rare luxury of thinking without interruptions.

The Garage Makeover

So, if your to-do list feels like a cluttered garage, delegation is your Marie Kondo moment. Start by asking, *Does this task spark joy—or can someone else do it better, faster, or with less frustration?* Then hand it off, step back, and watch as your workday transforms.

The ROI is clear: less clutter, more clarity, and a renewed sense of control over your time and energy. And while your garage may still need sorting, at least your business will be running like the well-oiled machine it was always meant to be.

Building Trust with Your Team

Trusting someone else with something you care deeply about is no small feat. It's why entrepreneurs often hesitate to delegate truly important tasks to their team. It's not that you don't like or respect your employees—it's just that handing over the reins of your beloved business can feel a bit like giving your prized bicycle to a toddler. There's an understandable fear that they might steer it straight into a wall or, worse, leave it in a ditch while they wander off to chase butterflies.

But here's the thing: just like that toddler, your team is far more capable than you might think. Sure, there's a chance they'll wobble at first, but with trust, guidance, and a bit of practice, they might just surprise you by riding off into the sunset like seasoned pros.

For entrepreneurs, the fear of trusting their team often boils down to three big concerns. First, there's the fear of losing control—the idea that if you're not involved in every decision, everything will spiral into chaos. Then, there's the fear of mistakes, which can feel catastrophic when your name is on the door. And finally, there's the fear of being let down, that nagging worry that no one will care about your business as much as you do.

These fears are understandable, even logical. After all, you've poured your heart, soul, and countless late nights into building this business. It's natural to want to protect it. But clinging too tightly can turn you into the bottleneck, and that doesn't serve anyone—not you, not your team, and certainly not your business.

Handing Over the Reins

The key to overcoming these fears is realizing that trust isn't an all-or-nothing proposition. It's a gradual process, like teaching someone to ride a bike. You start with training wheels—small tasks that allow your team to gain confidence and prove their capabilities. As they get better, you loosen your grip, allowing them to take on more responsibility.

Yes, there will be wobbles, and maybe even a scraped knee or two. But that's how people learn. The important thing is to resist the urge to hover or micromanage. Nothing stifles growth faster than a leader who refuses to let go of the handlebars.

When you trust your team, you're not just freeing yourself from the burden of doing everything—you're empowering them to take ownership of their work. This leads to better performance, higher morale, and a team that's genuinely invested in the success of the business.

And let's not forget the personal rewards. Delegating and trusting your team doesn't just make you a better leader; it makes your life easier. Imagine spending less time stressing over every detail and more time focusing on the big picture—or simply enjoying a well-earned break.

So, yes, trusting your team can feel a bit like handing over the reins of your beloved bicycle to a toddler. But with the right support and a little patience, that toddler grows into a confident cyclist. And before you know it, they're zipping along smoothly, leaving you free to focus on the road ahead—or take a moment to sit back and enjoy the ride.

Because the true beauty of trust isn't just what it does for your team; it's what it does for you.

Setting Your Team Up for Delegation Triumph

If delegation is an art, then training your team is the primer coat—it sets the foundation for something that not only works but shines. The secret? Clear instructions, achievable goals, and the unshakable resolve to avoid the perilously vague directive of *"make it amazing."* Because, let's face it, *"amazing"* is a wonderful word for fireworks and sunsets, but it's woefully unhelpful in a professional setting.

Start with clarity. There's a world of difference between *"fix the website"* and *"optimize the homepage for faster load times and improve the call-to-action placement."* The first is a cryptic puzzle that could lead anywhere; the second is a roadmap. When you're assigning a task, think of yourself as a GPS—provide detailed directions to ensure your team knows where they're headed and how to get there.

Next, let's talk about setting achievable goals. There's no faster way to demoralize your team than by handing them a task with expectations that rival a moon landing. Aim for stretch, not stress. For instance, instead of saying, *"Increase sales by 200% this week,"* try something more realistic: *"Let's test a new sales strategy and aim for a 20% increase this quarter."*

Achievable goals keep motivation high and anxiety low—plus, they provide a clear benchmark for success.

Avoiding the Vague Abyss

Ah, the danger of vagueness. We've all been guilty of it at some point—dropping phrases like, *"Make it pop,"* or *"I trust your judgment"* and then wondering why the end result looks nothing like we imagined. To prevent this, be specific. If you have a vision, spell it out. If there are examples of what you like (or don't like), share them.

Avoiding the vague abyss doesn't mean micromanaging—it just means giving your team the tools they need to deliver exactly what you're looking for.

Empowering Ownership

Once the instructions and goals are in place, it's time to empower your team to own the task. This means giving them the freedom to approach the work in their own way, make decisions, and bring their unique skills to the table. Think of it as handing them the ingredients for a cake and letting them bake it, rather than hovering over their shoulder and insisting they mix counterclockwise.

Feedback for Growth

Finally, set the stage for feedback—not just at the end of the task, but throughout the process. Constructive feedback helps your team grow, refine their skills, and feel confident in their abilities. And don't forget to celebrate their wins, big or small. A quick *"Great job!"* can go a long way in building trust and morale.

The Payoff

Training your team for delegation success isn't just about completing tasks; it's about building a culture of collaboration, accountability, and excellence. With clear instructions, achievable goals, and the occasional high-five, you'll find that delegation becomes less of a leap of faith and more of a calculated step toward freedom.

So, set the bar, point the way, and let your team surprise you—not with vague *"amazing,"* but with results that genuinely make your business shine. After all, a well-prepped team doesn't just meet expectations; it exceeds them—and has fun doing it.

Turning Employees into Owners of Their Work (Without Actually Handing Them the Keys)

Building a culture of ownership isn't about legally transferring shares or doling out titles like "Chief of All Things Awesome" (though the latter sounds fun). It's about creating an environment where your employees feel genuinely invested in their work—like their ideas, decisions, and efforts actually matter. When done right, this approach doesn't just lead to better results; it transforms your team into a group of proactive, problem-solving dynamos.

And the best part? You no longer have to answer every question or make every decision. Instead, you can watch your team take the lead—whether it's running a meeting, landing a client, or, yes, conquering the office printer (more on that in a moment).When employees feel ownership, they're not just completing tasks—they're taking pride in their work. It's the difference between someone saying, *"I fixed the problem"* versus, *"I solved the client's issue and streamlined the process for next time."* Ownership encourages initiative, creativity, and a sense of responsibility that no amount of micromanaging can achieve.

The Power of Praising Wins (Even Small Ones)

One of the simplest ways to foster ownership is to celebrate successes, no matter how small. Let's say someone on your team finally figures out the office printer—a notoriously temperamental beast that's baffled even the IT department. This might seem like a minor victory, but it's a golden opportunity to say, *"Great job! You've saved us from the brink of paper-jam-induced madness."*

Small wins create momentum, build confidence, and show your team that their efforts are noticed and appreciated. And when employees feel valued, they're more likely to step up and tackle bigger challenges with the same enthusiasm.

Encouraging Initiative

Another key ingredient in the ownership recipe is encouraging initiative. When employees come to you with a problem, resist the urge to swoop in with a solution (tempting as it may be). Instead, ask, *"What do you think we should do?"* This simple question shifts the focus from dependency to problem-solving, empowering your team to think critically and take action.

It's a bit like teaching someone to fish—not only do they figure out how to catch dinner, but they also stop calling you every time they're hungry.

Building Trust Through Responsibility

Trust is the backbone of a culture of ownership. This means giving your team the responsibility to make decisions and the freedom to learn from mistakes. Yes, mistakes will happen, but they're also where growth occurs. As long as the errors aren't catastrophic (no accidentally deleting the company's entire database, please), they're valuable learning opportunities that build confidence and competence.

When ownership becomes part of your company culture, it creates a ripple effect. Employees who feel empowered to take initiative inspire others to do the same. The result? A team that functions more like a well-tuned orchestra than a scattered collection of soloists.

And as the leader, you get the joy of watching your team shine—not because you micromanaged every note, but because you gave them the tools, trust, and encouragement to play their best.

So, the next time someone conquers a seemingly small task, like getting the office printer to finally spit out a double-sided report, don't dismiss it as trivial. Celebrate it, laugh about it, and use it as a springboard to cultivate even more initiative and ownership.

Because when employees feel empowered, they're not just working—they're building something they're proud of. And that, my friend, is how you create a team that doesn't just show up but takes charge.

The Magic of Letting Go: The Freedom to Trust and Truly Step Away

Letting go is one of those things that sounds impossibly simple in theory and terrifyingly difficult in practice—like riding a bike without training wheels for the first time. But once you master it, you realize it's not just liberating; it's downright magical.

Imagine this: It's a sunny afternoon, and you've decided to treat yourself to a long-overdue lunch at your favorite little café. The kind with mismatched chairs, fresh pastries, and a charmingly surly barista who knows your name. For the first time in ages, you're not clutching your phone like a lifeline, refreshing your email every thirty seconds or bracing for a panicked message from your team.

Instead, you're sipping coffee, savoring a sandwich that's far too delicious to eat in a hurry, and letting your mind wander. And here's the best part: back at the office (or across a series of remote workspaces), your team is handling everything. The emails are being answered, the projects are progressing, and the printer—dare we dream—might even be behaving itself.

When you trust your team, you're not just delegating tasks; you're reclaiming your life. You're making space for creativity, big-picture thinking, and those rare, precious moments when you can simply be present.

Letting go means you're no longer the default fixer, the all-knowing answerer, or the person who must oversee every detail. It means you can focus on the things that light you up, whether that's strategizing for the future, spending time with family, or finally learning how to make those perfect soufflés you've been dreaming about. The beauty of letting go is that it allows your team to rise to the occasion. When you trust them to take ownership, they don't just meet expectations—they exceed them. They solve problems you didn't even know existed, come up with ideas you hadn't considered, and keep the business humming along without you hovering like a helicopter on caffeine.

So, here's to that worry-free lunch—the ultimate symbol of a well-functioning, trust-filled team. It's a moment of peace, a reminder of why you started this business in the first place, and proof that letting go isn't about losing control; it's about gaining freedom.

Because when you finally step back and let your team take the reins, you're not just building a stronger business—you're creating a life where you can breathe, dream, and savor every bite of that impossibly good sandwich. And honestly, isn't that what it's all about?

Choosing the Right Partners: Outsourcing Without Regrets (or Nefarious Contractors)

Outsourcing is one of those words that tends to conjure a mix of excitement and trepidation. On the one hand, it promises to lighten your load and free up your time; on the other, it raises a nagging fear of entrusting your precious business tasks to someone who might mess it all up. It's a bit like handing over your house keys to a cleaner for the first time—equal parts hope and panic.

But here's the thing: just as hiring a professional cleaner can be the best decision you've ever made (goodbye, scrubbing bathroom grout!), outsourcing non-core business functions can be a total game-changer. It's not about giving away control; it's about strategically lightening your burden so you can focus on what you do best.

The Case for Outsourcing

Let's start with the big picture: why outsource at all? The answer is simple—because you can't (and shouldn't) do everything yourself. Certain tasks, while necessary, don't require your unique expertise. Things like bookkeeping, IT support, and managing social media are critical to your business's success, but they don't necessarily need your personal touch.

By outsourcing these functions to skilled professionals, you're essentially saying, *"I value my time and energy too much to spend it wrestling with QuickBooks or figuring out why the Wi-Fi won't connect."* Instead, you can direct your focus toward the areas where you truly shine—whether that's innovation, strategy, or building relationships with clients.

Think of outsourcing as the business equivalent of hiring someone to clean your house. Sure, you could spend your weekend scrubbing floors, dusting shelves, and vacuuming under the couch (where dust bunnies go to party). But what if you could pay a professional to handle all of that, leaving you free to spend your Saturday doing something you actually enjoy?

The same principle applies to your business. Outsourcing non-core functions isn't an indulgence; it's a smart investment in your productivity, peace of mind, and overall quality of life.

Where Outsourcing Shines

Outsourcing works best for tasks that are time-consuming, specialized, or just plain tedious. Need a beautifully designed website? Hire a web developer. Want to keep your financials in order without losing sleep? Bring in an accountant. Eyeing a sleek marketing campaign that doesn't look like it was made in PowerPoint circa 2005? Call a pro.

When you outsource to the right partners, you're not just offloading tasks—you're elevating the quality of work your business produces. And that, my friend, is worth every penny.

Outsourcing is about making smart choices that free you to focus on what truly matters. It's like handing over the mop and bucket so you can spend your time building, growing, and enjoying the business you've worked so hard to create.

So, embrace the magic of outsourcing—whether it's hiring a cleaner to make your house sparkle or bringing in experts to handle the nuts and bolts of your business. Either way, you'll thank yourself for the peace, efficiency, and freedom it brings. And who knows? You might even find time to finally tackle that hobby you've been putting off—without a mop in sight.

What to Outsource: Leave the Mystical Arts (and Payroll) to the Pros

Deciding what to outsource can feel a bit like deciding what to order at an overwhelmingly large buffet. There are so many options, and while it's tempting to just grab everything, you know you'll regret that later. Instead, focus on the areas where outsourcing can have the biggest impact—the tasks that are essential but don't require your personal expertise or, let's be honest, your frustration.

Let's start with a classic: IT support. If you've ever found yourself Googling *"Why won't my printer connect to the Wi-Fi?"* or staring blankly at an error message on your website like it's a riddle from an ancient sorcerer, it's time to call in the professionals. Fixing mysterious glitches, whether on your website or your office network, is best left to people who might as well be wizards.

The Perks of Passing Off Payroll

Next up: payroll. Ah, payroll—the task that strikes terror into the hearts of even the most confident entrepreneurs. Calculating taxes, keeping track of deductions, and making sure everyone gets paid on time is about as fun as herding cats through a field of laser pointers. Fortunately, there are payroll specialists who actually *enjoy* this sort of thing, and they'll handle it with far fewer expletives than you would.

Social Media Magic

Then there's social media management. Sure, posting the occasional photo or clever caption sounds easy enough, but keeping up with algorithms, hashtags, and the whims of an ever-changing digital audience is a full-time job. If your idea of a social media strategy is "post something and hope for the best," it's probably time to bring in a pro. They'll create content that actually engages your audience while you focus on the things you love—or at least the things that don't involve deciphering TikTok trends.

The Creative Conundrum

Graphic design, video editing, and other creative tasks are also prime candidates for outsourcing. If your attempts at designing a logo or editing a promo video look like they belong in a high school art project, do yourself a favor and hire someone who knows what they're doing. You'll end up with professional results and a lot less yelling at your computer screen.

Freeing Yourself for What Matters

Outsourcing isn't about shirking responsibility; it's about focusing your time and energy on the areas where you can make the biggest impact. Whether it's IT, payroll, social media, or creative projects, entrusting these tasks to experts doesn't just make your business better—it makes your life easier.

So, step back from the keyboard, put down the DIY how-to guides, and let the wizards, payroll pros, and social media mavens do what they do best. Because while you're busy running your business, they'll be behind the scenes making it shine. And honestly, isn't it nice to leave the mystical arts to someone else for a change?

Finding Outsourcing Solutions Without the Picasso Effect

Outsourcing can feel like a leap of faith. You're entrusting a part of your business to someone else, and the stakes feel high—after all, no one wants to request a sleek, professional website and end up with something that looks like Picasso took a stab at web design. The good news is that with a little due diligence and a dash of common sense, you can find outsourcing partners who deliver quality work without leaving you clutching your head in bewilderment.

The first step in vetting potential partners is to ask for references. A great outsourcing provider will have a list of happy clients who are more than willing to sing their praises. But here's the key: don't just take their word for it. Reach out to those references and ask specific questions about their experience. Did the provider deliver on time? Were they easy to work with? Did the final product look like a professional masterpiece or a first grader's finger painting?

A strong portfolio is like a crystal ball—it gives you a glimpse into what the provider is capable of before you hand over your hard-earned money. Look for examples of their previous work, and make sure it aligns with your vision. If their portfolio is full of avant-garde, edgy designs and you're looking for something clean and corporate, it's probably not a match made in outsourcing heaven.

Avoid the Magic Promisers

Beware of anyone who makes promises that sound too good to be true. If a prospective partner guarantees results that seem more like magic than hard work—think *"We'll triple your sales overnight!"* or *"Your website will rank #1 on Google by next Tuesday!"*—run, don't walk, in the opposite direction. Good outsourcing is rooted in expertise, strategy, and realistic expectations, not smoke and mirrors.

Test the Waters

If you're unsure about committing to a new partner, start with a small project. This trial run allows you to gauge their work quality, communication skills, and ability to meet deadlines without risking a major investment. It's the outsourcing equivalent of dipping your toe in the water before diving headfirst into the pool.

Communication Is Key

A good outsourcing partner is as much about collaboration as it is about execution. Look for someone who listens to your needs, asks clarifying questions, and keeps you updated throughout the process. If they respond to your emails with cryptic one-liners or seem as hard to pin down as a cat in a bath, it's a red flag.

The Picasso Test

Finally, remember the Picasso Test: Does the provider understand your vision? Before you hire someone, make sure they grasp exactly what you're asking for. If you want a photograph and they're planning to deliver a Cubist interpretation, it's better to sort that out upfront than to discover it after the work is done.

The Art of Choosing Wisely

Vetting outsourcing partners may take a bit of time, but it's worth every second to ensure you're working with someone who delivers quality, consistency, and results that align with your needs. By asking for references, reviewing portfolios, and avoiding anyone who promises to conjure miracles, you'll find the right partner to take your business to the next level—no abstract paintings required.

And when you do? You'll be free to focus on the big picture, knowing the finer details are in capable hands. Because outsourcing should feel like hiring a skilled craftsman, not a mystery artist.

Spotting Red Flags Before It's Too Late

Outsourcing can be a lifesaver—when you choose the right partner. But sometimes, despite the glowing promises and slick presentations, something just feels... off. Maybe it's the bafflingly complex contract, or perhaps it's the way every email they send feels like you're deciphering a secret code from a 1940s war movie.

Whatever the reason, knowing when to walk away is just as important as knowing when to say yes.

The Contract Labyrinth

Let's start with contracts. A clear, straightforward agreement is a sign of professionalism. But if the contract looks like it was drafted by a lawyer who moonlights as a cryptographer, it's time to pause. Overly complex contracts stuffed with jargon and endless clauses could be a red flag that the provider is more interested in tying you up in fine print than delivering results.

A good contract should outline what's being done, when it's being done, and how much it'll cost—without requiring a translator or a law degree to understand. If you're left scratching your head or, worse, suspecting they've hidden something, it's better to back out before you're knee-deep in legalese.

The Morse Code Communication Style

Clear communication is the backbone of a successful outsourcing partnership. If your prospective partner has a knack for sending cryptic, one-sentence responses—or worse, goes radio silent for days—consider it a warning sign.

Good outsourcing providers keep you in the loop with regular updates, respond promptly to questions, and make you feel like a valued client. If you're getting the conversational equivalent of smoke signals or find yourself decoding vague phrases like *"We'll see what's possible,"* it's probably best to move on.

Overpromising and Underexplaining

Beware the vendor who promises the moon but can't explain how they'll deliver it. If their pitch is full of lofty guarantees but short on details, that's a red flag waving furiously in the wind.

For example, if someone claims they'll double your website traffic overnight but can't articulate the strategy behind it, it's time to question their credibility.

Trustworthy providers will be transparent about their methods and set realistic expectations—not spin tales of overnight miracles.

The Gut Check

Sometimes, the biggest red flag is simply a feeling that something isn't right. Maybe they dodge questions about their past work, seem oddly cagey about pricing, or have reviews that feel a little too glowing to be genuine. Trust your instincts. If you wouldn't feel comfortable handing them the keys to your car, you probably shouldn't hand them the keys to your business.

The Escape Plan

Walking away from a potential outsourcing partner doesn't mean you're burning bridges—it just means you're protecting your time, money, and sanity. Whether it's the contract, communication style, or a general lack of trustworthiness, recognizing these red flags early can save you from a world of frustration down the line.

And remember, the right partner is out there—someone who will make your life easier, not harder. So, if you spot the warning signs, don't hesitate to walk away. After all, no one wants to end up locked into a partnership that feels more like a mystery thriller than a productive collaboration.

Keeping the Ship on Course Without Micromanaging the Crew

Finding the balance between oversight and autonomy is one of the trickiest parts of working with a team or an outsourcing partner. Lean too far in one direction, and you're the hands-off captain who doesn't realize the ship has hit an iceberg until it's too late. Lean too far in the other, and you're the hovering presence peering over the captain's shoulder, asking for hourly updates while they try to steer.

The trick, as with most things in life, is balance—enough involvement to ensure the ship stays on course, but enough trust to let the crew do their jobs without feeling micromanaged into oblivion.

The Art of Checking In Without Taking Over

Let's start with communication. Regular updates are key, but they don't need to border on obsessive. Think weekly status reports or milestone check-ins rather than a constant barrage of emails demanding to know *"where things stand"* every few hours.

Imagine you've hired someone to paint a mural on the side of your building. You don't need to inspect every brushstroke, but you *do* want to ensure they're painting a sunset and not an interpretive abstract that looks like spilled spaghetti. It's about maintaining a steady dialogue—enough to catch potential issues early, but not so much that it stifles creativity and progress.

Setting Clear Expectations Up Front

Oversight becomes much easier when you've laid the groundwork with clear expectations from the start. Define what success looks like, establish deadlines, and agree on how often and in what format updates will be provided. This eliminates the need for constant check-ins because everyone knows what's expected and when it's due.

Think of it as plotting a course on a map before setting sail. If the destination is clear and the route is marked, the crew can focus on getting there without needing you to point out every wave along the way.

Trusting the Crew to Steer

This is where autonomy comes in. Once you've provided direction, step back and let the crew do their jobs. Trust that they're capable of navigating the waters—whether it's designing a website, running a marketing campaign, or managing customer support.

Of course, there's always the risk that they'll hit a bump or make a mistake. But here's the thing: mistakes are part of the process. They're opportunities for learning, growth, and, more often than not, a good story to tell later.

Course Corrections, Not Takeovers

When things don't go as planned—and they won't, occasionally—it's tempting to grab the wheel and steer the ship yourself. Resist the urge. Instead, think of your role as a navigator, someone who provides guidance to get things back on track without taking over completely.

For example, if a project is veering off course, schedule a conversation to address the issue, outline adjustments, and ensure everyone is aligned moving forward. This approach keeps you involved without undermining your team's confidence or autonomy.

The Freedom of Balanced Leadership

Balancing oversight and autonomy isn't just about getting better results; it's about freeing yourself from the exhausting role of perpetual overseer. By trusting your team and providing just enough guidance to keep the ship steady, you create a work environment where everyone—yourself included—can thrive.

So, check the map, glance at the compass, and maybe even pop your head up to enjoy the view. Because when you strike the right balance, your ship doesn't just stay on course—it sails smoothly toward the horizon, leaving you free to focus on what's next. And that, my friend, is leadership done right.

Check In, Don't Hover

Let's face it: no one thrives under the watchful eye of a boss who checks progress so frequently that the only thing progressing is everyone's frustration. It's like asking a chef if dinner is ready every thirty seconds—eventually, they'll serve you a raw chicken out of spite.

Instead, the key to staying informed without being intrusive is setting regular, meaningful checkpoints. Think of these as well-placed mile markers on a road trip. They give you the reassurance that you're heading in the right direction without the need to constantly stop and ask, *"Are we there yet?"*

The Goldilocks Approach to Check-Ins

Not too often, not too infrequent—checkpoints should strike that perfect balance between staying in the loop and giving your team or outsourcing partners room to breathe. Weekly or bi-weekly updates often hit the sweet spot, but the frequency can vary depending on the project's complexity and timeline.

The goal is to establish a rhythm: a predictable schedule where everyone knows when updates are expected and can prepare accordingly. This avoids the dreaded *"Got a minute?"* interruptions that derail focus and progress.

Making Checkpoints Meaningful

A good checkpoint is more than just a "What's the status?" interrogation. It's a structured opportunity to share updates, address challenges, and clarify next steps. Whether it's a quick email summary, a scheduled call, or a dashboard that tracks progress in real time, the format should fit the task and the team's workflow.

For instance, if you've hired a graphic designer to create a new logo, an initial checkpoint might involve reviewing early sketches to ensure the concept aligns with your vision. Later checkpoints might focus on color palettes and typography choices, leading to a polished final design.

Avoiding the Hover Syndrome

The temptation to overcheck—especially when you're deeply invested in the outcome—is real. But resist it. Hovering not only disrupts productivity but sends an unspoken message that you don't trust your team. And trust, as we've established, is the secret sauce of any successful partnership.

So, instead of hovering, remind yourself that progress often happens in the quiet spaces between updates. Give your team room to work their magic, and you'll likely be pleasantly surprised by the results.

The Perks of Proper Checkpoints

When you establish clear, meaningful checkpoints, you get the best of both worlds: the peace of mind that comes from knowing the work is on track and the freedom to focus on your own priorities without constantly checking in.

And for your team or partners, it creates an environment where they feel trusted, respected, and empowered to deliver their best work. After all, no one does their finest work with someone peering over their shoulder and muttering, *"How's it going now? And now? What about now?"*

The Checkpoint Creed

So, set your checkpoints, trust the process, and let progress unfold. Because when you strike the right balance, everyone wins: your team stays motivated, your projects stay on track, and you get to enjoy the rare luxury of *not* feeling like you have to do everything yourself.

As the saying goes, "A watched pot never boils," but a properly timed check-in keeps everything simmering beautifully.

Tracking the Fruits of Delegation (and Fewer Monday Blues)

Delegation and outsourcing are only truly effective if they make your business—and your life—better. But how do you measure that? Is it about hitting key metrics, pleasing customers, or simply getting to the end of a Monday without fantasizing about becoming a hermit in the woods? The answer, happily, is all of the above.

Measuring the success of delegation and outsourcing isn't just about numbers—it's about results, efficiency, and the subtle yet glorious feeling of finally being able to breathe.

Key Performance Indicators (KPIs): The Metrics That Matter

Start with the measurable stuff. KPIs are like the dashboard of a car—they tell you if you're speeding ahead, stuck in traffic, or about to run out of gas. Depending on what you've delegated or outsourced, these metrics might include:

- **Sales growth** for that marketing campaign you handed off.

- **Project completion times** for those tasks your team now handles.

- **Error rates** (or the lack thereof) in areas like payroll or IT.

The beauty of KPIs is their objectivity. They offer a clear, unbiased picture of whether things are running smoothly or if there's a bottleneck lurking somewhere.

Customer Satisfaction: The Ultimate Litmus Test

Your customers' happiness is often the best indicator of whether your delegation efforts are working. Are response times faster? Are complaints down? Are customers suddenly praising your business like you've discovered the secret to perfect coffee?

A noticeable improvement in customer satisfaction usually means your team or outsourced partners are doing their jobs well—freeing you to focus on bigger-picture goals instead of putting out daily fires.

Now, let's talk about something less quantifiable but equally important: how you feel. If delegation and outsourcing are working as they should, you'll notice subtle but profound changes in your daily life.

For instance, Monday mornings might no longer fill you with existential dread. Instead, you'll feel a quiet sense of optimism as you sip your coffee and review your week—not because everything's perfect, but because you know you're not tackling it alone.

Likewise, the little moments of relief—like seeing a task expertly handled without your input—are a testament to the power of letting go. If you find yourself with more time for strategic thinking, creative pursuits, or even the occasional midweek nap, you're doing delegation right.

Efficiency Gains: Time as a Currency

Another sign of success is the efficiency gained. Are tasks being completed faster and with fewer headaches? Do you have more time to focus on the work that truly excites you, rather than the minutiae that once consumed your days?

Time, after all, is the ultimate currency. And if you're finding yourself with more of it, that's a clear indication that your delegation efforts are paying off.

Periodic Check-Ins

Measuring success isn't a one-and-done deal. Periodically review how delegation and outsourcing are performing, both for you and your business. Are there areas where processes could be improved? Tasks that need tweaking? Or partners who are excelling beyond expectations?

Take stock regularly, and don't hesitate to pivot if something isn't working. After all, the goal is continuous improvement—not perfection.

The Sweet Taste of Success

Ultimately, the effectiveness of delegation and outsourcing can be measured not just in numbers, but in the rhythm of your days. When your business feels less like a circus act and more like a well-oiled machine, when customers are happier and Mondays feel manageable, you'll know you've struck the right balance.

And that, dear reader, is the magic of delegation. It's not just about lightening your load—it's about transforming your business and your life into something that feels lighter, brighter, and infinitely more enjoyable.

The Art of Adapting: Business as a Living Recipe

Building a business, much like crafting the perfect recipe, is rarely a one-and-done affair. It starts with a plan—a dash of this, a pinch of that, and the hope that everything will come together in a harmonious symphony of flavor. But as any good cook knows, the first attempt is usually just that: an attempt. Perhaps the soup is too salty, the cake a bit dense, or the sauce mysteriously beige when it's supposed to be vibrant green. Adjustments are inevitable, and the same is true for your business blueprint.

Adapting over time isn't a sign of failure; it's proof that you're paying attention. You try something, see how it works, and tweak it until it fits just right. Maybe you discover that a particular process is more cumbersome than you expected, like realizing that whisking egg whites by hand is not, in fact, a charming nod to tradition but a surefire way to question your life choices. So, you upgrade to an electric mixer—or in business terms, you streamline the process.

The beauty of adaptation lies in its iterative nature. Each adjustment brings you closer to the ideal, even if it means scrapping parts of the original plan entirely. There's a bit of trial and error involved, sure, but that's where the fun comes in. You're not just running a business; you're experimenting, learning, and growing alongside it. And unlike baking, where a burnt batch can fill the house with smoke and regret, most business tweaks are far less catastrophic (though they might occasionally feel as dramatic).

The key is to keep refining, to embrace the process of improvement without fear of making a few metaphorical kitchen messes along the way. Because in the end, it's not about achieving perfection—it's about creating something that works for you, your team, and your goals. Something that feels sustainable, satisfying, and—dare I say it—delightful.

So, treat your business like your favorite recipe: experiment, adjust, and don't worry too much about the occasional spill. Just keep stirring, tasting, and tweaking until you've crafted something truly wonderful. And if along the way you happen to discover the perfect recipe for both business and brownies, well, consider that a win-win.

Delegation as a Superpower

Delegation and outsourcing, when you boil them down, are far from an abdication of responsibility. They're a strategic choice, a way of focusing on what only you can do—your unique talents, your big ideas—while empowering others to shine in their roles. Think of it as being the conductor of a symphony rather than attempting to play every instrument yourself. Not only does it sound better, but it also saves you from looking absurd trying to balance a trombone and a flute simultaneously.

When you embrace delegation, something magical happens. You discover that the tasks you've been clinging to—the ones you thought no one else could possibly manage—are often handled beautifully by others. What's more, they might even enjoy doing them, which is its own sort of marvel. Suddenly, you're free to focus on the parts of your business that truly excite you, the areas where you can make the most impact, and—dare I say it—maybe even have some fun.

And let's not overlook the liberation that comes with letting go. There's a distinct joy in stepping back from the spreadsheets, the inbox, or the eternal wrestling match with the office photocopier and entrusting those responsibilities to someone else. It's a bit like handing over a tangled ball of Christmas lights and coming back to find them neatly arranged and twinkling on the tree.

So, here's your call to action: put down the spreadsheets, step away from the photocopier, and let someone else handle it for once. Lean into the power of delegation, and watch as your business hums along more smoothly—and your stress levels drop accordingly. You might just find that delegation isn't only practical—it's downright liberating. And who knows? You might even discover a little extra time to enjoy the music of that symphony you've so expertly conducted.

Chapter Eight

Tools and Technologies

The Brave New World of Business Gadgets and Gizmos

LET ME TELL YOU about my brief and tempestuous affair with a fax machine. It was the kind of device that seemed purpose-built to test one's patience—an awkward contraption that whirred, beeped, and occasionally spat out crumpled sheets of paper as if it had aspirations of becoming a rebellious artist. I distinctly remember one instance when, after an hour of battling its paper tray and deciphering its cryptic error messages, I finally managed to send a document... to the wrong number. It was a thrilling mix of triumph and utter defeat, and it cemented my belief that technology is both a blessing and a menace.

Fast forward to today, and we've swapped clunky fax machines for a bewildering array of modern business tools. Every other day, it seems, a new app or gadget bursts onto the scene, promising to revolutionize productivity, streamline communication, and generally make you feel like a tech-savvy superhero. But more often than not, they leave you staring at a user interface that might as well be written in hieroglyphs, wondering if this new marvel will be your salvation or yet another item on your growing list of frustrations.

Navigating this digital labyrinth can feel like entering a tech obstacle course: passwords to remember, integrations to configure, and a dozen alerts pinging you into submission before your first sip of coffee. Even the names of these tools can be absurdly optimistic—names like "Workflow Wizard" or "Synergy Hub," as if just downloading the app will somehow grant you magical powers or cosmic balance.

But here's the thing: while tools and technologies have an uncanny ability to complicate life temporarily, when used wisely, they can be extraordinary allies. They're like the well-designed gadgets in a spy movie—intimidating at first but ultimately indispensable once you figure out which button to press. The key is finding the ones that fit your needs rather than trying to adapt your life to fit their quirks.

This chapter is your guide to sorting the wheat from the chaff—or, in this case, the truly helpful from the hopelessly overhyped. We'll dive into the gadgets and gizmos that actually deliver on their promises, and we'll explore how to harness their power without letting them take over your life. Because let's face it: the goal isn't to become a tech wizard. It's to find the right tools to free you up for the things that matter—like building your business, enjoying your downtime, and never, ever wrestling with a fax machine again.

Automation Essentials: Let the Robots Take the Wheel (For the Boring Stuff)

Picture this: it's late, you've been staring at your computer screen for hours, and you're knee-deep in a repetitive task that's equal parts soul-sucking and mind-numbing. Perhaps it's processing invoices, sorting emails, or updating a spreadsheet so complex it resembles an aerial map of a major city. It's the kind of work that makes you question your life choices and wonder why robots haven't taken over already. And then it hits you—robots *can* take over. At least, for the boring stuff.

Automation isn't some far-off sci-fi fantasy with blinking lights and humanoid machines with questionable ethics. It's here, it's real, and it's the secret sauce to reclaiming your time and sanity. Think of it as delegating your dullest, most repetitive tasks to a digital assistant that doesn't need coffee breaks, never forgets instructions, and doesn't complain about the monotony.

But let's be honest: the world of automation can feel intimidating at first. The sheer number of tools available, each promising to "revolutionize" your workflow, is enough to make even the savviest entrepreneur's head spin. You find yourself drowning in jargon like "AI-powered" and "cloud-based," wondering if you need a degree in computer science to send a simple invoice.

Fear not. The beauty of automation lies not in its complexity but in its simplicity. The best tools are the ones that seamlessly slip into your daily operations, quietly taking over the tedious bits while you focus on what really matters. It's like hiring an invisible assistant who never sleeps, never complains, and never sends you a resignation email on a Monday morning.

In this section, we'll explore the essentials of automation—what it is, why it matters, and how to make it work for you without turning your business into a scene from *The Matrix*. You'll discover the tools that can handle your repetitive tasks, freeing up hours in your day to tackle bigger, more meaningful projects—or, dare I say it, take a proper lunch break.

So, let the robots take the wheel for the boring stuff. You'll not only save time and energy but also avoid the dreaded monotony of tasks that seem designed to test your patience. And who knows? You might even start to enjoy watching your digital helpers work their quiet magic while you sip your coffee and dream a little bigger. Because automation isn't just a productivity boost—it's a sanity saver. And really, who couldn't use a bit more of that?

Why Automate? A Practical Take on Friendly Robots

When most of us think of robots, our minds immediately drift to science fiction. Perhaps it's an image of gleaming metal humanoids plotting world domination or zipping around in spaceships with unsettling efficiency. The robots we imagine are either frighteningly brilliant or hilariously inept—think less *Star Wars'* R2-D2 and more the clunky creations that stumble around in low-budget films, bumping into walls. But here's the thing: the real-life robots in your business are much less dramatic. They don't have existential crises or dreams of overthrowing humanity. Their main goals? To send emails, schedule appointments, and save you from the tedious grind of repetitive tasks.

Imagine, for a moment, a robot that exists solely to make your life easier. It doesn't beep ominously or demand a power source that requires NASA-level ingenuity. Instead, it's an unassuming bit of software that quietly takes over the boring, repetitive parts of your day. Need invoices sent out automatically? Done. Want reminders sent to clients without lifting a finger? No problem. It's like having a silent, hyper-efficient assistant who handles the grunt work while you focus on more exciting—and human—tasks.

So, why automate? Because life is too short to spend it wading through the endless swamp of administrative details. Automation frees you from the small stuff, those little tasks that pile up and drain your energy without adding much value. Think of it as delegating to a team of invisible helpers who don't need lunch breaks, never make typos, and definitely won't roll their eyes at your workflow preferences.

The beauty of automation lies in its practicality. It's not about replacing humans; it's about giving them the tools to thrive. By automating the routine, you create space for creativity, strategy, and maybe even a bit of breathing room. And let's be honest: wouldn't you rather spend your day dreaming up the next big idea or catching up on that hobby you've been neglecting than triple-checking email lists?

In this brave new world, robots aren't here to take over—they're here to lend a hand (or a circuit). And while they might not be the intergalactic explorers of science fiction, their quiet efficiency makes them the real heroes of your business. So go ahead, let them handle the boring bits. You'll thank yourself later—and so will your inbox.

Tasks Begging for Automation: Freeing Up Your Time (and Your Sanity)

If your daily to-do list feels like a relentless game of Whack-a-Mole, it's time to consider automating the tasks that are quietly devouring your time and energy. These aren't the creative, big-picture jobs that make your heart sing—they're the repetitive, soul-sucking chores that, if left unchecked, could turn even the cheeriest entrepreneur into a frazzled husk of their former self. Fortunately, these are precisely the tasks that automation was born to conquer.

Take invoicing, for example. If you've ever spent hours chasing down unpaid invoices, you'll know the unique frustration of trying to be a polite yet persistent debt collector. It's a delicate dance—reminding clients they owe you money without resorting to menacing all-caps emails. Automation can take the awkwardness out of this process entirely, sending out gentle reminders on your behalf, so you don't have to. Think of it as having a relentlessly polite assistant who never forgets to follow up—and who will never accidentally add a passive-aggressive emoji.

Then there's email marketing, a task that can quickly spiral into chaos if left to its own devices. From crafting the perfect subject line to timing your sends with the precision of a NASA launch, email campaigns require more effort than they often seem worth. But with automation, you can schedule emails, segment your audience, and track results without lifting a finger—leaving you free to focus on writing that perfect newsletter that makes readers laugh, cry, or (ideally) hit "Buy Now."

And let's not forget customer follow-ups, the unsung hero of relationship-building. Whether it's thanking a client for their purchase, checking in on a service request, or sending a birthday discount to make their day, these small gestures make a big impact. But manually keeping track of them? A recipe for missed opportunities and mild panic. Automation swoops in here too, ensuring every customer feels seen and appreciated, without you needing to glue yourself to your CRM dashboard.

The beauty of automating these tasks is not just the time it saves but the consistency it brings. Your invoices go out on time, your emails hit the right inboxes, and your follow-ups never fall through the cracks. It's like hiring an entire administrative team, only they don't require salaries, snacks, or pep talks.

So, if you're tired of juggling tasks that don't spark joy—or even mild interest—consider handing them over to automation. Because life's too short to spend it chasing invoices or micromanaging email lists. Let the robots handle the boring bits, and reclaim your time for something far more fulfilling—like running your business, enjoying your life, or perfecting your latte art.

Top Automation Tools to Explore: Your New Digital Sidekicks

Let's dive into the glittering toolbox of automation, where apps and software gleam like shiny new gadgets at a tech expo. These are the trusty companions that take on the mundane tasks of your business, freeing you to focus on the bigger picture—or to binge-watch your favorite series without a twinge of guilt. Here's a quick look at some of the stars in the automation galaxy and why you might want to invite them into your workflow.

First up, we have **Zapier**, the digital wizard of "connecting the dots." Think of Zapier as the backstage crew at a play, seamlessly moving props and cues without anyone noticing. It links different apps together, automating repetitive actions so you don't have to. For instance, imagine you get an email inquiry that automatically triggers a task in your project management app, updates your CRM, and sends a thank-you response—all while you're out enjoying your lunch. Zapier works quietly behind the scenes, making your life look effortlessly organized.

Then there's **Mailchimp**, the granddaddy of email marketing. Sure, there are other platforms out there, but Mailchimp remains a favorite for its user-friendly interface and cheeky little mascot that makes email campaigns feel just a tad more fun. Whether you're sending out newsletters, promotions, or follow-ups, Mailchimp helps you automate the entire process. Picture this: you schedule a week's worth of email campaigns in one afternoon, then spend the rest of the week smugly knowing your audience is being nurtured without you lifting another finger.

And let's not overlook the charm of scheduling assistants like **Calendly**. These are the unsung heroes of appointment setting. No more exhausting back-and-forth email threads trying to find a time that works for everyone. Calendly takes care of it all, showing your availability, syncing with your calendar, and confirming the details. Imagine this: you're watching your favorite series when, without lifting a finger, Calendly schedules a meeting with a client. You press "Next Episode" while it takes care of the logistics. Magic, right?

Each of these tools is like hiring a specialized assistant, only they don't need lunch breaks or pep talks, and they definitely won't complain about office snacks. They're here to do the grunt work, streamline your operations, and, most importantly, make you look like you have everything together—even when you're secretly catching up on *The Great British Bake Off*.

So, take a moment to explore these automation marvels. You might just find that with the right tools in your corner, running your business feels a little less like herding cats and a little more like having your own personal tech-powered dream team. And if that's not magic, I don't know what is.

Pitfalls to Avoid: Don't Let Gerald Take Over

Automation, while a brilliant invention, is not without its quirks and hazards. Like all powerful tools, it needs to be handled with care—or you risk tipping into a dystopian future where your customers feel like they're trapped in an endless loop of robotic replies, wondering if "Gerald" is a chatbot, a disgruntled call center agent, or perhaps a rogue AI plotting its escape.

Here's the thing: customers crave efficiency, yes, but they also want to feel seen and valued. Over-automating your interactions can quickly turn what should be a smooth, delightful experience into a robotic nightmare. Imagine a customer sends a heartfelt message about how your product changed their life, only to receive a cold, automated reply that says, *"Thank you for your inquiry. Your ticket has been escalated to Tier 2 Support."* Gerald might think that's a perfectly adequate response, but your customer? Not so much.

Automation works best when it enhances, not replaces, the human connection. It's perfectly fine to use a chatbot to handle routine inquiries or to automate appointment reminders. In fact, it's a lifesaver for many businesses. But the moment you automate empathy, you've crossed into dangerous territory. People can spot a robotic response from a mile away, and nothing says "we don't care" like an email that feels like it was written by a toaster.

The key is balance. Let automation handle the boring, repetitive stuff, like sending order confirmations or scheduling follow-ups. But for the moments that matter—resolving a complaint, celebrating a milestone, or responding to a personal message—make sure a real, warm-blooded human is at the helm. Think of it as automation setting the stage, while you and your team step into the spotlight for the starring roles.

So, by all means, let the robots work their magic, but don't let Gerald run the show. Keep a healthy dose of humanity in your interactions, and your customers will not only stick around—they'll sing your praises (and hopefully never have to ask, *"Who, or what, is Gerald?"*). Balance is everything, after all, and when done right, automation can be the ultimate supporting act to your business's human heart.

Communication Solutions: Bridging the Digital Divide Without Losing Your Mind

Let's talk about communication in the digital age. It's a marvel, really—messages zipping around the globe in an instant, meetings happening across time zones, and the ability to send emojis to express everything from delight to existential despair. But with all this convenience comes a curious downside: the sheer chaos of keeping it all straight.

Picture this: you're juggling emails, text messages, Slack channels, and the occasional carrier pigeon (or at least it feels that way). Each platform has its quirks, each conversation its urgency, and somewhere along the way, you've completely lost track of where you promised to follow up on that all-important client request. Welcome to the digital divide—where communication options abound, but clarity? Not so much.

This is where the right communication solutions come in, acting as the bridges that span the digital chaos. The trick isn't to adopt every shiny new platform that promises to revolutionize your workday. Instead, it's about finding the tools that make sense for your business, streamline your interactions, and—this is key—help you keep your sanity intact.

Effective communication tools are like well-organized filing cabinets for your conversations, ensuring nothing important gets lost in the shuffle. They bridge the divide between instant messaging and email, between formal updates and casual chats, and even between teams separated by oceans (or at least the odd lunch break). The right tool can be the difference between a team that's always on the same page and one that's frantically flipping through the book, wondering where the plot went.

In this section, we'll explore some of the top communication solutions that can transform your workflow from a tangled web of missed messages into a symphony of streamlined coordination. Whether it's project management platforms, unified inboxes, or video conferencing apps that don't make everyone look like they're broadcasting from a potato, we'll uncover the best ways to bridge the digital divide without losing your mind—or your inbox.

So, if you've ever wished for a magical app that could sort your messages, prioritize your tasks, and maybe even order you a coffee while it's at it, you're in the right place. Let's dive into the tools that will keep your business connected, your conversations clear, and your sanity blissfully intact.

The Perils of Poor Communication

Ah, miscommunication—the silent saboteur of so many well-intentioned projects. It sneaks in when you least expect it, taking a perfectly straightforward plan and turning it into a comedy of errors. I once heard a tale—let's call it *The Great Reply-All Fiasco*—that perfectly illustrates just how quickly things can go awry.

It began innocently enough. A team was working on a big presentation for an important client, and someone decided to send out a group email to gather feedback. Fairly routine, right? But instead of sending it to just the project team, the sender—let's call them Greg—accidentally included the entire company on the email. All 200 employees, from interns to executives, suddenly had front-row seats to a conversation they were never meant to join.

What followed was a chain reaction worthy of a disaster movie. One person hit "reply all" to politely point out the mistake. Then another responded, also hitting "reply all," to say, "Please stop replying all." This, of course, prompted someone else to chime in with, "Can everyone stop saying 'stop replying all'?" Within minutes, inboxes were flooded with increasingly exasperated (and occasionally creative) messages, including one brave soul who suggested, "Let's all meet in the break room and discuss this in person."

Meanwhile, the actual project—the one this email was supposed to facilitate—was entirely forgotten in the chaos. Deadlines slipped, tempers flared, and poor Greg earned a dubious new nickname: Reply-All Greg.

The moral of the story? Poor communication can derail even the best-laid plans. Whether it's a simple misunderstanding or a full-blown email apocalypse, the consequences can range from mildly inconvenient to downright catastrophic.

Good communication tools and practices are the antidote to these perils. They help ensure everyone stays on the same page—or at least in the same book—avoiding the kind of confusion that turns an email thread into a digital shouting match. So, before your next project spirals into its own Reply-All Incident, take a moment to consider how you can streamline your communication and save your inbox (and your sanity) from unnecessary chaos.

Finding the Right Communication Tools

In the sprawling jungle of modern work life, communication tools are the trusty machetes that carve a path through the thicket of confusion. Done right, they're like digital watercoolers—keeping your team connected, collaborative, and up to speed. And unlike the real office watercooler, you don't have to endure that one colleague's dissertation on last night's reality TV.

Let's start with **Slack**, the undisputed champ of instant messaging for teams. Think of Slack as a high-tech message board for everything from urgent project updates to lighthearted banter about whose turn it is to bring donuts. Channels keep conversations organized (no more hunting through a dozen email threads), and integrations with other apps mean you can check calendars, review files, or even schedule a reminder—all without leaving the platform. It's the digital equivalent of an open office space but without the awkward eye contact.

Then there's **Microsoft Teams**, the Swiss Army knife of communication tools. Like Slack's slightly more formal cousin, Teams combines messaging, file sharing, and video calls in one tidy package. It's perfect for companies already entrenched in the Microsoft ecosystem, seamlessly syncing with Outlook and other Office apps. Picture it as the office conference room, always ready for a meeting, but this time with fewer "Can everyone hear me?" moments.

And, of course, there's the ever-reliable **Zoom**, the video conferencing hero of the modern era. Whether it's a team check-in or a client presentation, Zoom ensures you can see and hear your colleagues, assuming your Wi-Fi cooperates. With breakout rooms, screen sharing, and a gallery view that resembles a digital Brady Bunch, Zoom makes it easy to connect, even when you're miles apart. Just don't forget to double-check your background—no one needs to see your laundry pile during a sales pitch.

The beauty of these tools is that they eliminate the guesswork. Instead of shouting across the office (or worse, sending a "Just circling back" email), you can hop into a quick Slack channel, fire up a Teams video chat, or schedule a Zoom call with a few clicks. They bring your team together no matter where they are, helping everyone stay on the same page—or at least in the same chapter.

So, say goodbye to confusing email threads and miscommunication-induced migraines. With the right communication tools, your team can stay in sync, collaborate seamlessly, and maybe even have a little fun along the way. And while they might not replace the camaraderie of a shared coffee break, they'll certainly save you from the questionable quality of office java.

Streamlining Messaging Overload: Turning Chaos Into Clarity

Let's face it: modern communication can feel like an unending tidal wave of pings, emails, and notifications, each demanding your attention like a toddler in a candy aisle. One moment, you're deep in a project, and the next, you're navigating a digital cacophony of chat messages, email threads, and, inexplicably, a flood of cat GIFs in the team chat. While we all love a well-timed meme, there's a fine line between staying connected and drowning in communication clutter.

The key to managing messaging overload is setting some simple yet effective guidelines. First up: designate clear roles for your communication channels. Email should be reserved for long-form, formal updates—the kind of messages where you'd rather not include a dancing banana GIF. Chats, on the other hand, are best for quick questions, updates, and collaborative brainstorms, assuming everyone agrees not to spam the channel with "reaction memes" at the slightest provocation.

Another lifesaver is creating a culture of mindful messaging. Before hitting "send," ask yourself, "Does this really need to be shared?" If the answer is yes, make sure it's going to the right audience. Not everyone in the company needs to know that Susan's printer is on the fritz again. A little forethought can go a long way in reducing inbox bloat and ensuring that truly important messages don't get lost in the shuffle.

And then there's the golden rule of workplace chats: keep the GIFs to a reasonable minimum. Sure, a well-placed clip of a dancing penguin can brighten a Monday, but when every third message is a looping video of someone dramatically fainting, your work chat starts to resemble a comedy club more than a productivity tool. Save the humor for the designated #watercooler channel or the Friday afternoon wind-down session.

Lastly, establish boundaries for when communication is necessary—and when it's not. Encourage team members to disconnect after hours unless it's truly urgent. No one should feel obligated to respond to a Slack message about quarterly goals at 11 p.m. unless the world is on fire. And even then, let's hope it's not because someone misread an emoji.

Streamlining your messaging systems isn't about cutting back on connection—it's about making sure the right messages reach the right people at the right time. With a little structure and some shared discipline, you can transform your team's communication from a chaotic flood into a steady, manageable stream. And who knows? You might even find that fewer distractions mean more time for the work—and the occasional, perfectly timed GIF.

The Art of Balancing Connectivity and Peace: When to Log Off and Breathe

Ah, connectivity. It's the double-edged sword of modern business. On one hand, it's a marvel—you can answer a client's question at the speed of light, collaborate with your team across time zones, and order office supplies with a tap on your phone. On the other hand, it can feel like you're perpetually tethered to your devices, like a very diligent dog walker holding twenty leashes at once.

Finding the balance between staying connected and preserving your sanity is a skill worth mastering. It's not about throwing your smartphone into the ocean (tempting as that might sound during a particularly relentless week). Instead, it's about creating intentional pauses, moments when you can step away from the digital noise and, for a while, just... exist.

Let's talk about *tech-free hours*. Think of these as little slices of tranquility carved out of your otherwise plugged-in day. It might mean setting a hard stop in the evening—devices down, emails ignored, notifications silenced. Imagine it as taking a quiet walk in the woods, only without the risk of tripping over a rogue tree root or encountering an overly curious raccoon. Instead, you can savor the blissful silence of a tech-free hour, perhaps with a book, a cup of tea, or a lively debate with your cat (a fine companion for such moments).

Another trick is to schedule dedicated "connectivity windows" during the day. These are times when you're fully available to tackle emails, respond to messages, and handle whatever the digital world throws at you. Outside those windows? You focus on work, or better yet, on life—real, non-digital life. The kind that includes people, hobbies, and the occasional afternoon nap.

You might also consider leaving your devices behind for a while. No, not forever—just for an hour or two. Take a walk, enjoy a meal, or simply sit on the porch and watch the world go by. The emails will still be there when you return, I promise. And you'll likely feel calmer, sharper, and a lot less like a character in a dystopian novel about overworked humans controlled by their devices.

Balancing connectivity and peace isn't about disconnecting completely; it's about reclaiming your time and attention. By creating boundaries and embracing the joy of occasional disconnection, you'll find it's possible to stay engaged with your business without feeling like you're constantly tethered to it. And who knows? You might discover that the quiet moments—the ones free of screens and pings—are where the real magic happens.

Project Management Tools: Keeping Your Projects Organized Without Needing a PhD in Overwhelm

Managing a project can often feel like juggling flaming torches while riding a unicycle—difficult, precarious, and likely to end in singed eyebrows. Tasks multiply like rabbits, deadlines creep closer, and before you know it, you're buried under a mountain of half-remembered priorities and sticky notes that mysteriously migrate to places they don't belong. Enter project management tools, the digital equivalent of a superhero cape for frazzled entrepreneurs.

These tools are designed to transform chaos into clarity, breaking sprawling projects into neat, manageable chunks. Think of them as the conductor of your business orchestra, keeping everyone in harmony and on schedule. With the right tool, you'll not only know who's doing what but also when, how, and why—without the stress of second-guessing yourself into oblivion.

Take **Trello**, for instance. It's like having a giant corkboard where you can pin your tasks and shuffle them around with satisfying ease. Trello's colorful cards and simple interface make it approachable even for the most tech-averse, while its flexibility ensures it can handle everything from a product launch to your holiday shopping list.

Then there's **Asana**, the overachiever of the group. It thrives on precision, offering detailed timelines and progress updates that give you the warm, fuzzy feeling of being on top of everything. Its features are robust enough for large teams managing complex workflows, yet intuitive enough not to feel like you're piloting a spaceship. And let's not forget the little celebratory bursts of confetti when you tick off a task—it's the digital equivalent of a pat on the back.

Finally, meet **Monday.com**, the Swiss Army knife of project management. If Trello is a corkboard and Asana a meticulous timeline, Monday.com is the customizable all-in-one dashboard. Whether you're tracking client deadlines, managing budgets, or simply figuring out where on earth the stapler went, Monday.com adapts to your needs with seamless integrations and a layout so logical you'll wonder how you lived without it.

The true magic of these tools isn't just in their features but in how they centralize communication and accountability. No more digging through endless email chains or awkwardly texting teammates at odd hours. Instead, your project dashboard becomes a one-stop shop for updates, assignments, and progress checks. It's like opening the blinds in a cluttered room—suddenly, everything is illuminated, and you can actually see what needs attention.

Choosing the right tool depends on your personal style and the needs of your business. If you're a visual thinker, Trello's dynamic boards will feel like a dream. For those who thrive on structure and detail, Asana's timelines and task dependencies are a perfect match. And if you're juggling diverse projects and crave versatility, Monday.com will handle it all with aplomb.

By streamlining your workflow with one of these digital lifesavers, you're not just organizing your projects—you're reclaiming time, sanity, and the energy to tackle the work that truly matters. No one needs to feel like they're one missed deadline away from a meltdown. So pick your tool, dive in, and let the chaos of unorganized projects become a distant memory. And yes, if it comes with confetti, consider it a bonus.

Why You Need a Digital Command Center

Let's talk about the allure of a good project management tool, or as I like to think of it, the digital command center for your business. On paper, these tools are a dream come true. They promise order, clarity, and the kind of streamlined efficiency that makes you feel like a CEO genius. But, much like the cluttered desk you swore you'd keep tidy, they're only as good as your commitment to actually *using* them.

Picture this: you invest in a shiny new project management tool, eagerly set up all your boards, tasks, and deadlines, and then promptly forget about it. Weeks later, you log back in to find it stuffed with outdated tasks and overdue alerts, like a digital junk drawer bursting with random receipts and expired coupons. It's the modern equivalent of stacking papers on your desk in neat piles and pretending you've organized them—except the papers are now virtual, and the clutter is even harder to ignore.

Here's the thing: a well-maintained project management tool is a thing of beauty. It's your personal headquarters, where you can see everything from today's to-dos to next month's deadlines in one tidy, accessible place. But when neglected, it quickly devolves into a chaotic wasteland of forgotten tasks and cryptic notes like, *"Fix the thing before Thursday!"* (What thing? Which Thursday? We'll never know.)

The trick to making your digital command center work is discipline. Check in regularly, update it religiously, and use it consistently. Think of it as your loyal assistant, always ready to keep your projects on track—provided you actually let it. With a little effort, it can turn the overwhelming mess of running a business into something almost, dare I say, enjoyable.

And the best part? Unlike your desk, you'll never lose your coffee mug under it.

Avoiding Tool Overload: The Too-Much-of-a-Good-Thing Trap

Ah, the allure of shiny new tools. Each one promises to revolutionize your workflow, solve all your problems, and make you feel like the most productive person in the room. It's easy to get swept up in the excitement—adding a new platform here, downloading an app there—until suddenly, you're managing more tools than tasks. It's like buying a dozen planners because each one seemed perfect in the store, only to still forget your dentist appointment because you never actually used any of them.

The truth is, more tools don't always equal better organization. In fact, juggling too many platforms can create an entirely new layer of chaos. You'll find yourself switching between dashboards, resetting forgotten passwords, and wondering why you've spent half the day troubleshooting an integration that was supposed to save you time in the first place.

The key to avoiding tool overload is restraint. Start small. Pick one or two platforms that align with your biggest needs and learn to use them well. If Trello covers your task management and Zoom handles your team meetings, do you really need three other apps promising slightly different versions of the same thing? Probably not.

It's also worth considering the learning curve. Adding a new tool means getting your team on board, training them to use it, and then actually sticking with it. If you're not careful, you'll end up with a graveyard of abandoned logins and half-implemented systems that no one remembers how to use.

The goal isn't to become a tech aficionado with a dozen tools at your fingertips. It's to find the right tools that simplify your workflow, not complicate it. Think quality over quantity. A single, well-chosen platform that integrates seamlessly into your daily routine will do far more for your productivity than a scattershot approach that leaves you clicking and cursing your way through a maze of tabs.

So, resist the temptation to try every shiny new app that comes your way. Remember, the best tools are the ones you'll actually use. After all, it doesn't matter how sleek a platform looks if it's just sitting there, gathering virtual dust while you scramble to find your to-do list on a sticky note. Choose wisely, keep it simple, and let your tools work for you—not the other way around.

Getting the Team Onboard: Turning Skeptics into Enthusiasts

Introducing new tools to a team can feel a bit like coaxing a cat into a bath. There's often skepticism, a hint of resistance, and maybe even some muttered grumbling. But with the right approach—gentle persuasion and perhaps the occasional metaphorical treat—you can turn even the most hesitant team members into enthusiastic users of your shiny new platforms.

First, start with the "why." No one likes being handed a new tool without understanding how it will make their life easier. Take the time to explain what the tool does and, more importantly, how it solves problems they've been facing. For example, if your team has been drowning in email chains or losing track of deadlines, show them how a project management tool can cut through the chaos and make their workload more manageable. It's not about adding another layer of complexity; it's about removing existing frustrations.

Next, keep the rollout simple. Instead of overwhelming your team with every bell and whistle the tool has to offer, focus on the core features they'll need right away. Think of it as a soft launch—like teaching someone to drive in an empty parking lot rather than throwing them into rush hour traffic. Once they're comfortable with the basics, you can gradually introduce more advanced features.

Training sessions can also work wonders, but keep them short, engaging, and to the point. Nobody wants to sit through a three-hour tutorial that feels like a college lecture. Instead, opt for quick demonstrations and real-life examples that show how the tool will make their specific tasks easier. And if you can make it fun—maybe with a little friendly competition or the promise of snacks—so much the better.

Encourage experimentation. Give your team time to play around with the tool, ask questions, and discover its quirks. Mistakes will happen (just like the occasional cat claw in a bath scenario), but that's part of the learning process. Be patient and supportive, emphasizing that it's okay to fumble a bit at first.

Finally, don't forget the treats—metaphorically speaking. Celebrate small wins, like when someone successfully uses the tool to streamline a task or solve a problem. A little recognition goes a long way in building enthusiasm and momentum. Before you know it, the tool will go from "new and intimidating" to "indispensable" in their daily routine.

Getting your team onboard with new tools doesn't have to be a struggle. With clear communication, a gentle rollout, and a dash of humor, you can turn even the most reluctant adopters into loyal fans. And who knows? They might even start wondering how they ever managed without it—like a cat finally realizing the bath wasn't so bad after all.

Choosing Scalable Technology: Today's Tools, Tomorrow's Superpowers

Ah, technology. It's like a double-edged sword—gloriously helpful when chosen wisely, but a bit of a nightmare when it feels outdated before you've even mastered the user manual. For entrepreneurs, choosing scalable technology is one of those deceptively simple tasks that turns out to be the cornerstone of long-term success. The right tools don't just serve you today; they evolve with your business, adapting to future needs like a superhero learning new powers just in time to save the day.

Let's face it: many tools are built to impress during the honeymoon phase, dazzling you with features you never knew you needed. But not all are built to last. You want tech that can handle your growing workload, expanding team, and inevitable pivot to something slightly different than what you originally planned. After all, it's not just about where you are now—it's about where you're headed.

Imagine, for instance, investing in a project management system that feels perfect while you're running a small, tight-knit team of three. It's simple, streamlined, and does the job. But fast-forward two years, and your team has tripled in size, your projects have become exponentially more complex, and that once-perfect tool now feels about as sturdy as a rickety chair at a family reunion. That's the danger of choosing tech that doesn't scale—it's a temporary fix for a long-term challenge.

Scalable technology, on the other hand, is like a favorite pair of jeans that somehow fits whether you've gained or lost a few pounds. It grows with you, expands to accommodate new demands, and never feels stretched too thin. Think cloud-based systems that can handle data increases, apps with multi-tiered plans that grow with your budget, or software platforms designed to integrate seamlessly with others as your tech stack inevitably expands.

Take customer relationship management (CRM) tools, for example. Choosing one that works for your current client base but has the capacity to handle a database ten times its size will save you endless headaches (and possibly a tearful midnight migration session) down the road. Similarly, accounting software that accommodates a single user might feel cozy now, but you'll thank yourself later for picking one that supports multiple team members and even automates tax season.

The key to choosing scalable technology is thinking ahead. Picture your business a few years down the line—bigger, busier, and bursting with potential. Will the tools you choose today still hold up, or will they leave you scrambling for replacements just when you need them most?

Of course, there's a fine line between planning for growth and drowning in features you won't use for years. The trick is to find tools that are robust but not overwhelming, flexible but not riddled with unnecessary complexity. And don't be afraid to test the waters. Most platforms offer free trials or demos, so take the time to kick the tires and see how they handle under pressure.

Scalable technology isn't just an investment in convenience—it's an investment in your sanity. With the right tools, you'll not only keep your business running smoothly today, but you'll also be ready to seize tomorrow's opportunities without breaking a sweat. And when that day comes, you might just feel like a superhero yourself, cape optional.

Think Big (But Start Small)

When it comes to choosing scalable technology, the mantra should always be: think big, but start small. Picture it like planting a sapling. At first, it's a modest little thing, fragile and unassuming, but with the right care—water, sunlight, and the occasional bit of pruning—it grows into a mighty oak, its roots deep and branches wide, capable of weathering storms and providing shade for generations.

The same philosophy applies to technology. You don't need to outfit your business with the digital equivalent of a fully grown forest right out of the gate. Instead, start with tools that meet your immediate needs but have the potential to expand as your business does. This way, you're not overwhelmed by complexity you don't yet require, nor are you left scrambling to replace systems when growth inevitably kicks in.

For instance, if you're managing a small team, a simple project management tool like Trello might be just the ticket. It's intuitive, easy to set up, and perfectly suited for straightforward workflows. But as your team grows and your projects become more intricate, you'll want something that can handle dependencies, timelines, and multi-tiered collaboration—features you might find in tools like Asana or Monday.com. By choosing a platform that scales, you ensure a smooth transition from sapling to sturdy oak without uprooting everything in the process.

The same goes for communication tools. A basic chat app might suffice when it's just you and a couple of team members, but what happens when you're juggling remote employees, international clients, and a growing need for integration with other systems? Starting with a scalable platform means you're not tethered to a tool that feels more like a shrub when you need a treehouse.

The beauty of starting small and thinking big is that it allows you to focus on what matters now without losing sight of what lies ahead. You can test tools, refine processes, and make adjustments as you grow—all without the panic of realizing your current setup can't handle the business equivalent of a growth spurt.

So, when selecting technology, look for tools that feel like saplings—small, manageable, but brimming with potential. Choose platforms that grow with you, adapting to your needs and ensuring you're never stuck chopping down what doesn't work to start fresh. With the right choices, your tech stack will stand tall, steady, and capable of supporting even your most ambitious goals.

And who knows? One day, as you gaze at the towering oak that started as a humble sapling, you might just feel a bit like a proud gardener—albeit one whose garden is filled with beautifully efficient, wonderfully scalable tech.

Key Features of Scalable Tech

When scouting for scalable technology, it's all about finding tools that grow alongside your business, adapting to its needs without throwing you into a spiral of panic midway through an expansion. Think of it like planning a cross-country road trip: the last thing you want is to realize halfway through that your car only seats two, and you've somehow picked up three more passengers along the way. A little foresight goes a long way in avoiding those "Well, this is awkward" moments.

One of the hallmarks of scalable tech is **cloud-based storage**. Forget clunky servers and the anxiety-inducing need to manually back up files; cloud-based systems let you scale up effortlessly. Need more space? It's as simple as upgrading your plan—no wrestling with outdated hardware required. Plus, the beauty of accessing your data from anywhere means you can work seamlessly whether you're in the office or sipping a latte in a café that's entirely too proud of its artisanal foam art.

Next, look for **customizable options**. Scalable tech should feel like a tailored suit—not the one-size-fits-all kind that somehow fits no one. Customization ensures that as your workflows evolve, the tool evolves with them. Maybe you start out needing a simple task tracker, but six months later, you need dashboards, analytics, and a way to color-code everything within an inch of its life. Customization means your tool doesn't just keep up—it keeps you ahead.

And then there are **integrations**. Oh, glorious integrations—the feature that stops your tech stack from resembling a patchwork quilt stitched together with duct tape and wishful thinking. A scalable tool should play nicely with others, connecting seamlessly to your existing platforms. Imagine your project management software automatically syncing with your calendar, your CRM talking to your email marketing tool, and your invoicing system linking up with your accounting software. It's like assembling a jigsaw puzzle where all the pieces actually fit, instead of hammering them into place out of frustration.

The beauty of these features is how they future-proof your business. When the inevitable growth spurt arrives, you're not left scrambling to migrate to a new system in the middle of a critical project (or, heaven forbid, tax season). Instead, your tech adjusts effortlessly, making the transition as smooth as possible—unlike cramming extra passengers into a tiny car.

So, when choosing scalable tech, think beyond today. Ask yourself, "Can this grow with me? Will it adapt as my needs change?" With the right features—cloud storage, customization, and integrations—you're not just investing in a tool; you're investing in your sanity. And let's be honest, that's worth every penny.

Balancing Cost and Functionality

Choosing scalable technology is a lot like shopping for hiking boots: you want something comfortable, durable, and reliable enough to carry you through the journey without leaving you blistered, limping, or filled with regret halfway up the trail. But let's be honest—much like hiking gear, tech tools can range from "bargain bin" to "do I need to sell a kidney for this?" Finding the sweet spot between cost and functionality is an art worth mastering.

The first step is understanding your needs. Just as you wouldn't buy mountaineering boots for a stroll through a city park, you don't need to invest in a tech platform designed for Fortune 500 companies if you're running a lean, nimble startup. Start by listing the features that are essential to your current operations and growth plans. These are your "must-haves"—the non-negotiables that make a tool truly valuable.

Next, weigh those essentials against the price tag. A tool might promise the moon and stars, but if the cost requires you to take out a second mortgage, it's probably not the right fit. Look for platforms that offer a balance: they deliver on core functionality without drowning you in features you won't use for years. Many tools offer tiered pricing plans, so you can start with an entry-level package and scale up as your needs (and budget) grow.

Then there's the matter of durability—or in tech terms, reliability. Just as you wouldn't trust hiking boots that fall apart after a single trek, you don't want software that's glitchy, prone to outages, or notorious for terrible customer support. Do your homework. Read reviews, test free trials, and don't be afraid to ask questions about uptime, security, and usability. A slightly higher price tag is worth it if it comes with peace of mind.

Finally, consider the long-term investment. The cheapest option might save you money upfront, but if it doesn't scale with your business or requires frequent replacements, you'll end up spending more in the long run. Conversely, the most expensive tool might have every bell and whistle imaginable, but if you're only using 10% of its features, you're essentially paying a premium for bragging rights.

Remember, the goal is to find a tool that feels like a natural extension of your business. It should fit seamlessly into your workflow, provide the functionality you need, and leave you room to grow—all without breaking the bank. Because much like a trusty pair of hiking boots, the right tech tool should support you every step of the way, letting you focus on the journey ahead rather than the blisters you've acquired along the way.

Case Studies of Scalable Success

Let's take a moment to highlight a few success stories—businesses that started small with tools perfectly suited for their humble beginnings and scaled up seamlessly as they grew. Think of these as the tech equivalent of planting a tiny sapling that eventually grew into a sprawling, shade-providing oak.

Take **QuickBooks**, for example. For countless small businesses, QuickBooks is the ultimate financial sidekick—a straightforward, user-friendly platform to track expenses, send invoices, and keep taxes from becoming a yearly nightmare. It's perfect for a one-person operation or a tight-knit team managing modest revenues. But here's the beauty of it: as businesses grow, QuickBooks scales right alongside them. From automating payroll to managing multi-currency transactions for global ventures, it evolves to meet increasingly complex needs without requiring a painful software migration.

Then there's **Shopify**, the go-to platform for entrepreneurs diving into the world of e-commerce. Starting a small online store with Shopify is as simple as clicking a few buttons, uploading your products, and basking in the glow of your first sale. But its scalability is where it truly shines. As your business grows, Shopify's features expand—offering integrations with inventory management systems, customer analytics, and even international shipping solutions. What starts as a side hustle selling handmade candles can transform into a global enterprise, all without outgrowing the platform.

Or consider **Slack**, the beloved communication tool. It's ideal for startups with a handful of employees who need a quick, efficient way to stay connected. But as those startups morph into larger teams with multiple departments, Slack's scalable features—custom channels, integrations with project management tools, and robust search capabilities—ensure it remains an indispensable part of the workflow.

The common thread in these stories is that each business chose tools designed to grow with them. There were no dramatic pivots or frantic searches for replacements; their tech simply scaled to meet new challenges and opportunities.

The takeaway? The tools you choose today don't have to be grandiose or overly complex. They just need to have the potential to grow alongside your ambitions. With the right technology in your corner, your business can evolve without the stress of reinventing your systems every time you hit a growth milestone. And who doesn't love a happy ending where everyone—business owners and customers alike—wins?

Embracing Technology Without Letting It Take Over

Technology is a bit like hiring a well-trained butler. When it works as intended, it quietly and efficiently handles the tedious tasks, leaving you free to focus on the things you truly enjoy. It schedules your meetings, reminds you about invoices, and keeps your projects running smoothly—essentially, the digital equivalent of someone saying, "Don't worry, I've got this," while you sip tea and dream big.

But let's be honest: even the best tools can sometimes feel like overly enthusiastic butlers who, despite their best intentions, occasionally rearrange your entire kitchen while you're out. The key to embracing technology is finding the right balance. Tools and apps are there to support your entrepreneurial journey, not overwhelm it. They're meant to streamline your day, not leave you tangled in a labyrinth of logins and integrations.

The right technology won't just save you time—it'll give you freedom. Freedom to focus on the parts of your business that excite you, whether it's brainstorming bold new ideas or nurturing relationships with clients and colleagues. Freedom to enjoy the life you've been working so hard to create. And yes, freedom to step away from your screen every once in a while and do something refreshingly analog—like a walk on the beach, a chat with a friend, or finally mastering the art of that perfect cup of tea.

So, as you wade through the myriad of tools and technologies out there, remember that the goal isn't to use *everything*. It's to find the few that truly make a difference—the ones that feel less like a chore and more like an invisible hand, quietly lifting the load. And if you ever find yourself overwhelmed, take a step back. Even the fanciest app in the world can't replace the clarity that comes from a deep breath, a clear head, and a well-deserved moment of calm.

Your entrepreneurial journey is yours to design, and with the right tools in your corner, you'll have all the support you need to make it truly extraordinary. Just don't forget to enjoy the ride—and maybe let the butler handle the dishes.

Chapter Nine

Harmonizing Growth with Lifestyle

Growing Without Becoming a Victim of Your Own Success

A GOOD FRIEND OF mine once decided to build a treehouse for his son. It was supposed to be a simple weekend project—just a basic platform in the branches where his boy could let his imagination run wild. Nothing fancy. But, as these things often do, it quickly escalated.

Initially, it was just a few planks and a ladder, but then his son started chiming in with requests. Could it have a trapdoor? How about a telescope for spying on squirrels? And wouldn't it be even better with a zipline? My friend, being the enthusiastic type, agreed to all of it. Before long, what started as a humble treehouse morphed into a multi-level engineering feat, complete with a pulley system, a fireman's pole, and a questionable plan to attach a hammock "somewhere cool."

By the end of it, he was knee-deep in wood shavings and battling a ladder that seemed determined to overthrow him. His son, of course, thought the whole thing was marvelous. But my friend? He looked like a man who had seen too much. The joy of building the treehouse had been overshadowed by the sheer magnitude of the project.

This, I realized, is what scaling a business can feel like. It starts with a great idea—a spark of excitement about growing and reaching new heights. But then the extras creep in: more clients, bigger goals, grander plans. Before you know it, you're not just building a business—you're juggling ten projects at once, balancing on a metaphorical ladder, and wondering why your dream now feels so exhausting.

This chapter is about avoiding that fate. Growth doesn't have to mean chaos or burnout. With the right approach, you can expand your business while still enjoying the journey. It's not about saying no to ambition—it's about pursuing it in a way that keeps you grounded and aligned with what matters most.

Just like my friend eventually had to pause, regroup, and remind himself why he started the treehouse in the first place, you'll need to find balance in your business. Because growth should be exciting and fulfilling, not overwhelming.

In the pages ahead, we'll look at how to scale your business in a way that complements your lifestyle rather than overrunning it. From setting boundaries to managing expectations, you'll discover strategies to help you build something remarkable—without feeling like you're about to topple off the ladder.

Because in the end, success shouldn't feel like survival. It should feel like standing back, looking at what you've built, and knowing it's everything you hoped for—whether it's a treehouse or a thriving business.

Defining Balanced Growth: The Sweet Spot Between Too Much and Not Enough

Imagine you're baking a cake. Not just any cake, mind you—a showstopper worthy of applause and second helpings. You start with the perfect amount of flour, eggs, and sugar. But then you think, *What if I added a little more butter? Or maybe another egg? Or perhaps just a touch more sugar for good measure?* Before long, you're standing in front of a batter that's overflowing the bowl and a nagging suspicion that the cake might emerge from the oven resembling a science experiment gone awry.

Growing a business can feel remarkably similar. There's a fine line between expanding just enough to achieve your goals and piling on so much that everything feels precariously unbalanced. Too little growth, and you stagnate, missing opportunities and watching others pass you by. Too much growth, and you risk overwhelming yourself, your team, and the very systems that are supposed to support your success.

Balanced growth, as it turns out, is that elusive sweet spot—a Goldilocks zone where progress is steady, manageable, and in tune with your life. It's about embracing opportunities without letting them run wild, ensuring that every step forward feels intentional rather than chaotic.

This isn't about playing it safe or staying in your comfort zone. Far from it. Balanced growth means challenging yourself while maintaining a solid foundation. It's about recognizing when to push, when to pause, and, perhaps most importantly, when to say no.

In the world of business, the allure of "more" is constant—more clients, more revenue, more expansion. But growth for the sake of growth can leave you spinning your wheels, chasing goals that don't actually serve your vision. Balanced growth, on the other hand, allows you to build a business that thrives sustainably, without requiring you to sacrifice your health, happiness, or sanity along the way.

In this section, we'll delve into what balanced growth looks like and how to achieve it. You'll learn how to set realistic goals, prioritize effectively, and find that delicate equilibrium between ambition and peace of mind. Because at the end of the day, a well-baked cake—and a well-balanced business—should leave you feeling satisfied, not stressed.

What is Balanced Growth?

Balanced growth is not the entrepreneurial equivalent of a 100-meter dash, where you push yourself to the brink, collapsing triumphantly across the finish line. No, balanced growth is more akin to a leisurely hike through the hills—steady progress, mindful pacing, and plenty of time to take in the view.

Imagine setting out on a beautiful trail. The goal isn't just to reach the summit as quickly as possible but to enjoy the journey. You stop to admire the wildflowers, take a breather on a sunlit rock, and maybe even snap a few photos of the breathtaking vistas along the way. You're moving forward, yes, but you're doing so in a way that feels enriching rather than exhausting.

In business, balanced growth follows a similar rhythm. It's not about grabbing every opportunity that comes your way or trying to double your revenue overnight. Instead, it's about growing at a pace that feels sustainable and aligned with your values. It's about making thoughtful decisions, savoring the wins, and ensuring you don't burn out before you reach the next milestone.

This kind of growth requires clarity and intention. You need to know what you're aiming for—not just in terms of numbers, but in how your business fits into the bigger picture of your life. Are you building something that supports your personal goals, or are you scaling so fast that it feels like your business is dragging you up the mountain by your shoelaces?

Balanced growth also leaves room for adaptability. Just like a hiker adjusts their pace based on the terrain, you'll need to be flexible as your business evolves. There will be times to push harder and times to ease back, moments to celebrate progress and moments to reassess your direction.

The beauty of balanced growth is that it allows you to thrive without losing yourself in the process. It's about creating a business that doesn't just grow—it grows in harmony with the life you want to lead. And when you find that balance, the journey becomes as rewarding as the destination.

Why Balance Matters

Let me tell you about a friend of mine—we'll call him Dave—who launched a business with all the gusto of a rocket leaving the launch pad. Within months, his company was booming. Clients were pouring in, revenue was climbing, and Dave had become the poster child for entrepreneurial success. But there was one tiny problem: Dave hadn't seen sunlight in weeks.

When I finally caught up with him, he looked like a mole that had wandered out of its burrow for the first time. His skin had taken on a pale, bluish tint, and he squinted at the world as if daylight were some foreign concept. "How's business?" I asked, knowing full well the answer.

"Oh, it's incredible," he said, holding up his phone to show me the latest sales charts. "I'm crushing it." Then he paused, scratching his head. "But, uh, when was the last time it rained? Has it rained? What month is it?"

You see, Dave had been so consumed by his skyrocketing success that he'd lost track of, well, everything else. Meals were replaced by hastily devoured protein bars. Sleep had become a distant memory. And his social life? Let's just say the office plants were his only regular companions.

Sure, Dave's business was thriving, but at what cost? His rapid growth had turned into a hamster wheel of obligations—round and round he went, unable to stop, let alone enjoy what he'd built.

This is why balance matters. Growth without balance might bring short-term wins, but it often leads to long-term misery. Success should enhance your life, not consume it. If your achievements leave you feeling like a pale, overworked shadow of yourself, it's time to rethink the approach.

Finding balance ensures that as your business grows, you grow too—in health, happiness, and the ability to appreciate all the good things success brings. It's not just about working hard; it's about working smart, leaving room for sunlight, laughter, and maybe even the occasional meal that doesn't come in bar form.

So let Dave be a cautionary tale. Success is wonderful, but it's infinitely better when it comes with a side of fresh air and a full night's sleep. Let's make sure you thrive in every sense of the word.

Finding Your Balance: A Reflection Exercise

Before we dive into the How-Tos of balanced growth, let's pause for a moment of self-reflection. Imagine this as the entrepreneurial version of sitting on a park bench with a good cup of coffee, taking stock of what really matters.

Balance, after all, is deeply personal. For some, it's carving out time to pick up that long-forgotten guitar or tending to the herb garden that's slowly being overtaken by weeds. For others, it might be as simple—and as profound—as reclaiming the sacred act of eating dinner without answering emails mid-bite.

So, here's your task: Ask yourself what balance looks like for *you*. If you could wave a magic wand and create more space in your life, what would it be for? Would it be more time for hobbies? The luxury of a lazy Sunday? Or perhaps just a chance to finish a book that doesn't have the words "business strategy" in the title?

Take a moment to jot down your thoughts. Don't overthink it—this isn't a test, and no one's grading your answers. The goal here is to reconnect with what you value and to start imagining what a more balanced life might feel like.

And if your first thought is, *I'd like to breathe more,* well, that's a perfectly valid place to start. Balance isn't about grand gestures; it's about reclaiming the little joys that make all the hard work worthwhile.

So go ahead, reflect. The email notifications can wait.

Flexible Growth Models: Scaling Without Breaking (or Breaking Down)

Let's talk about growth that bends and stretches but doesn't snap like an over-worked rubber band. Scaling a business can feel like inflating a balloon—you want to see it expand, but push too hard, and you're left holding the sad remnants of what could have been. Flexible growth models are the antidote to that kind of high-pressure peril.

The beauty of a flexible approach lies in its adaptability. It's about designing your business to grow in a way that fits your life, not the other way around. Think of it like building a sandcastle near the tide: you don't fight the waves; you adjust your castle's height and distance to keep it intact while enjoying the scenery.

These models allow you to scale without sacrificing your sanity or the things you value most. Whether it's creating a subscription-based service that grows steadily or developing a product line that doesn't require you to personally pack every box, flexibility gives you room to breathe. It's about finding that sweet spot where your business thrives without turning you into its frazzled caretaker.

But here's the kicker: flexible growth isn't just about keeping you happy—it's also about future-proofing your business. The world changes, markets shift, and life throws the occasional curveball. A business built with flexibility in mind can roll with the punches, adapting to new opportunities and challenges without falling apart.

In this section, we'll explore different growth models that balance ambition with sustainability. You'll learn how to scale thoughtfully, manage resources effectively, and build a business that grows with you rather than against you. Because growth should feel like progress, not pressure—more like adding rooms to a cozy house than frantically building a skyscraper that sways in the wind.

Let's dive into the practical magic of scaling without breaking—or breaking down.

Finding the Right Model for Your Business

Picking the right growth model for your business is a bit like shopping for shoes. Sure, those glittery, sky-high stilettos might look fantastic in the store, but will they still feel fabulous after an afternoon of walking? Probably not. You need something that supports your goals without pinching your sanity—a business model that fits just right.

Flexible growth models are your business's comfortable-yet-stylish footwear, designed to help you move forward without blisters or regret. They're scalable, sustainable, and adaptable to your lifestyle. Let's take a moment to slip a few options on for size.

Take subscription services, for example. They're like the sneakers of the business world—reliable, steady, and perfect for a comfortable jog toward growth. Whether it's a monthly delivery of artisan coffee or an ongoing software service, subscriptions create predictable revenue and the kind of routine your bank account will thank you for. Plus, once they're up and running, they free you to focus on the next big thing.

Or consider online courses. These are more like a good pair of hiking boots: a bit of effort to break in, but once you've set them up, they can take you to incredible places. Whether you're sharing your expertise in graphic design, yoga, or the finer points of underwater basket weaving, online courses allow you to reach a global audience without adding endless hours to your workweek.

And then there are scalable product lines—the loafers of growth models. Polished, practical, and always ready to slip into action, scalable products can grow with demand without requiring you to personally assemble each widget or hand-pack every order. With the right processes in place, they let you expand your reach while keeping the workload manageable.

The key to finding the right model is knowing what fits your goals and lifestyle. Are you looking for steady, predictable growth? A subscription service might be your best bet. Want to leverage your expertise? Start developing that online course. Need a way to grow your brand without cloning yourself? A scalable product line could be the answer.

Whatever you choose, remember: the right model should support you, not pinch. It should feel like a natural extension of your business, propelling you forward without dragging you down. After all, the journey is just as important as the destination—and no one enjoys a journey in the wrong pair of shoes.

Adapting to Your Lifestyle

Designing a business model that fits your life is a bit like choosing between a hammock and a hamster wheel. One lets you sway gently in the breeze, enjoying the fruits of your labor with a lemonade in hand. The other keeps you running in circles, panting furiously while getting precisely nowhere. Spoiler alert: you want the hammock.

The beauty of flexible growth models is their ability to adapt to your personal priorities. If location independence is at the top of your list, an online course or subscription service could let you run your business from a sun-drenched beach—or the comfort of your couch, whichever you prefer. If your goal is to cut back on hours, scalable product lines or digital downloads could help you work smarter, not harder, freeing up time for the things you love.

The trick is to start by asking yourself, *What kind of life do I want my business to support?* Are you craving the freedom to travel without being tethered to your phone? Or is your dream a little closer to home—like spending evenings with your family instead of your inbox?

Once you know what you want, you can design a growth model that works with your lifestyle, not against it. This isn't about building a business just to prove you can hustle—it's about building a life where your work fits seamlessly into the bigger picture.

Of course, this doesn't mean you'll be lounging in that metaphorical hammock 24/7. Even the most balanced business models require effort, especially in the beginning. But with the right setup, your efforts will feel purposeful rather than punishing—like tending a garden that grows steadily, rather than running on a hamster wheel that never stops spinning.

So, take a moment to picture your ideal business model. Does it look like a steady, location-independent subscription service? A creative product line that thrives while you sleep? Or something entirely unique to your passions and priorities? Whatever it is, aim for the hammock—not the wheel. Life's too short for endless running in place.

Success Stories: Growth Without the Grind

Let me introduce you to Rachel, a graphic designer who once thought success meant pulling all-nighters fueled by caffeine and sheer determination. Her business was booming, but her life? Not so much. Her dream of "making it" turned into a nightmare of endless deadlines and no time to even think about anything outside of work—let alone do it.

Then one day, while staring at her perpetually overstuffed planner, she decided enough was enough. Rachel took a hard look at her business model and realized she could shift from custom projects to selling pre-designed templates. It was a risk—letting go of the one-on-one work that she thought defined her brand. But once she set up her online shop and automated her sales process, something magical happened: her income grew steadily, and her hours shrank.

With her newfound time, Rachel did something she'd never imagined: she took up pottery. Now, when she's not creating stunning design templates, she's crafting misshapen vases and mugs that she proudly displays in her home. "My work still makes me happy," she says, "but it's not the only thing that makes me happy anymore."

Then there's Mark, a fitness trainer who used to juggle back-to-back sessions from dawn until dusk. His income was solid, but his knees? Not so much. He realized that his in-person model wasn't scalable unless he cloned himself, and that seemed, well, impractical.

Mark pivoted by launching an online training program with pre-recorded videos and a subscription-based community. Within a year, his income had doubled, and his schedule finally allowed for things like sleep and an occasional weekend hike. "I still get to help people reach their fitness goals," Mark says, "but now I have the energy to reach my own."

And then there's Linda, who ran a small bakery and dreamed of expanding without turning her kitchen into a 24-hour production line. Instead of opening a second location, she leaned into selling her signature cookies online, shipping them nationwide. With the help of a streamlined fulfillment process, Linda scaled her business and found the freedom to spend her evenings reading novels instead of rolling dough.

These stories remind us that growth doesn't have to mean sacrificing everything else in your life. With the right model and a bit of strategic thinking, you can build a thriving business and still have time to explore hobbies, spend time with loved ones, or simply enjoy a quiet moment with your coffee.

Because let's face it: success isn't just about the numbers. It's about how you feel when you finally have the space to breathe—and maybe even take up pottery.

Strategic Outsourcing for Growth

Outsourcing often conjures images of reluctantly handing over your most cherished tasks to someone else, like letting a stranger carry your grandmother's delicate antique vase across a slippery floor. It feels risky, unnatural, and maybe even a little wrong. But done right, outsourcing isn't about losing control—it's about reclaiming your time and energy to focus on what really matters.

Let's start with an uncomfortable truth: you can't do everything. Sure, you might be a master multitasker, juggling invoices, marketing campaigns, and the occasional office plumbing disaster like a circus performer on a unicycle. But sooner or later, even the best jugglers drop a ball—or all of them.

Delegating Like a Pro (Instead of a Reluctant Control Freak)

Enter strategic outsourcing. It's not about throwing random tasks at people and hoping for the best. It's about thoughtfully delegating the things that don't require your unique expertise, allowing you to focus on the areas where you truly shine. Think of it as building a symphony where you conduct, rather than play every instrument.

Start by identifying the tasks that sap your time and sanity. Is it bookkeeping that makes your eyes glaze over? Social media scheduling that feels like an endless black hole? Or perhaps the technical glitches on your website that might as well be written in hieroglyphics? These are prime candidates for outsourcing—tasks that others can do faster, better, and with far less frustration than you.

But outsourcing isn't just about offloading the tasks you despise. It's also about bringing in experts who can elevate your business in ways you never could alone. A skilled graphic designer can make your brand shine, a savvy virtual assistant can streamline your operations, and a marketing pro can help you reach new heights—all while you focus on steering the ship.

Of course, trusting someone else with your precious work takes a leap of faith. It's natural to worry, "Will they do it right? Will they care as much as I do?" But when you approach outsourcing strategically—by vetting professionals, setting clear expectations, and maintaining open communication—you'll find that your business not only survives but thrives.

So, embrace the art of delegating like a pro. Outsourcing doesn't mean you're stepping away from the helm; it means you're building a team that keeps the ship sailing smoothly, freeing you to focus on the horizon ahead. Who knows? You might even discover that letting go isn't just practical—it's downright liberating. And as a bonus, you'll finally have time to fix that leaky faucet—or hire someone else to do it.

What to Outsource

There are tasks in every business that, while crucial, don't exactly set your soul on fire. You know the ones—hours spent tweaking social media posts, responding to the same customer queries for the hundredth time, or wrestling with spreadsheets until your eyes cross. These are the tasks begging to be outsourced, the unsung heroes of growth that don't actually need your fingerprints on them.

Start with social media management. Sure, it's fun to post the occasional quirky update, but crafting a consistent online presence? That's a full-time job in itself. Handing this over to a professional not only saves you hours but ensures your brand voice remains charming and cohesive, rather than descending into the panicked chaos of late-night posting.

Then there's customer support. While you might feel compelled to answer every email personally (because, who else can explain your return policy with just the right blend of empathy and wit?), the reality is that trained support staff can handle these interactions beautifully—and probably faster than you can. Plus, you'll finally get a break from those 3 a.m. "Where's my order?" messages.

And let's not forget bookkeeping. Unless you're one of those rare creatures who genuinely enjoys reconciling accounts and calculating quarterly taxes, this is a prime candidate for outsourcing. A skilled bookkeeper can transform your financial chaos into clean, comprehensible order, leaving you free to focus on growing your business—or enjoying a spreadsheet-free afternoon for once.

The magic of outsourcing these tasks lies in the freedom it brings. By letting go of the everyday essentials that don't require your personal touch, you create space to focus on the areas where you truly add value—whether that's developing new products, connecting with key clients, or dreaming up your next big idea.

So, take a deep breath and hand over those spreadsheets, email templates, and scheduling calendars. You'll be amazed at how much lighter your workload—and your mood—feels when you let someone else wrestle with the day-to-day. Outsourcing isn't just practical; it's a gift to your future self—the one who finally has time for a second cup of coffee.

Finding Reliable Partners

Outsourcing is a bit like hiring someone to paint your house. Sure, it sounds simple—grab a brush, splash on some color, voilà! But if you're not careful, you might end up with a ceiling that looks like a Jackson Pollock original or walls that scream "oops" instead of "elegant retreat." The same holds true for finding reliable partners to handle the essential tasks in your business: you need to do a little homework to ensure they know what they're doing—and that they'll do it well.

Start with the basics: vetting. Whether you're hiring a freelance graphic designer, an agency for customer support, or a virtual assistant to keep your calendar from resembling a game of Tetris, take the time to look at their work. Ask for samples, reviews, or references, and pay attention to the details. If their portfolio feels polished and their past clients rave about them, you're probably onto a winner. If their samples look like they were created during a power outage, well, maybe keep looking.

Next, have a conversation. A good working relationship is built on clear communication and mutual understanding. Ask them about their approach, their turnaround times, and how they handle challenges. If they respond with enthusiasm and clarity, great. If they seem confused or evasive, it might be a red flag—after all, you wouldn't hire a house painter who can't explain what a primer is.

And let's talk about alignment. The best outsourcing partners will not only have the skills to do the job but will also understand your vision and goals. Think of them as an extension of your team. If you're outsourcing your social media, for instance, you want someone who gets your brand voice—not someone who thinks "on fleek" is still a trendy phrase.

Finally, test the waters. Before committing to a long-term contract, start with a smaller project or trial run. It's like letting a house painter tackle one room before unleashing them on the entire house. This gives you a chance to see their work in action and ensure they're a good fit for your needs.

Outsourcing isn't just about handing off tasks; it's about building trust with people who can help your business grow. So, take your time, do your research, and choose partners who not only meet your standards but exceed them. Because the last thing you want is a metaphorical ceiling that looks like it was painted by a blindfolded amateur.

Balancing Cost and Value

Outsourcing is a bit like deciding where to eat on a busy weeknight. Do you swing through the drive-thru for something quick and budget-friendly, or do you opt for a gourmet meal that promises a dining experience you'll savor? Both choices have their place, but knowing when to go fast and cheap versus when to invest in quality is key.

When it comes to outsourcing, the same principle applies. Some tasks—like basic data entry or routine scheduling—can be handed off to cost-effective providers without compromising your business's integrity. These are your metaphorical fries and nuggets: functional, no-frills, and perfect for when you just need to get the job done.

But for more complex or high-impact tasks, like branding, strategic marketing, or customer-facing roles, you'll want to invest in gourmet-level quality. The pay-off for spending more on an expert or specialist often comes in the form of fewer headaches, better results, and the satisfaction of knowing it's been done right. You wouldn't hire a bargain-rate chef to cater your wedding, and you probably shouldn't trust the cheapest option with your business's core operations.

The trick is to assess the return on investment (ROI) for each task. Ask yourself: How much time will outsourcing this save me? How much better (or faster) will someone else do it? And most importantly, what impact will this have on my bottom line? For example, outsourcing social media management might cost more than doing it yourself, but if it drives significant customer engagement and revenue, it's worth every penny.

However, not every task requires a Michelin-starred approach. For routine, low-impact jobs, a dependable, budget-friendly option can be just the ticket. Think of it as balancing your menu: a mix of fast, efficient solutions for the everyday stuff and premium choices for the big-ticket items.

The goal isn't to spend as little as possible or splurge on everything—it's to find the sweet spot where cost meets value. And remember, it's okay to experiment. Start small, track the results, and adjust your strategy as needed.

Because whether you're outsourcing your bookkeeping or your website re-design, the goal is the same: to free up your time and energy for what truly matters. And if you save a little extra cash to treat yourself to an actual gourmet meal now and then, well, that's just smart business.

The Freedom of Letting Go

There's something profoundly liberating about finally letting go of the tasks that have been tethering you to your desk like a modern-day ball and chain. It's like setting down a heavy backpack after a long hike or delegating the Thanksgiving turkey to someone else so you can focus on perfecting your pumpkin pie. Outsourcing isn't just about efficiency—it's about reclaiming your time, your sanity, and maybe even your weekends.

When you offload the day-to-day minutiae, you create space for what truly matters. Suddenly, you have the bandwidth to focus on high-impact activities—the ones that drive growth, spark innovation, or simply remind you why you started this business in the first place. Instead of fretting over invoices or struggling to schedule social media posts, you can direct your energy toward big-picture strategies, creative projects, or building meaningful relationships with your clients and team.

And let's not forget the most tempting benefit of all: the possibility of a real holiday. Yes, you heard that right—a holiday where you actually leave your laptop at home and don't spend your afternoons surreptitiously answering emails by the pool. With the right outsourcing in place, you can step away from your business without the nagging fear that it will implode in your absence. Imagine this: sipping a tropical drink, toes in the sand, while your well-oiled team handles everything back at the office. Bliss, isn't it?

But the freedom of letting go isn't just about work; it's about life. It's about reclaiming the hours to reconnect with hobbies, spend quality time with loved ones, or simply breathe without the constant hum of "What's next?" running through your head.

So, take the leap. Let go of the spreadsheets, the scheduling apps, and the endless to-do lists. Hand them over to capable hands and trust that the world won't crumble without you micromanaging every detail. Because the freedom of letting go isn't just a perk of outsourcing—it's the ultimate reward. And who knows? You might even find time to plan that holiday after all.

Mindful Growth Decisions: Choosing the Right Path

(Without Falling Into the Rabbit Hole of Regret)

Growing a business often feels like standing at a fork in the road, each path promising riches, success, and possibly a slightly smug LinkedIn post about your achievements. The problem is, not every route is paved with gold. Some turn out to be detours into chaos, while others lead to dead ends adorned with regret and unnecessary expenses. The key to avoiding these pitfalls? Mindful growth decisions—choosing your next step with clarity, purpose, and just the right amount of caution.

Mindful growth is not about jumping on every shiny opportunity that comes your way. It's about pausing to ask yourself: Does this align with my goals? Does it serve my business *and* my life? Imagine it's like picking a hiking trail. Sure, that steep climb might look thrilling, but if it leaves you gasping for air and questioning your life choices, was it really the best option?

Start by examining your priorities. Growth for the sake of growth is rarely sustainable—or enjoyable. Ask yourself what kind of business you want to build and, just as importantly, what kind of life you want to live alongside it. Are you aiming for an empire or a boutique operation? Do you crave a bustling team or a streamlined solo endeavor? These answers will act as your compass, guiding you toward opportunities that fit, rather than overwhelm.

It's also wise to consider the ripple effects of each decision. Adding a new product line or opening a second location might sound exciting, but what will it require in terms of time, resources, and energy? And more importantly, what will it cost you in terms of balance and sanity? Growth doesn't have to mean burning the candle at both ends—it can mean smarter, more intentional choices that allow you to scale without setting your hair on fire.

Mindful growth also means learning to say no, even to seemingly good ideas. Not every opportunity is the right one, and it's okay to let a few pass by. Saying no is less about shutting doors and more about protecting the ones that truly matter.

After all, every "yes" you give takes time and energy away from something else. Choose wisely.

Finally, be prepared to adjust. Even the best-laid plans can hit unexpected snags—a detour, a flat tire, or in business terms, a sudden market shift. Staying flexible and willing to pivot is part of the journey. Mindful growth isn't a straight line; it's a winding path that adapts to the terrain, taking you where you need to go without losing sight of the view.

So, as you stand at that fork in the road, take a moment. Consider your priorities, weigh your options, and don't be afraid to turn back if something doesn't feel right. Growth is not a race; it's an evolution, and when done mindfully, it's a journey that enriches not just your business but your entire life. And if all else fails, remember: the best path is the one that lets you sleep at night—and maybe even take the occasional afternoon nap.

Evaluating Opportunities

In the whirlwind of entrepreneurial life, opportunities often present themselves like eager street performers—dazzling and hard to ignore. A new partnership, a promising expansion, a trend that everyone else seems to be jumping on—how could you possibly say no? But as tempting as it is to leap at every shiny prospect, not all opportunities are created equal. Some will align beautifully with your goals, while others will leave you wondering why you signed up for a juggling act you never wanted.

This is where a simple, lifestyle-focused framework can save the day—and your sanity. Before you dive headfirst into any new venture, pause and ask yourself a few grounding questions. Start with the most essential one: *Will this add joy or just stress?* If the thought of taking on this new opportunity makes you sigh rather than smile, it might be worth reconsidering. After all, what's the point of growing a business if it feels like it's shrinking your happiness?

Next, consider whether this aligns with your long-term vision. Picture your ideal future: Does this opportunity fit into that vision like a perfect puzzle piece, or does it feel like cramming a square peg into a round hole? For example, if you dream of a flexible schedule but this new project requires you to be tethered to your desk at all hours, it's a clear mismatch.

Another useful question to ponder is: *What will this cost me—in time, energy, or other opportunities?* Every "yes" has a trade-off, whether it's skipping a family dinner, cutting into your leisure time, or sidelining another project you're passionate about. Think of your time and energy as a finite budget—spend them wisely.

Finally, don't forget to ask: *What's the upside?* Not just in financial terms, but in fulfillment, creativity, or personal growth. The best opportunities are the ones that pay dividends in multiple areas of your life, leaving you feeling energized rather than drained.

Evaluating opportunities isn't about being overly cautious or shutting every door—it's about being intentional. When you take the time to consider how a new venture fits into your life and business, you're not just avoiding stress; you're creating space for the opportunities that truly matter. And when those come along, you'll be ready to embrace them with open arms—and maybe even a little enthusiasm. After all, the best decisions are the ones that feel like a gift, not a chore.

Avoiding the Shiny Object Syndrome

Entrepreneurs are naturally drawn to new ideas. It's part of the charm—like magpies collecting shiny trinkets. But chasing every glimmering opportunity that crosses your path can quickly turn your business into a cluttered garage of half-finished projects and regrettable decisions. Welcome to the world of Shiny Object Syndrome, where every new trend or fad promises success but often delivers chaos.

Picture this: You hear about a hot new business strategy sweeping the industry. Everyone is raving about it, from your competitor down the street to that influencer who seems to run their empire from a hammock. Inspired by their glowing testimonials, you dive in headfirst, investing time, money, and maybe a little of your dignity, only to realize it's as practical for your business as buying a jet ski for a desert adventure. Sure, it's flashy and fun to talk about, but where exactly are you supposed to use it?

Shiny Object Syndrome doesn't just waste resources; it distracts you from what truly matters. It's like trying to build a sturdy treehouse while abandoning your blueprint every time a new design trend pops up. Before long, you're left with a hodgepodge of ideas that don't quite fit together—and probably a structure that wobbles more than you'd like.

The key to avoiding this tempting trap is staying anchored to your goals. When a new opportunity arises, pause and ask yourself: *Does this align with my long-term vision? Will it support my priorities or simply create more noise?* If the answer is no—or even a hesitant maybe—it's worth stepping back and reconsidering.

Another trick is to remind yourself that trends come and go, but your values and vision are your true north. Just because everyone else is jumping on a particular bandwagon doesn't mean it's the right ride for you. Sometimes the best decision is to admire the shiny object from afar and continue building your business with intention and focus.

Finally, don't be afraid to test the waters cautiously. Dip a toe in, assess the results, and only commit fully if it genuinely enhances your business. This approach keeps you agile without throwing you into the deep end of an uncharted pool.

Remember, not all that glitters is gold—sometimes, it's just a distraction in a sparkly wrapper. Stay true to your path, and you'll find that the opportunities worth pursuing are the ones that shine steadily, not the ones that flare up and fizzle out. And if you're ever tempted by a particularly gleaming prospect, just ask yourself: *Is this my jet ski in the desert?* If the answer is yes, you'll know what to do.

Staying True to Your Vision

Running a business often feels like navigating a long, winding road trip. You've got your map (or at least a vague idea of your destination), a tank full of ambition, and a playlist of motivational anthems to keep you going. But along the way, temptations arise—those tantalizing detours promising quick success, exciting adventures, or at least a break from the grind. They're the business equivalent of roadside attractions: shiny, alluring, and occasionally disastrous.

Picture this: You're driving toward a picturesque beach retreat (your vision, of course), when a hand-painted sign appears, advertising the "World's Largest Ball of Yarn" just 20 miles off-route. Intrigued, you veer off the highway, only to find yourself hours later in the middle of nowhere, staring at a tangled mess that wasn't worth the detour. Meanwhile, the beach? Still waiting.

Sticking to your vision is like staying on that well-planned route. It doesn't mean you can't explore or adapt along the way—just that you should always keep your ultimate destination in mind. When a shiny opportunity pops up, tempting you to stray, ask yourself: *Does this get me closer to where I want to be, or am I just chasing distractions?* If it's the latter, it's time to tighten your grip on the steering wheel and drive on.

Staying true to your values and goals also acts as a safeguard against regret. It keeps you grounded, ensuring that every decision aligns with the business and life you're trying to build. Sure, those glittering fads and detours might seem exciting in the moment, but if they don't align with your map, they're more likely to leave you lost, frustrated, or—worst of all—stuck in the world's most boring tourist trap of a decision.

And here's the beauty of staying the course: it allows you to enjoy the journey. When you're not constantly second-guessing or chasing after distractions, you can focus on what matters—your goals, your growth, and maybe even the view out the window.

So, the next time a dazzling new opportunity beckons, pause and ask yourself: *Is this helping me reach my beach, or am I about to take a detour into the land of oversized yarn balls?* Stick to your map, and you'll not only arrive at your destination—you'll enjoy the ride there.

Course Corrections Along the Way

No matter how meticulously you plan your journey, life—and business—has a way of tossing in unexpected twists. Maybe your "surefire" marketing strategy fizzles, or that partnership you were banking on veers off course. It's a bit like following GPS directions on a road trip, only to hear the dreaded, *"Recalculating..."* just as you realize you've missed the turn and are now heading toward a questionable dirt road.

But here's the thing about detours: they're rarely the end of the world. In fact, they often lead to valuable lessons or surprising opportunities—like discovering a charming roadside café when you were just trying to get back on the highway. The key is to embrace the recalibration process with grace (and maybe a touch of humor) rather than panic.

Adjusting plans doesn't mean abandoning your vision. It's more like tweaking the route to avoid unnecessary roadblocks or take advantage of a smoother path. Think of it as recalibrating your GPS—not because you're lost, but because the road ahead has shifted. The destination remains the same; you're just navigating smarter.

Of course, some course corrections feel less like charming detours and more like flat-out disasters. A campaign flops, a product launch tanks, or a big client jumps ship. It's tempting to view these moments as failures, but they're really just part of the journey. Even the best-laid plans need a little flexibility—after all, what's a road trip without a few wrong turns? As long as you keep moving forward, every setback becomes a story to tell and a lesson to learn.

So, how do you handle these inevitable adjustments? Start by taking a deep breath (or several) and assessing the situation. What's the reality of where you are versus where you wanted to be? What's working, and what's not? Once you've got a clear picture, you can recalibrate your efforts and steer back on track—or onto a better track you hadn't considered before.

Remember, the journey isn't about perfection; it's about progress. And some of the most rewarding paths are the ones you never planned to take. So, when life throws you a detour, don't despair. Adjust your course, enjoy the unexpected scenery, and trust that you'll find your way—even if it's not quite the way you envisioned. After all, a good GPS (and a good mindset) always knows how to get you there in the end.

Growing Gracefully (Without Losing Your Marbles)

Growth can be a truly beautiful thing, much like planting a garden. You start with seeds of potential—your ideas, your ambitions, your goals—and then you nurture them. You water consistently, make sure they get enough sunlight, and yes, prune what doesn't work. Over time, you begin to see the results: vibrant blooms, sturdy stems, and fruits ripe for picking. It's rewarding, yes, but only if you don't collapse in a heap from the sheer effort of trying to grow everything at once.

Much like gardening, harmonizing business growth with your lifestyle isn't about frantic, unchecked expansion. It's about intention—deciding what to grow, what to let go, and how to manage the process without losing your sanity. Maybe you don't need a sprawling orchard; maybe a tidy, thriving herb garden is exactly what fits your life. The trick is to focus on what matters most to you and ignore the temptation to compare your garden to someone else's vineyard.

It's easy to get caught up in the whirlwind of "bigger is better" thinking. Business magazines and motivational speakers love to spotlight explosive growth stories—the entrepreneur who scaled overnight or the company that hit seven figures before breakfast. What they don't tell you is how often these stories come with a cost: burnout, strained relationships, and a life so overstuffed with work there's no room for joy. But here's the good news: you don't have to grow that way. You can grow gracefully.

Growing gracefully means embracing balance, strategy, and the occasional deep breath. It means knowing when to delegate and when to step back, trusting your team to handle their part while you focus on what you do best. It's about choosing growth that aligns with your values and enhances your life, not growth for growth's sake.

And yes, it's about letting go of the small stuff. Not every task, opportunity, or idea deserves your attention. Think of it as weeding your garden—removing what doesn't serve the greater good so the important things have room to flourish.

So, as you nurture your business, remember this: growth doesn't have to come at the cost of your well-being. With a little balance, a dash of strategy, and a willingness to trust the process, you can create a business that grows beautifully—and a life you actually enjoy living. After all, what's the point of a garden if you're too exhausted to sit back and admire the view?

Chapter Ten

The 80/20 Lifestyle Principle

The Curious Magic of Doing Less (and Getting More)

ONE AFTERNOON, A FRIEND of mine, in a fit of ambition, decided to tackle everything on his to-do list at once. And I mean *everything*. Reorganizing the sock drawer, creating a color-coded calendar of the next decade, and finally learning Italian—all crammed into a single afternoon. He envisioned himself gliding effortlessly from one task to the next, ending the day as a paragon of productivity, possibly even bilingual.

Instead, the afternoon predictably unraveled into chaos. The sock drawer was emptied but left in disarray, the calendar became an indecipherable rainbow of sticky notes, and his attempt at Italian ended with a vaguely accurate pronunciation of *ciao*. The only real accomplishment was the rediscovery of a long-lost pair of socks, which, to his credit, did spark a moment of joy.

We've all been there, haven't we? Overloaded with tasks and convinced we can do it all, only to find ourselves drowning in the minutiae and barely making a dent in the mountain of work. Enter Pareto's Principle, the brilliantly simple idea that 80% of results often come from just 20% of efforts. It sounds almost too good to be true—like finding out you can eat pizza and still lose weight or skip the gym and somehow get fitter.

But here's the thing: it works. Named after the Italian economist Vilfredo Pareto, who noticed that 80% of Italy's wealth was held by 20% of the population, this principle applies far beyond economics. It shows up in all aspects of life: 80% of a business's profits often come from 20% of its customers, 80% of your wardrobe rotation probably consists of 20% of your clothes (yes, the comfy ones), and 80% of your daily stress stems from just 20% of your email inbox.

The beauty of the 80/20 Principle lies in its simplicity. It's a roadmap for cutting through the noise and focusing on what truly matters. It doesn't mean ignoring the rest but rather shifting your energy toward the high-impact tasks, relationships, and decisions that yield the most meaningful results.

This chapter is all about embracing that mindset—not just in your work, but in your life. It's about doing less but doing it better and feeling like you've actually accomplished something at the end of the day (even if that *something* doesn't involve sock drawers or Italian flashcards).

So, let's dive into the curious magic of doing less and getting more. You might just discover that by narrowing your focus, you can unlock an abundance of time, energy, and maybe even a few long-lost socks.

Understanding Pareto's Principle:

Meet Pareto, the Pea-Loving Economist

Vilfredo Pareto was the kind of man who could see patterns where others saw chaos—a rare gift that would cement his place in history as the godfather of what we now call the 80/20 rule. Picture this: It's the late 19th century in Italy, and Pareto, an economist with an eye for detail and, as legend might have it, a fondness for both espresso and eccentric experiments, notices something curious. A whopping 80% of Italy's land is owned by just 20% of its population. This discovery would have been interesting enough to jot down in his ledger and call it a day, but Pareto wasn't one to leave a pattern unexplored.

No, Pareto's investigative mind led him to his garden, of all places, where he noticed a similarly lopsided reality: 80% of his peas came from just 20% of his pea pods. Let's take a moment to appreciate the whimsical absurdity of this—an economist uncovering a universal truth by observing legumes. From his garden to the grand economic stage, Pareto's discovery would eventually transcend both wealth and vegetables to find its way into virtually every corner of human activity.

The 80/20 Rule: Everywhere You Look

Pareto's Principle has since revealed itself in the most unexpected places. Think about it: 80% of the time, you probably wear the same 20% of your clothes (the ones that don't require ironing or tugging at awkward seams). And 80% of your joy likely comes from 20% of your favorite people—the ones who never say things like, "Let's circle back to that," and actually mean it. Even your playlist adheres to this curious ratio—20% of your songs dominate 80% of your streams, leaving the other 200 tracks gathering digital dust.

But here's the thing: Pareto's Principle isn't just an observation; it's a strategy. It's not about lamenting life's imbalance—it's about leveraging it. It's about identifying that golden 20% that drives the lion's share of your results, whether you're running a business, planning your week, or figuring out which Netflix show to binge next.

Breaking It Down: The Buffet of Life

Let's imagine your daily to-do list is a buffet table. There are tasks that matter, tasks that are mildly important, and tasks that, let's face it, could be skipped entirely—like color-coding your email folders or alphabetizing your spice rack. Pareto's Principle is like a kindly buffet chef nudging you toward the high-value dishes and away from the parsley garnish. Load up on the steak of meaningful work, and leave the decorative distractions behind.

This isn't about cutting corners or doing the bare minimum. It's about focusing your energy on what truly moves the needle. The beauty of Pareto's Principle is that it forces you to question: What are the 20% of efforts creating 80% of your success? And just as importantly, what's the 80% that's simply spinning your wheels?

A Life Lived by Pareto

The magic of Pareto's Principle is that it's not confined to business. It applies to everything. What activities bring you the most fulfillment? What relationships energize you? What projects deliver the biggest wins? Life, much like Pareto's garden, thrives when you nurture the most productive pods.

So here's the takeaway: You don't have to do it all. Focus on the right things—the tasks, people, and passions that truly matter—and let the rest fall by the wayside. Pareto may have discovered a truth about inequality, but in doing so, he also handed us a guide to balance, focus, and maybe even a little sanity. And who knows? If you start applying Pareto's Principle, you might just find a few metaphorical peas worth celebrating in your own garden.

Why the 80/20 Rule Works

The brilliance of the 80/20 rule lies in its almost infuriating simplicity: a small fraction of your efforts tends to generate the lion's share of your results. It's the kind of concept that feels so obvious once it's pointed out, you can't help but wonder why you didn't notice it yourself—like discovering you've been opening bananas from the wrong end your entire life (Google it and let me know if you've been doing this right).

Think about it: a handful of your clients probably account for most of your revenue. A fraction of your products or services brings in the bulk of your sales. Even in your personal life, just a few of your daily activities likely contribute the most to your happiness or sanity (coffee, for instance, is practically a one-item Pareto Principle all on its own).

So why does this work? Because not all efforts are created equal. Some tasks, decisions, or relationships pack a disproportionate punch when it comes to outcomes. The trick isn't about working harder; it's about working smarter—figuring out which 20% of what you're doing is moving the needle and doubling down on that, while letting the other 80% fade into the background.

And yet, knowing this, what do we do instead? We spend hours meticulously reorganizing email folders, perfectly aligning the fonts on a PowerPoint slide, or deciding which shade of beige is best for the office walls—tasks that might be satisfying in the moment but ultimately make no meaningful dent in our overall success.

The 80/20 rule is your friendly wake-up call, nudging you to step back and rethink your priorities. It doesn't mean you ignore the little things altogether—after all, those email folders aren't going to color-code themselves—but it does mean recognizing that your time and energy are precious. Spend them where they count, and let the rest take care of itself (or not—it's probably not that important anyway).

Because really, wouldn't you rather sip your coffee, knowing you've tackled the tasks that matter most, than spend another afternoon debating whether that fourth sub-folder should be labeled "Miscellaneous" or "General"?

Examples in Real Life

The 80/20 rule isn't just a handy concept for business—it's woven into the very fabric of our everyday lives, quietly governing everything from our closets to our phone screens. Once you start spotting it, you'll wonder how you ever missed it.

Take your wardrobe, for instance. Despite owning enough clothing to outfit a small theater troupe, you probably rotate between the same four shirts, two pairs of pants, and one pair of sneakers. That's 20% of your wardrobe doing 80% of the heavy lifting. The rest? A motley collection of "maybe someday" outfits, like that dress you wore once to a wedding or the jacket that seemed like a good idea before you remembered you lived in a tropical climate.

Or consider your smartphone. You might have 50 apps installed, but let's face it: most of your screen time is spent on the same two or three. Your email app?

That's a given. Social media? Naturally. That random meditation app you down-loaded in a burst of optimism about "mindful mornings"? Probably untouched since the day it was installed.

Even your kitchen isn't immune to Pareto's Principle. Think about your uten-sils drawer. Out of the dozens of spoons, knives, and mismatched forks, you probably reach for the same trusty spatula and that one non-stick pan 80% of the time. The rest are there for moral support—or to fill up the dishwasher when you've run out of the good stuff.

The beauty of the 80/20 rule is that it doesn't just reveal inefficiencies; it gives you permission to let go of the unnecessary. Why clutter your life—or your wardrobe, apps, or kitchen—with things you rarely use when you could focus on the 20% that actually brings you value? By identifying the essentials and embracing them, you're not just decluttering your physical spaces—you're clearing up mental space, too.

So, the next time you're overwhelmed by choice, remember Pareto and his peas. Whether it's deciding what to wear, which app to tap, or which skillet to grab, life often boils down to a few key players. Embrace them, and you'll be surprised how much smoother—and simpler—things become.

Finding the Gold in the Gravel

Focusing on the core 20% is a bit like panning for gold. Most of what you sift through is ordinary gravel—tasks, clients, or projects that consume time but don't add much value. The trick is finding those glittering nuggets that make all the effort worthwhile. And, unlike actual gold panning, you don't need to stand knee-deep in a freezing river to do it.

In business, the "gold" might be your top clients, the best-performing prod-ucts, or the most impactful activities. These are the things that generate the majority of your success, whether that's revenue, customer satisfaction, or plain old peace of mind. The key is figuring out what they are—and then devoting your time and energy to them like they're your favorite snacks.

Start by taking a step back and asking yourself: *What really moves the needle?* Maybe it's the one client who consistently brings in high-value projects or the product that outsells everything else combined. Or perhaps it's a recurring task—like weekly strategy sessions—that has a ripple effect across your entire operation. These are your gold nuggets, the things that deserve your attention.

Now, contrast that with the gravel. These are the activities that fill up your day but don't add much to the big picture. Responding to every non-urgent email? Gravel. Spending hours debating font choices for a proposal? Gravel. Perfecting the art of coffee brewing when a machine could do it in half the time? You guessed it—gravel.

The beauty of identifying your core 20% is the clarity it brings. Once you've unearthed the gold, you can start reallocating your time and resources accordingly. Say goodbye to the endless slog of trying to do everything and hello to the satisfaction of doing the right things exceptionally well.

When you put your energy into the gold, the returns are not only bigger—they're also more fulfilling. After all, wouldn't you rather polish a nugget of gold than shovel through endless piles of gravel? Exactly.

Identifying High-Impact Activities

Finding your high-impact activities—the golden 20%—is a bit like discovering that your morning coffee habit is what keeps you human: eye-opening and life-changing. These are the tasks that actually move the needle, the ones that yield significant results for the effort invested. The trick is spotting them amidst the clutter of your to-do list, which often resembles a never-ending game of Whac-A-Mole.

Let's start with the obvious candidates. Think about your workday. Are there tasks that consistently lead to tangible, positive outcomes? For instance, maybe it's crafting one thoughtful, tailored client proposal rather than blasting out 100 generic emails that sound like they were written by a robot on a caffeine break. Quality often trumps quantity, especially when you're targeting clients, customers, or projects that genuinely matter.

Or consider your marketing efforts. You might find that spending an hour creating one engaging blog post brings in far more leads than scattering your energy across ten half-hearted social media updates. It's like making one great pot of soup instead of trying to serve everyone a thin gruel—people notice the effort, and it pays off.

High-impact activities also tend to align with your strengths. If you're great at building relationships, focus on networking or client calls rather than agonizing over spreadsheets. If creative problem-solving is your jam, prioritize brainstorming sessions instead of getting bogged down in mundane administrative tasks.

The beauty of identifying these golden tasks is the freedom it brings. Once you've pinpointed your 20%, you can focus your energy where it really counts—on the actions that make you feel accomplished and your business thrive. The rest? Delegate, automate, or, in some cases, let it fall into the abyss of "nice to have but not necessary."

In the end, high-impact activities aren't just about efficiency—they're about fulfillment. They're the things that remind you why you started your business in the first place. And when you focus on them, you're not just doing more with less; you're doing better with less. That's the kind of math we can all get behind.

The 20% of Clients You Actually Like

Ah, clients. The lifeblood of your business, the reason your lights stay on, and, occasionally, the reason you consider taking up a career in competitive napping. Let's face it: not all clients are created equal. Some are a joy to work with—respectful, enthusiastic, and excellent at paying invoices on time. Others? Well, let's just say they make you wonder if you've accidentally entered a reality show titled *Survivor: Entrepreneur Edition.*

This is where the 80/20 rule comes in handy yet again. Chances are, 20% of your clients bring in 80% of your revenue, satisfaction, or sanity—sometimes all three. These are the dream clients, the ones who make you remember why you started your business in the first place. The ones who reply to your emails with concise answers instead of essays, or who don't turn every minor revision into a six-hour ordeal.

The challenge is identifying them. Start by looking at your client list. Which names make you smile instead of groan? Which projects feel energizing rather than soul-draining? Bonus points if they also pay promptly and don't ask for "just one more tiny change" fifteen times in a row.

Then, of course, there's the other 80%—the ones who make you question every life choice that led to this moment. Maybe they're perpetually late with payments or have an uncanny ability to turn even the simplest task into a logistical nightmare. These clients are your metaphorical gravel. Sure, they fill the bucket, but at what cost to your time, patience, and general will to live?

Once you've identified your golden 20%, the goal is simple: focus on them. Nurture those relationships, prioritize their needs, and—here's the big one—don't be afraid to let go of the clients who consistently bring chaos. Yes, it's scary, but the rewards are worth it. When you clear space for the clients who truly align with your values and goals, you'll not only boost your revenue but also rediscover the joy in your work.

Because let's be honest: life's too short to spend it dreading client calls. So go ahead, embrace the 20% who make your business—and your days—infinitely brighter. And for the others? Wish them well and let them be someone else's gravel.

The Pareto Principle in Action: My Own Journey from Chaos to Clarity

Now, I know what you might be thinking—this all sounds lovely in theory, but what about real life? How do you actually go about letting go of clients when you're staring at your revenue numbers and feeling that familiar pang of panic? Well, let me tell you, this isn't just theory for me. I've done it.

Let me take you back to a time when my IT company had reached a critical point—the sort of point where everyone, myself included, was on edge. We'd gotten to a place where every time the phone rang, my team would visibly tense. No one wanted to answer it because we all knew it was probably one of three clients. You know the ones.

These particular clients were like human versions of storm clouds. Their issues were relentless, and they ate up time like termites in an old house. The biggest culprit? A company using a 20-year-old piece of software that required every user to have local administrator access on their computers. Now, if you're not familiar with IT best practices, let me just say—this is a giant neon sign flashing *"Disaster Ahead."*

Because of this outdated setup, their system constantly needed repairs. We had to restore backed-up data, troubleshoot endless issues, and generally perform what felt like digital CPR on a near-daily basis. It was exhausting. And this wasn't an isolated case—two other clients were just as bad, each with their own unique flavor of chaos.

I took a step back and applied the Pareto Principle. It hit me like a ton of bricks: 80% of our time was being consumed by these three clients. Three! And it wasn't just the time—it was the emotional drain, the stress, and the growing dread whenever their names popped up on the caller ID.

So, I did something that felt both terrifying and oddly liberating. I "released them to industry." In other words, I fired them.

Now, I won't sugarcoat it—that decision came with a sting. I took a hit to our monthly recurring revenue (MRR) to the tune of over $13,000. That's not chump change. But here's the thing: once we let go of those clients, it was as if a weight had been lifted from the entire team. The phones rang less, but when they did, the conversations were far more pleasant. The stress level dropped noticeably, and suddenly we had time to focus on the clients who didn't make us want to pull our hair out.

And the best part? That $13,000 loss was replaced within 90 days. Three months. The space we'd created by cutting out the chaos allowed us to grow quickly and attract new clients who didn't require a full-time team of firefighters.

Looking back, I can confidently say it was one of the best decisions I've made. Sure, letting go of revenue feels risky, but in reality, I wasn't letting go of revenue—I was letting go of *gravel*. And with that gravel out of the way, we had room to focus on the clients who were golden.

So, trust me when I say: life is too short to spend it dreading client calls. Your time, your sanity, and your team's morale are worth far more than any client who brings nothing but chaos. Wish them well, release them to industry, and let someone else take on the gravel.

And for you? Focus on the clients who make your business brighter. Because the moment you do, you'll rediscover why you started this entrepreneurial journey in the first place—and maybe even find yourself smiling when the phone rings again.

By the way, I've read a book by Mike Michalowicz called "The Pumpkin Plan". I highly recommend this book. I haven't read this book in several years, but I have read it several times. It is from this book that I learned to thin out troublesome clients. Do read this book!

Double Down on the Winners

In business, as in gardening, the secret to flourishing isn't found in desperately trying to revive every struggling seedling. Instead, it lies in nurturing the healthiest, most vibrant plants—the ones that promise the greatest blooms for your efforts. Similarly, the key to sustainable success is doubling down on your winners: the activities, relationships, and strategies that yield the highest rewards.

Think about your business like a garden. You wouldn't waste gallons of water and precious daylight on a plant that's already half-eaten by caterpillars, would you? No, you'd focus on the ones thriving in the sunlight, producing those juicy tomatoes or fragrant blossoms. The same principle applies to your business.

Identify what's already working—the clients who adore your work, the products that fly off the shelves, or the services that bring in rave reviews—and give them the attention they deserve.

For example, if you've got a handful of clients who are not only profitable but also an absolute joy to work with, why not invest in strengthening those relationships? Reach out more often, offer them exclusive perks, or brainstorm ways to expand the work you're already doing together. They're your sunflowers, standing tall and bright, ready to bring you more than their fair share of joy and income.

The same goes for your core business activities. If writing detailed, personalized proposals consistently lands you the best clients, put more energy into perfecting that process rather than scattering generic emails into the digital void. Or if a particular product or service consistently outperforms the others, consider refining and scaling it instead of spreading your resources thin across underperformers.

And what about the wilting plants—the activities or relationships that sap your time and energy without much return? It's time for some tough love. Cut back, delegate, or, when necessary, let them go entirely. Freeing up that space allows you to devote your best efforts to the things that truly matter.

The beauty of doubling down on the winners is how it shifts your perspective. Instead of feeling overwhelmed by all the "shoulds" vying for your attention, you can focus on the "musts" that bring you success and satisfaction. It's not just a strategy for growth; it's a recipe for balance, clarity, and a business that thrives.

So, grab your metaphorical watering can and tend to your best blooms. Your garden—and your business—will thank you with results that are as beautiful as they are bountiful.

Marie Kondo-ing Your Workload

Ah, the art of simplification—business-style. Imagine for a moment you're tackling an overflowing closet, except instead of mismatched socks and questionable fashion choices, it's filled with redundant tasks, bloated processes, and responsibilities that haven't sparked joy since the Clinton administration. Streamlining your workload isn't just about tidying up; it's about creating space for what truly matters, the things that make you feel alive and productive rather than overworked and cranky.

In business, as in closets, complexity tends to creep in. A process gets a new step here, an extra spreadsheet there, and suddenly what was once a straightforward workflow now resembles a spaghetti diagram worthy of an art installation. The result? You spend more time untangling the mess than actually getting things done.

Let's start with the basics: identifying what's cluttering your business life. Take a long, hard look at your daily tasks and ask, "Does this actually contribute to my goals, or is it just busywork masquerading as productivity?" Spoiler alert: a lot of it is probably the latter. That weekly report you've been painstakingly creating for months? If no one's reading it, it's time to thank it for its service and let it go.

Next, assess your processes. Where are things slowing down or duplicating unnecessarily? If a task requires three sign-offs and a ceremonial blessing to move forward, it might be time to trim some steps. Think of it as decluttering your business operations—paring things down to the essentials that keep everything running smoothly without bogging you down in minutiae.

And then there's the delicate art of delegation. Streamlining isn't just about what you stop doing; it's about redistributing tasks to people or systems better suited for them. That monthly reconciliation you dread? Hand it off to your accountant or a trusty piece of software. The endless back-and-forth emails about scheduling? Automate it with a tool that handles the details while you focus on work that actually excites you.

The magic of streamlining lies not just in what you remove but in the clarity and calm you gain. Suddenly, your workload feels lighter, your days less chaotic. It's like walking into a well-organized room—peaceful, functional, and not a single stray paperclip in sight.

So, embrace the Marie Kondo method for your business: keep what sparks joy and ditch what doesn't. You'll find yourself with more time, more focus, and maybe even a little extra energy for that passion project you've been putting off. And who knows? You might just rediscover that running your business can actually be, dare I say it, enjoyable.

Eliminating the Low-Impact 80%: Why Nobody Cares About Your PowerPoint Animations

There's a peculiar phenomenon in work life where we invest in tasks that consume inordinate amounts of time but deliver approximately the same return as planting a garden in the shade—nothing much happens. These are the infamous low-impact 80%, the tasks that clutter our schedules while barely making a ripple in the grand scheme of things.

Picture this: you're preparing for an important presentation. Naturally, you want it to shine. So, you spend three hours perfecting the "fly-in" animation for a single bullet point. You tinker with the timing, test different sound effects (all of which are equally cringeworthy), and agonize over whether the bullet should swoop in from the left or the right. By the time you've finished, it's midnight, you've missed dinner, and here's the kicker—no one in the room tomorrow will even notice. They'll be too busy checking their emails on their phones.

This is the essence of the low-impact 80%. They're the tasks that demand far more energy and attention than they deserve, sneaking into our schedules disguised as productivity but ultimately stealing time from work that actually matters. The trick to eliminating them lies in a ruthless yet liberating act of triage: asking, "Does this task directly contribute to my goals, or is it just filler?"

Start with a simple audit of your day. Where are you spending time that feels busy but not productive? Is it endlessly formatting spreadsheets? Attending meetings that could've been emails? Re-reading and rewording the same client message six times before hitting send? These tasks are the culprits, the low-impact time thieves that keep you trapped in the hamster wheel of busyness.

Once you've identified the offenders, the solution is blissfully straightforward: cut them loose. Simplify processes, delegate where possible, and for heaven's sake, stop obsessing over the font choices in your email signature. By clearing out these unnecessary distractions, you reclaim precious hours to focus on high-impact activities—the ones that drive revenue, build relationships, and move your business forward.

The beauty of eliminating the low-impact 80% isn't just in the time saved; it's in the mental clarity that follows. Your to-do list feels lighter, your priorities sharper, and your workday less like a chaotic sprint and more like a purposeful stroll. So, embrace the power of letting go, and remember: no one ever won a contract because their bullet points did a perfect backflip.

Passing the Baton (and the Spreadsheet)

Delegation, they say, is an art—and if that's true, many of us are still doodling stick figures. It's not that we don't want to delegate; it's just that we get stuck in the mindset that no one else could possibly handle our work with the same level of care, precision, and downright stubbornness. But here's the thing: some tasks are begging—absolutely pleading—to be handed off. And if you're spending your time formatting spreadsheets to the point where you know Excel's color palette by heart, it's time to let someone else take the reins.

Delegation isn't about admitting defeat; it's about making the smart choice. Think of it as a relay race: you're still on the team, but you've got to pass the baton if you want to win. Low-impact tasks like calendar wrangling, social media scheduling, or tweaking the alignment on a presentation slide are perfect candidates for delegation. These are the bits and bobs of business life that need doing but don't require your unique brilliance to get done.

Picture this: you've finally decided to outsource your weekly reporting task to a trusted team member. At first, it's nerve-wracking—like watching a toddler attempt to carry a glass of milk across a carpeted room. But then, a miraculous thing happens. Not only do they manage it, but they also come up with a clever shortcut you never thought of. Suddenly, the task you dreaded becomes their moment to shine, and you've just freed up an hour to tackle something that truly matters—or, dare I say it, to take a leisurely coffee break.

The key to effective delegation is clarity. Be specific about what needs to be done, why it's important, and what the final outcome should look like. And then—and this is the hardest part—let them do it their way. Resist the urge to hover, nitpick, or demand updates every ten minutes. Trust them to handle it, and more often than not, they'll rise to the occasion.

Delegation doesn't just lighten your workload; it builds your team's confidence, fosters collaboration, and creates a sense of shared responsibility. And if it means you'll never again have to wrestle with spreadsheet margins at 2 a.m., then it's a win for everyone involved. So, hand over that task list, take a deep breath, and remember: letting go isn't losing control—it's gaining sanity.

Simplifying Processes: Streamlining Without Losing Your Mind

If there's one thing modern business tools excel at, it's promising to simplify your life while secretly conspiring to complicate it. You know the ones—they boast sleek interfaces, cheerful tutorials, and names like "Effortless Sync" or "ZenFlow." Yet somehow, an hour in, you're still reading the user manual, feeling less Zen and more like you're decoding ancient hieroglyphics.

But fear not, because streamlining processes doesn't have to be an exercise in frustration. In fact, when done right, it's less about wrestling with tech and more about creating a workflow that's as smooth as a freshly paved road (minus the occasional pothole).

Let's start with the basics: automating recurring tasks. Think about all those repetitive chores that quietly siphon away your time—sending invoices, following up on emails, or scheduling meetings. Automation tools, like Zapier or Calendly, are your unsung heroes here. They quietly hum along in the background, handling the mundane so you don't have to. It's like hiring a diligent assistant who never takes coffee breaks or complains about Mondays.

Next up, consolidating tools. If you've ever found yourself juggling five different apps to manage one project, it's time for an intervention. The goal isn't to collect digital gadgets like they're Pokémon; it's to find a few versatile tools that play well together. Platforms like Notion or Monday.com can combine task management, communication, and file sharing in one tidy package, sparing you the ordeal of hopping between tabs like a caffeinated rabbit.

Streamlining also means taking a good, hard look at your current processes and asking, "Does this actually need to be this complicated?" Maybe there's a team approval process that resembles a bureaucratic labyrinth, or a client onboarding checklist that's longer than War and Peace. Simplify, condense, and cut out the fluff. Because the truth is, no one's impressed by how intricate your workflow is; they're impressed by how effective it is.

The beauty of simplifying processes is that it not only saves time but also clears mental space. Suddenly, you're not bogged down by the minutiae of day-to-day operations. You can focus on the bigger picture—or, dare I say, take an afternoon off without fear that your business will implode.

And if you're still tempted to download that new "life-changing" app, remember this: the best tool is the one you'll actually use. So, pick what works, ditch what doesn't, and simplify your way to a saner, smoother workday. After all, life's too short to spend it troubleshooting a login page.

Decluttering Your Workload and Rediscovering the Good Stuff

There's a peculiar delight in decluttering a closet. You pull out heaps of forgotten items—pants that haven't fit since the last Olympics, shirts that went out of style so long ago they might be retro again—and then, like a gift from the universe, you stumble upon that one jacket you love. You slip it on, realize it still fits, and suddenly, life feels just a little more together.

The same principle applies to your workload. Trimming the unnecessary isn't just practical; it's downright satisfying. It's like reclaiming bits of yourself that had been buried under the chaos of doing too much. And let's face it, most of us are guilty of treating our to-do lists like a collection of "shoulds" rather than "needs."

The joy of doing less lies in its simplicity. By shedding the tasks, commitments, and projects that don't truly serve your goals, you make room for the things that do. You stop frantically multitasking, juggling priorities like a circus act, and instead focus on what actually moves the needle—or, better yet, brings you joy.

Think about the meetings that could've been emails, the emails that could've been a quick phone call, and the phone calls that probably didn't need to happen at all. By eliminating these time-suckers, you're left with a day that feels lighter, clearer, and infinitely more manageable.

And the best part? Once you've done a proper purge, you might rediscover tasks that you actually enjoy—the creative work, the strategic planning, or the small wins that remind you why you started your business in the first place. It's like finding that favorite jacket, but for your career.

So, embrace the joy of doing less. Clear out the clutter, reclaim your energy, and focus on the things that truly matter. Because, as anyone who's ever cleaned out a closet knows, life is far better when you're not weighed down by unnecessary baggage—and when you can finally see the good stuff you had all along.

Sustaining the 80/20 Lifestyle: A New Way to Look Busy (Without Actually Being Busy)

There's a peculiar art to looking busy. You know the drill—typing furiously, shuffling papers, maybe even throwing in an exasperated sigh for good measure. The problem is, being busy doesn't always mean being productive. And if you're serious about living the 80/20 lifestyle, it's time to trade the illusion of busyness for the reality of balance.

The 80/20 lifestyle isn't just a passing fad or a one-time productivity hack. It's a philosophy—a way of working and living that focuses on doing less but achieving more. But like any good philosophy, it requires maintenance. Without regular check-ins, it's all too easy to slide back into old habits, drowning in tasks that add little value but make you feel like you're "getting things done."

To sustain the 80/20 lifestyle, start by treating it like a regular garden. Yes, a garden. Every so often, you'll need to prune the weeds (those pesky low-value tasks that creep back into your schedule), water the flowers (the high-impact activities that keep your business thriving), and plant a few new seeds (those exciting projects that align with your long-term vision).

Another key to sustaining this lifestyle is resisting the siren call of perfectionism. Perfectionism has a way of turning the simplest tasks into Herculean labors. If you find yourself spending an hour tweaking the font on a presentation no one will notice, take a breath. The goal isn't to make everything perfect; it's to focus on what actually matters.

And then there's the all-important art of saying no. Mastering this single skill can save you countless hours of unnecessary meetings, distractions, and commitments. It's not about being rude—it's about protecting your time for the 20% of activities that truly move the needle.

Finally, let's talk about the beauty of boundaries. To live the 80/20 lifestyle, you need to set firm limits on when and where work happens. Think of these boundaries as the fence around your garden—Sustaining the 80/20 lifestyle is about being deliberate—choosing where to invest your energy and reaping the rewards of a life that feels purposeful and productive without the constant grind.

So, here's to the new way of "looking busy." It's less about appearances and more about priorities. It's choosing to work smarter, live fuller, and enjoy the rare satisfaction of a to-do list that doesn't make you want to hide under the nearest desk. Because at the end of the day, the 80/20 lifestyle isn't just a better way to work—it's a better way to live.

The Importance of Regular Reviews: Keeping Your Garden Free of Weeds (and Your Calendar Free of Clutter)

Picture a garden in full bloom—vivid flowers, lush greenery, maybe even a hummingbird or two flitting about. It's a slice of paradise, carefully cultivated and pruned to perfection. Now, imagine leaving that same garden unattended for a few months. What happens? The weeds take over, the flowers wilt, and you're left wondering where all your hard work went.

The same thing happens with your 80/20 lifestyle if you don't tend to it regularly. It might feel pristine and productive at first, but priorities shift, tasks creep in, and before you know it, your carefully pruned schedule is overrun with weeds in the form of low-impact tasks and unnecessary commitments.

That's why regular reviews are so important. Life changes, businesses evolve, and what was once a high-impact activity might no longer pack the same punch. A client that used to bring in significant revenue may now require more effort than they're worth. A project that seemed promising six months ago might have turned into a time-suck with no clear payoff. Without taking the time to reassess, you risk pouring your energy into areas that no longer serve your goals.

Treat these reviews like a quarterly garden-tending session. Pull out the weeds—those tasks and commitments that have snuck back into your life but aren't yielding results. Water the flowers—your core 20% of activities that bring the most value. And don't forget to plant something new—a fresh idea or project that aligns with your evolving goals.

Regular reviews don't have to be a daunting process. Start with a simple question: What's working? Then ask: What's not? Be brutally honest. If you find that some activities have become more about habit than impact, it's time to reevaluate.

And remember, just like a garden, your 80/20 lifestyle doesn't require perfection—it thrives on care and attention. You don't have to eliminate every single weed, but keeping the clutter in check allows the important things to flourish.

So, make a habit of stepping back, reassessing, and adjusting as needed. Your business—and your peace of mind—will thank you. And the best part? You'll spend less time tangled in low-value tasks and more time enjoying the fruits of your labor, whether that's a thriving business, a balanced life, or a garden free of dandelions.

The 80/20 Guide to Happiness (and Dodging Unnecessary Meetings)

The 80/20 principle isn't just for work; it's a secret weapon for life itself. Think about it: much like your business, your personal life is filled with activities, relationships, and commitments. Some bring immense joy and fulfillment, while others—let's be honest—feel like obligations that exist purely to test your patience.

Take a moment to apply the 80/20 lens to your calendar. Are there activities that you genuinely look forward to? Maybe it's a Friday evening game night with friends or a solo hike that clears your head. These are your golden 20%—the moments that fuel your spirit and make life rich. Now, think about the other 80%. The errands, the never-ending PTA meetings, or, dare I say, those weekly neighborhood watch gatherings where the most action involves debating the appropriate height of a garden fence.

Here's the beauty of the 80/20 principle in your personal life: you're allowed to let some of that 80% go. Yes, really. You don't have to say yes to everything or be everywhere at once. In fact, saying no to the things that don't truly matter frees up time and energy for the things that do.

Balancing work and life is about making deliberate choices. It's choosing to spend Saturday morning playing catch with your kids instead of reorganizing the garage for the third time this year. It's deciding that dinner with a close friend will always take priority over scrolling through endless emails. It's realizing that your personal life, just like your business, deserves its own curated list of priorities.

By focusing on the relationships and activities that bring you the most joy and fulfillment, you'll find yourself with a life that feels less like a series of obligations and more like an adventure. And if that means bowing out of the occasional neighborhood watch meeting, so be it. After all, life is too short to spend it debating the finer points of lawn decor.

The 80/20 principle in personal life isn't about shirking responsibilities—it's about nurturing what matters most. When you give yourself permission to focus on the golden 20%, you're not just improving your life; you're creating a ripple effect of positivity that benefits everyone around you. So go ahead, prune the unnecessary, and savor the moments that make your life truly yours. And who knows? Maybe you'll even find the time to start that long-overdue novel—or just enjoy a really good walk on the beach.

Staying Disciplined: Resisting the Siren Song of Busywork

Ah, busywork—that seductive mistress of the modern world. It's everywhere, waiting to pounce the moment you feel a twinge of uncertainty or boredom. It's the color-coded spreadsheet no one asked for, the endless reshuffling of Post-it notes, and the compulsive email-checking that somehow feels productive even when it's not. Let's face it: "looking busy" might as well be a national pastime, but it rarely leads to anything meaningful.

Staying disciplined in your commitment to the 80/20 principle requires a bit of vigilance, a dash of willpower, and perhaps a smidgen of humor. First, recognize busywork for what it is: a distraction disguised as productivity. It loves to masquerade as important but offers little in return. Sure, you might feel accomplished after spending an hour tweaking the font on your PowerPoint presentation, but does it really move the needle? Spoiler alert: it does not.

One way to resist the temptation is to set clear, purposeful goals for each day. Before diving into your to-do list, identify the tasks that truly matter—the ones that align with your golden 20%. Write them down, stick them on your desk, or tattoo them on your forearm if necessary. The point is to keep them front and center, so you don't get sidetracked by the siren song of reorganizing your desktop icons.

Another trick is to schedule your high-impact work during your peak productivity hours. Are you a morning person? Tackle your core 20% before the rest of the world starts demanding your attention. Night owl? Save your best work for when the house is quiet and you're in the zone. When you anchor your day around what matters most, there's less room for busywork to creep in.

And finally, give yourself permission to stop "performing" productivity. You don't need to look busy to justify your existence—real impact doesn't require a flurry of activity. In fact, some of the most successful people in the world are experts at doing less, better. Take a page from their playbook, and embrace the quiet confidence of someone who knows exactly where their time is best spent.

Staying disciplined isn't about perfection—it's about consistency. Sure, you'll have days when busywork sneaks past your defenses. But as long as you return to your 80/20 principles, you'll find that discipline becomes second nature. And who knows? You might even discover that doing less is the ultimate superpower. Because let's be honest: no one ever changed the world by perfecting their email folder system.

Living the 80/20 Life

Embracing Pareto's Principle isn't about becoming lazy or neglectful—it's about working smarter, not harder. Think of it as wandering through a buffet line where 80% of the food is uninspiring filler, and 20% is downright delightful. Would you really waste your plate on limp salads and overcooked pasta when you could head straight for the tender roast beef and the chocolate fountain at the end? Of course not. Life, like that buffet, is best enjoyed when you focus on the good stuff and skip the rest (unless they bring out crème brûlée, in which case all bets are off).

The 80/20 lifestyle invites you to rethink the way you approach your time, energy, and effort. It's not about abandoning your ambition or cutting corners. Quite the opposite—it's about identifying what truly moves the needle and channeling your efforts there. Imagine clearing out the mental clutter of busywork and replacing it with meaningful tasks that not only yield great results but also align with your passions and goals.

The beauty of Pareto's Principle is its inherent simplicity. You don't need a PhD in time management to apply it. Start small: take a good, hard look at your to-do list and ask, "What here really matters?" Chances are, you'll find a few golden tasks hidden among the mundane. These are your 20%. Nurture them, prioritize them, and let them lead you to success.

And the other 80%? Well, let's just say you're under no obligation to keep juggling every plate. Delegate, automate, or simply let go of the things that don't serve your bigger picture. Your time is too precious to be spent perfecting PowerPoint transitions or organizing a filing cabinet that no one will ever open again.

So, here's your cheerful nudge: The 80/20 lifestyle doesn't dictate that you do less—it redirects you to do less of what drains you and more of what drives you. It directs your work back to purpose, creating space for joy, and rediscovering what it feels like to have room to breathe.

Now, go find your 20%. It's probably waiting patiently behind all those less important tasks on your to-do list, wondering when you're finally going to notice it. Spoiler alert: it's the chocolate fountain of your life's buffet, and trust me, it's worth every bite.

Chapter Eleven

Resilience as a Business Strategy

The Rubber Band Principle of Entrepreneurship

ENTREPRENEURSHIP, AS IT TURNS out, has a knack for taking simple expectations and turning them into highly creative chaos. One day, you're cruising along, thinking you've got everything under control, and the next, the metaphorical soul on your shoe suddenly starts flopping wildly with each stride, and you're left hobbling toward the nearest safe spot.

That's where resilience comes in. In business, as in life, things break. Plans go awry. Clients disappear. Tech glitches crop up at the worst possible moments. And no matter how carefully you've built your vacuum—or your business—something, somewhere, is bound to fail spectacularly at some point. But here's the thing: it's not about avoiding those moments. It's about how you bounce back when they happen.

Enter the Rubber Band Principle. A rubber band, as you'll recall from idle office days of shooting them at coworkers, has a remarkable ability to stretch, sometimes to ridiculous lengths, and then snap back into shape. That's the kind of spirit every entrepreneur needs. Resilience isn't about pretending nothing ever goes wrong or gritting your teeth through endless catastrophes. It's about staying flexible, adapting to the unexpected, and—this is key—bouncing back stronger, preferably with your sense of humor intact.

Think of this chapter as your guide to becoming the rubber band in your business. We'll explore how to weather setbacks, learn from them, and maybe even emerge with a few entertaining war stories to tell. After all, what's entrepreneurship without a bit of chaos and a lot of creative recovery? Let's dive in, shall we? And if your shoelace snaps along the way, don't worry—we've got that covered, too.

Why Resilience is the Entrepreneur's Superpower

Resilience, much like a superhero cape, is an essential accessory for any entrepreneur. Unlike the capes of comic book lore, however, this one doesn't help you fly or render you impervious to disaster. Instead, it equips you with something far more useful: the ability to adapt, recover, and keep moving forward, even when it feels like the world—or your email inbox—is conspiring against you.

Picture this: You've poured your heart into launching a new product. The marketing is on point, the team is hyped, and you're already envisioning the glowing reviews and sales figures rolling in. Then, the launch day comes, and the website crashes. Or the delivery gets delayed. Or, in a particularly cruel twist of fate, your competition unveils an eerily similar product the same morning.

These moments can feel crushing, but resilience steps in like a trusty sidekick, whispering, "Okay, that didn't go to plan. Now what?" It's this ability to pivot and find a way forward that separates those who succeed in the long run from those who crumble at the first sign of trouble.

Resilience isn't just about bouncing back; it's about growing stronger through the process. It's the superpower that turns setbacks into steppingstones, missteps into moments of learning, and disasters into, well, mildly entertaining anecdotes for future dinner parties. Think of every challenge as a plot twist in your entrepreneurial origin story. Sure, it's frustrating now, but someday, it might make you seem downright heroic.

In this section, we'll delve into how resilience fosters growth, both personal and professional. You'll discover how to channel your inner superhero, complete with the ability to stretch, adapt, and recover without losing sight of your goals—or your sanity. So, grab your metaphorical cape (or rubber band), and let's explore the art of turning trials into triumphs.

Resilience Defined

Resilience, at its core, is like a well-maintained suspension bridge: strong enough to bear heavy loads, flexible enough to sway with the winds, and expertly designed to withstand the storms that will inevitably come. It's not about being unbreakable—that would be brittle and risky. Instead, resilience is about being adaptable, bending without breaking, and remaining functional even when the weather (or the market) gets particularly rough.

For entrepreneurs, resilience is the bridge that connects challenges to opportunities. It's what keeps you standing when the unexpected happens—like a product launch that flops, a key client who decides to jump ship, or a team meeting that spirals into chaos over the merits of almond milk versus oat milk in the office fridge. It's the quality that helps you absorb the shock, recalibrate, and keep moving forward without losing sight of the end goal.

Resilience isn't just a trait you're born with; it's something you build and maintain over time, like a sturdy bridge that gets stronger with each storm it weathers. It's about learning how to handle the turbulence of entrepreneurship without feeling like you're going to collapse into the metaphorical river below. And, as with any bridge, the key lies in the design: a balance of strength, flexibility, and a foundation deeply rooted in purpose and perspective.

In this chapter, we'll explore how to cultivate resilience in your entrepreneurial journey—how to strengthen your bridge, so to speak. Because while you can't control the storms, you can absolutely control how well you're prepared to face them. And who knows? You might even find that the view from your suspension bridge, swaying gracefully in the wind, isn't so bad after all.

Why Resilience Matters

Resilience is, without a doubt, the unsung hero of long-term entrepreneurial growth. It's the thing that lets you face market shifts, economic downturns, and even those spectacularly ill-conceived product launches that seemed brilliant in the brainstorming phase but turned out to be about as useful as a chocolate teapot.

At its heart, resilience is what keeps you moving forward when the ground beneath your feet feels less like a sturdy path and more like quicksand. It's not just about weathering the storm—though that's certainly part of it—it's about finding a way to dance in the rain without, as fate would have it, ending up electrocuted by a rogue puddle and a poorly insulated wire. It's the fine art of turning setbacks into setups for your next great leap forward.

Consider the entrepreneurial rollercoaster: one moment, your product's flying off the shelves; the next, your new marketing campaign is about as popular as a wasp at a picnic. Resilience is the quality that stops you from throwing in the towel—or worse, using it to mop up your tears. Instead, it gives you the ability to analyze, adapt, and move on, armed with the knowledge that even the best plans sometimes hit a snag or ten.

But resilience isn't just for the big, dramatic moments. It's also what helps you handle the day-to-day hiccups with grace (or at least without shouting into the void). It's what gets you through the endless maze of red tape, the occasional no-show at a pitch meeting, or the team brainstorming session that turns into an argument about whether cats or dogs make better mascots.

The beauty of resilience is that it's a muscle you can build. Each time you recover from a setback, you add another layer of strength, another strand to your entrepreneurial safety net. And as you flex that muscle, you'll find that the very challenges you once dreaded become the proving grounds for your success. After all, it's not the calm seas that make a great sailor—it's the storms that teach you how to navigate with skill and, when necessary, a hearty laugh at the absurdity of it all.

The Cost of Burnout

Burnout is the silent saboteur of entrepreneurial dreams, sneaking up on you like a dodgy Wi-Fi connection right when you're about to hit "submit" on something important. It doesn't announce itself with fanfare or flashing lights—it creeps in slowly, setting up shop in the corner of your life until you're working harder than your coffee machine and breaking down just as often.

Imagine a business owner, let's call them Chris, who starts every day with enthusiasm and at least two cups of espresso. At first, Chris is all systems go, tackling emails, managing the team, and drafting grand plans for expansion. But somewhere along the line, the to-do list becomes a to-survive list, and the excitement of running a business starts to feel more like juggling flaming swords—minus the applause.

Soon, Chris's days blur together, marked by late nights, early mornings, and the alarming realization that the concept of a "weekend" is now as mythical as unicorns. The coffee machine gets a workout that would make a marathon runner blush, while Chris stumbles through meetings with the dazed look of someone who hasn't slept since Y2K was a concern.

And then it happens: the crash. One morning, Chris finds that no amount of caffeine can jump-start his motivation. Tasks that once felt invigorating now seem insurmountable. He's hit the wall—not figuratively but with the full force of exhaustion that leaves even the thought of getting out of bed a monumental task.

The cost of burnout is more than just fatigue; it's the erosion of creativity, productivity, and joy. It's the missed opportunities, the strained relationships, and the feeling that the business you once loved has turned into an insatiable monster. And for many entrepreneurs, it's a wake-up call that comes too late, forcing them to rebuild not just their business but their mental and physical well-being.

This is why resilience isn't just a nice-to-have—it's a must. It's the safety net that catches you before you reach the burnout stage, helping you recover from setbacks without sacrificing your health or happiness. Because let's face it: no one starts a business dreaming of becoming its most overworked, underappreciated employee. Resilience is the key to staying in the game—not just surviving but thriving, with your sanity (mostly) intact.

Building Emotional Resilience: Mindset Shifts for Staying Strong Without Losing Your Marbles

Entrepreneurship has a way of testing your mental fortitude in ways you never imagined. It's not just about handling a tricky client or a product launch that fizzles—it's about keeping your cool when everything seems to go sideways all at once. Think of emotional resilience as your internal shock absorbers, smoothing out the bumps on the entrepreneurial road before you end up careening into a ditch.

At the heart of emotional resilience is your mindset—the way you process challenges and setbacks. Now, this isn't about gritting your teeth and pretending everything's fine while your metaphorical house is on fire. No, resilience is about learning to reframe the chaos and find strength in the unexpected. It's like that moment you realize the IKEA bookshelf instructions are in Swedish, but instead of despairing, you think, *Well, this will be an adventure.*

Start by embracing the idea that failure isn't a personal indictment but a rite of passage. Resilience isn't about avoiding mistakes; it's about laughing at them later (and hopefully learning something along the way).

Then there's the power of perspective. When you're knee-deep in a crisis, it's easy to feel like the sky is falling. But take a step back, and you might find that it's not the apocalypse—it's just a thunderstorm, inconvenient but survivable. A handy trick is to ask yourself, *Will this matter in five years?* If the answer is no, congratulations: you've just deflated your problem into something far more manageable.

Another crucial element of emotional resilience is knowing your limits. You're not a superhero, and even if you were. Superman took breaks too (though probably not enough). Pay attention to the warning signs—fatigue, irritability, an alarming consumption of chocolate—and give yourself permission to step back. Resilience doesn't mean running on fumes; it means refueling before you hit empty.

Finally, surround yourself with people who lift you up, not weigh you down. Whether it's a mentor, a supportive partner, or a friend who knows when to deliver a pep talk or a pint of ice cream, having a solid support system makes all the difference. Resilience might start within, but it thrives in connection with others.

Building emotional resilience isn't about pretending you're unshakable. It's about acknowledging the challenges, shifting your mindset, and bouncing back with a bit of humor intact. After all, if you can't laugh at the absurdities of entrepreneurship, you're missing half the fun. And isn't that what resilience is all about? Finding strength in the storm—and maybe even enjoying the rain.

Reframing Challenges: Turning Potholes into Opportunities

Imagine driving along the entrepreneurial highway, feeling pretty good about yourself. The sun is shining, the radio is playing your favorite tunes, and then—BAM—you hit a pothole the size of a small swimming pool. Suddenly, your journey is less "joyful road trip" and more "emergency roadside repair."

This, my friends, is the essence of entrepreneurship: an adventure full of unexpected bumps. The trick isn't avoiding the potholes—they're practically a feature of the road—it's learning how to navigate them without losing your wheel alignment or, worse, your sense of humor.

Reframing challenges is about seeing these entrepreneurial potholes not as disasters, but as opportunities. Sure, it's easier said than done when you're knee-deep in a mess that feels more like quicksand than a minor inconvenience. But with the right mindset, those bumps in the road can become lessons, stepping stones, or at the very least, anecdotes to entertain your friends later.

For instance, that delayed product launch might teach you patience and the importance of preparation. The miscommunication with a major client might push you to sharpen your processes. Even that catastrophic attempt at designing your own logo (why is Comic Sans even an option?) might lead you to discover the value of outsourcing.

It's all about perspective. Instead of throwing up your hands and shouting, "Why me?" when things go awry, try asking, "What can I learn from this?" Think of it as a mental suspension system, absorbing the jolts and keeping you moving forward. And if you can find a little humor in the chaos—well, that's like upgrading to luxury shocks.

Of course, not every challenge will feel like an opportunity in the moment. Some will just feel like a pain in the proverbial neck. That's where resilience comes in. By practicing the art of reframing, you start to see challenges for what they truly are: temporary, navigable, and occasionally even useful.

So, next time you hit a pothole, take a deep breath, steady the wheel, and remind yourself: this, too, shall pass. And who knows? By the end of the journey, you might even look back at that particular bump and smile—if only because it didn't completely derail you.

The Power of Perspective: Turning Today's Crisis into Tomorrow's Cocktail Party Story

Perspective is a magical thing. One minute, you're knee-deep in chaos, convinced your business is moments away from imploding, and the next, you're recalling the same ordeal over drinks, laughing so hard you nearly spill your martini. This isn't just the soothing passage of time at work—it's the power of perspective. And, as an entrepreneur, learning to harness it is like discovering a hidden superpower.

The beauty of perspective is that it allows you to take a step back from whatever fresh disaster has landed on your plate. Didn't land the big client? Think of it as a chance to refine your pitch. Spilled coffee on your laptop during a virtual presentation? You've now got an icebreaker for every meeting going forward. Perspective doesn't erase problems, but it does shrink them down to manageable, laugh-about-it-later size.

One of the best ways to develop perspective is to reflect on past successes. Think back to a time when everything seemed impossible—yet somehow, you made it through. Maybe it was that product launch where the boxes arrived labeled in Portuguese (and your customers decidedly did not speak Portuguese), or the time your website crashed during your biggest sale of the year. At the moment, it felt like the end of the world. But here you are, battle-tested and still standing. If you handled that, you can handle this.

Another trick is to imagine how today's crisis will make for a fantastic anecdote a few years down the road. Picture yourself at a dinner party, recounting the time your meticulously planned event was nearly derailed by an accidental double-booking with a Zumba class. ("And that's how we invented networking on the move!") It's remarkable how much easier it is to cope with chaos when you frame it as future material for a good story (O.K., that might be just a bit optimistic).

And, of course, there's journaling. Now, I know what you're thinking: "I barely have time to answer emails—why would I write a diary?" But hear me out. Journaling isn't just about recording the day's events; it's about giving yourself a chance to process them. Think of it as talking to yourself without alarming coworkers or family members. Jotting down thoughts, fears, and even small wins can provide clarity and, over time, show just how much you've grown.

Perspective, in the end, is about realizing that the mountain in front of you is probably more of a molehill—or at least a moderately sized hill with an excellent view once you reach the top. It's about remembering that crises are temporary, resilience is permanent, and you're far more capable than you give yourself credit for.

So, the next time disaster strikes, pause for a moment. Reflect on how far you've come, think about how good this story will sound later, and maybe even scribble down a few thoughts for posterity. Because in the grand scheme of things, today's mess is just tomorrow's material for laughter—or, maybe a cautionary tale.

Self-Care Without the Fluff: Keeping Your Sanity (and Your Sense of Humor) Intact

Let's talk about self-care, shall we? Not the kind that involves cucumbers on your eyes or aromatherapy candles that smell like a mystical forest, but the kind that actually keeps you functional as a human being. You know, boring but essential things like getting enough sleep, moving your body, and occasionally stepping away from the omnipresent glow of your laptop screen. Keep in mind, "just one more email" does not count as self-care, no matter how you try to justify it.

First, let's address the big one: sleep. It's free, it's restorative, and it's probably the most underrated performance enhancer out there. Yet somehow, entrepreneurs treat it like a luxury item reserved for holidays or bouts of the flu. If you find yourself saying things like, "I'll sleep when I'm successful," I have news for you: you'll get there faster—and in one piece—if you let your brain recharge nightly. Think of sleep as your operating system update. Skip it, and you're bound to crash, probably mid-presentation.

Then there's exercise, the thing we all know we should do but often relegate to the bottom of the priority list, somewhere below reorganizing the junk drawer. Here's the thing: you don't need to train for a marathon or join an intimidating CrossFit cult. A brisk walk around the block, a yoga class that doesn't involve pretzel poses, or even a solo dance party in your kitchen can do wonders for your mood and energy levels. Plus, nothing clears your head quite like a stroll—or a poorly executed rendition of "Stayin' Alive."

Now, hobbies. Remember those? Things you do purely for fun, with no ROI or performance metrics involved? Whether it's painting, gardening, or assembling impossibly tiny model ships, a hobby lets your brain breathe. And no, doom-scrolling social media or tweaking your website for the 15th time this week doesn't count. Choose something that lets you unplug, unwind, and, dare I even hope, smile without a hint of work guilt.

Finally, let's address the sneaky little voice that whispers, "Just one more email." That voice is a liar. No email, no matter how urgent it seems, is worth sacrificing your mental and physical well-being over. Step away from the screen, pour yourself a cup of tea (or a stronger beverage if the day has truly tested you), and remind yourself that the world will not implode if you take a breather.

Real self-care isn't about indulgence—it's about sustainability. It's the stuff that keeps you from becoming a frazzled, over-caffeinated shadow of your former self. So, go ahead: sleep, move, and rediscover the joys of doing something utterly frivolous. Your spreadsheets—and your sanity—will thank you.

Connecting with Others: Building Your Lighthouse Maintenance Crew

Entrepreneurship, for all its thrilling highs and inevitable lows, can sometimes feel like standing alone on a windswept cliff, valiantly waving your metaphorical lantern at the world. You're the lighthouse keeper, guiding your ship—your business—through choppy waters. But here's the thing: even the sturdiest lighthouse needs a maintenance crew. Without support, even the brightest beacon risks going dim.

Let's start with your inner circle—family and friends. These are the people who remind you to eat something that isn't prepackaged, who listen patiently as you rant about supply chain delays, and who somehow manage to look genuinely interested when you describe your latest marketing strategy. They're your rock, your grounding force, and the ones who love you even when you're pacing the room at 2 a.m. muttering about quarterly projections.

Then there's the magic of connecting with fellow entrepreneurs. No one quite understands the peculiar joys and absurd challenges of running a business like someone else who's been there. They're the ones who won't bat an eye when you confess you've accidentally sent an email to the wrong mailing list or that you've spent the afternoon debating logo fonts. These connections are more than networking—they're camaraderie, a shared understanding that helps lighten the load.

Think of these relationships as the crew that keeps your lighthouse shining. They'll polish the glass, tighten the bolts, and occasionally remind you to step outside and enjoy the view. But remember, lighthouses aren't built in isolation—they stand as part of a larger network, each supporting the other to guide ships safely home.

Even the most introverted among us need connection, especially when navigating the stormy seas of entrepreneurship. A trusted conversation, a hearty laugh, or simply knowing someone else is cheering you on can do wonders for your resilience.

So, reach out, lean on your crew, and let them help you stay bright and steady. After all, even the most resilient lighthouse can't shine alone forever.

Practical Strategies for Tough Times: How to Prepare Without Stockpiling Canned Goods

When it comes to weathering storms—whether in business or life—having a plan beats sheer panic every time. Of course, the term "preparation" might conjure images of a bunker filled with canned beans and bottled water, but fear not: we're talking about a more sophisticated survival strategy. This is about resilience with a touch of finesse, the kind that keeps your business afloat and your sanity intact, no hard hats required.

Let's start with **financial buffers**, the unsung heroes of tough times. Think of them as your business's raincoat—boring when the sun is shining but an absolute lifesaver in a downpour. A few months of cash reserves can mean the difference between navigating a rough patch with grace or frantically bailing water from a sinking ship. If you're currently operating on a "just-in-time" cash flow strategy, consider this your gentle nudge to tuck away a bit for a rainy day. (Yes, this might mean fewer impulse purchases of shiny office gadgets.)

Next, there's the **power of adaptability**. Businesses that survive tough times aren't necessarily the strongest—they're the ones that pivot gracefully, like a ballerina dodging a rogue spotlight. Whether it's tweaking your product line, adjusting your pricing model, or exploring new markets, the ability to change direction quickly can be your greatest asset. Think of it as swapping sails mid-storm—nerve-wracking, yes, but infinitely better than stubbornly heading straight into a squall.

Then there's the underestimated brilliance of **open communication**. In challenging times, keeping your team in the dark is about as effective as steering a ship blindfolded. Instead, share the realities and rally their support. You'll find that a united crew can solve problems you'd never crack alone—and they'll appreciate being treated as part of the solution rather than just passengers.

Finally, let's talk about **mindset maintenance**. Tough times have a way of clouding judgment and making every decision feel like the weight of the world rests on your over-caffeinated shoulders. That's where resilience-building habits come in: taking breaks, seeking advice, and, most importantly, remembering that no setback is permanent. If nothing else, think of your current crisis as future storytelling gold. "Remember that time we survived *that*?" is always a hit at reunions.

With these practical strategies in hand, you'll find that tough times aren't insurmountable—they're manageable. And while they might still come with a bit of drama (because when doesn't life?), you'll be prepared to face them with a clear head and, ideally, without resorting to canned beans.

The Resilience Toolkit: Packing for Life's Business Earthquakes

Resilience isn't just a state of mind; it's also a state of preparation. Think of it as putting together an emergency kit for your business—not with flashlights and canned beans, but with strategies that can absorb the shocks of life's inevitable business earthquakes. Let's dive into what should be in your resilience toolkit.

First up, **contingency plans**. These are like the emergency escape maps you find on the back of hotel room doors—rarely exciting but invaluable when things go sideways. A good contingency plan covers key "what if" scenarios: What if sales drop? What if a major client disappears? What if your website crashes at the worst possible moment? Crafting answers to these questions now, while your stress levels are manageable, is much better than scrambling for solutions mid-crisis.

Next, we have **diversifying revenue streams**, a fancy way of saying, "Don't put all your eggs in one basket." Relying on a single source of income is a bit like investing all your savings in lottery tickets—thrilling, perhaps, but risky beyond reason. Whether it's introducing a new product line, launching an online course, or dipping your toes into a different market, diversification cushions you against surprises. It's the financial equivalent of having more than one route home when traffic is backed up.

Then there's the perennial favorite: **cash reserves**. Imagine your business as a hiker venturing into unknown terrain. Without a financial reserve, you're trekking without a water bottle—fine until it isn't. A rainy-day fund gives you breathing room to address challenges without frantic scrambling. Building one might mean tightening your belt temporarily, but the peace of mind it brings is worth every skipped fancy latte.

Finally, let's talk about **building strong relationships**—because in tough times, a solid network is as valuable as gold. Clients, colleagues, and mentors who believe in you and your business can be the lifeline you need to weather storms. Think of these relationships as the sturdy tent poles in your resilience kit: essential for holding everything up when the wind picks up.

When combined, these strategies make up a toolkit that's practical, adaptable, and far more satisfying than trying to patch things up with duct tape when the ground starts to shake. By packing your business's emergency kit now, you're setting yourself up to face challenges with confidence—and maybe even a bit of swagger. After all, when you're prepared, even life's biggest business earthquakes can feel more like a gentle tremor.

Embracing Flexibility: When Plans Catch Fire

If there's one universal truth about plans, it's this: they look fantastic on paper, but life has a habit of setting them alight at the worst possible moment. That's where flexibility comes in—not as a sign of failure, but as your secret weapon for resilience. After all, sticking rigidly to a plan that's clearly crumbling is like continuing to follow GPS directions straight into a lake: admirable commitment, but not terribly wise.

Flexibility in business isn't about abandoning goals or values; it's about navigating the detours with grace (and perhaps a few muttered expletives). It's the ability to pivot when circumstances demand it, whether that means adjusting your product line, rethinking your marketing strategy, or, occasionally, deciding that Plan B—or even Plan Q—is the way to go.

Take, for instance, the classic case of launching a new product. You've done the research, prepped the marketing materials, and told everyone who will listen that it's going to be *the next big thing*. Then launch day arrives, and sales trickle in at the rate of a leaky faucet. Now what? Flexibility means stepping back, analyzing what went wrong, and tweaking the approach instead of doubling down on a doomed strategy.

Adaptability also applies to the little things—those daily curveballs that keep entrepreneurs on their toes. A key supplier goes MIA? Time to call in a backup. A client needs an urgent change? Find a way to accommodate without derailing your entire week. It's less about rolling over and more about rolling with the punches, keeping your eye on the ultimate goal while staying light on your feet.

Of course, flexibility requires a certain amount of humility—the ability to admit when something isn't working and try something else. It's like cooking without a recipe: sometimes the soufflé collapses, but other times you discover a brilliant new dish. The important thing is to stay open to possibilities and willing to make adjustments when needed.

So, the next time life hands you a flaming plan, don't panic. Channel your inner firefighter: assess the situation, grab a metaphorical hose, and adapt. In the long run, being flexible isn't just key to survival—it's how you uncover unexpected opportunities and keep your business (and sanity) intact. And who knows? You might just end up with a better plan than the one you started with.

Streamlining in a Crisis: Clearing the Garage Without Losing the Unicorn

There's something about a crisis that has a way of bringing clarity—or at least, it should. Unfortunately, it often starts with the mental equivalent of opening a cluttered garage: you're overwhelmed by the sheer volume of "stuff" and have no idea where to begin. Business crises are much the same, except instead of dust-covered lawn chairs, you're dealing with overflowing to-do lists, panicked emails, and a growing sense of dread.

The key to surviving—and thriving—during challenging times is knowing what to keep and what to set aside. It's not about throwing everything out (including the inflatable unicorn you're inexplicably attached to), but about prioritizing the essentials that will keep your business running smoothly while you weather the storm.

Start by identifying your critical operations. These are the things that keep the lights on—literally and figuratively. For most businesses, this means focusing on revenue-generating activities, maintaining customer relationships, and ensuring your team has the resources they need to do their jobs. If it's not directly contributing to your survival or long-term stability, it can probably wait.

Once the essentials are clear, it's time to tackle the "nice-to-haves." These are the projects and tasks that are important but not urgent—the proverbial unicorns. They're lovely and might even be useful someday, but they won't make or break your business in a crisis. Set them aside temporarily, knowing you can revisit them once things have settled down.

Streamlining also means letting go of perfectionism. In a crisis, "good enough" is often exactly that—good enough. It's better to move forward with a functional solution than to waste time polishing something until it sparkles. Remember, your goal is to stabilize the ship, not install gold-plated railings while it's still leaking.

Lastly, don't be afraid to ask for help. Whether it's delegating tasks to your team, outsourcing a specific project, or leaning on your support network for advice, you don't have to do everything yourself. Clearing out a garage is much faster with an extra pair of hands—and the same goes for navigating a business crisis.

Streamlining during challenging times isn't just about survival; it's an opportunity to rethink and refine your approach. And when the dust settles, you'll find that focusing on what truly matters not only helped you through the crisis but also left your business (and your metaphorical garage) in better shape than before. Just don't forget to bring the inflatable unicorn back out when you're ready—it's far too fun to leave behind permanently.

The Role of Humor in Survival

If there's one thing that has the power to turn a sinking ship into a tolerable paddleboat ride, it's humor. Not the belly-aching, tears-down-your-cheeks kind of laughter (although that helps), but the sort of wry chuckle that takes the sting out of adversity. Humor, when applied correctly, is like WD-40 for the entrepreneurial spirit—helpful, versatile, and surprisingly effective at easing those grating moments.

Take, for instance, the time an entrepreneur I once met accidentally shipped 500 mismatched shoes to a retailer. Faced with what could have been a catastrophic business blunder, he instead quipped, "At least we're halfway to solving everyone's 'lost sock' problem!" The joke didn't magically pair up the shoes, but it did break the tension, allowing the team to approach the issue with a clearer head—and a fresh determination to double-check shipping labels.

Humor doesn't fix the crisis, but it does wonders for the soul. It shifts the focus from panic to perspective, reminding everyone that while the current situation might feel dire, it's rarely the end of the world. Even in the toughest times, a lighthearted moment can be a reset button for morale. It's hard to brood when someone cracks a joke about how your latest "disaster" might just make for an excellent chapter in your future memoir.

For teams, humor serves as a powerful connector. Shared laughter reinforces camaraderie, making the trenches of problem-solving feel less like a pit of despair and more like a quirky escape room. Plus, it creates an environment where people feel safe to make suggestions, even if they're offbeat. Who knows? That offbeat idea might just be the key to turning things around.

So, when you're waist-deep in chaos and feel like all is lost, try laughing about it. No, it won't file that overdue tax form or magically reschedule a missed deadline, but it will give you and your team the mental space to tackle the challenge head-on. And hey, you might even emerge with a story so ridiculous, it becomes a legend in your entrepreneurial journey.

How to Turn Lemonade Back Into Lemons (for a Profit)

Setbacks are the entrepreneurial equivalent of stepping on a Lego—painful, unexpected, and likely to provoke a string of creative language. But here's the thing: setbacks also have a curious way of teaching us lessons we wouldn't have learned otherwise, provided we're willing to stop hopping on one foot long enough to take a closer look.

Take Jake, for example. Jake started a custom furniture business with high hopes and a penchant for overpromising. One fateful week, he managed to book so many simultaneous orders that his workshop resembled the aftermath of a lumber hurricane. Deadlines were missed, a client complained loudly on social media, and Jake's stress level soared to a record-breaking altitude.

At first glance, this seemed like an unmitigated disaster, the kind of situation that sends one Googling "stress-free careers in small towns." But Jake did something remarkable: he leaned into the chaos. Instead of focusing solely on damage control, he dissected the mess to figure out what went wrong. And what he discovered wasn't just helpful—it was transformative.

For starters, he learned that not all clients are created equal. By identifying the ones who brought him joy and steady work (versus the ones who haggled endlessly and still paid late), he refined his client list. Then, he revamped his scheduling system to prevent future overbooking, even hiring a part-time assistant to manage incoming requests. Jake didn't just bounce back; he came out stronger, smarter, and, yes, more relaxed.

This, my friends, is the alchemy of setbacks. They're frustrating, yes, but they're also invaluable sources of data—if you're willing to mine them. Every failure, flop, or fumble contains a nugget of wisdom just waiting to be unearthed. Maybe your target market isn't quite who you thought it was. Maybe your processes need streamlining. Or maybe you just need to stockpile extra coffee for crunch time.

The key to learning from setbacks is to reframe them as experiments. Instead of labeling a failure as a dead end, think of it as an unexpected plot twist in your entrepreneurial narrative. Ask yourself: What went wrong? What went right (if anything)? And most importantly, what can I do differently next time?

And don't forget to celebrate your resilience along the way. Sure, things didn't go according to plan, but you're still here, still learning, and still building something remarkable. That, in itself, is a victory worth savoring—preferably with a lemonade. Or, in Jake's case, a sturdy new workbench and a much lighter client roster.

The Value of Failure

Failure often feels like the unwelcome guest at a dinner party, barging in uninvited and spilling red wine on the carpet of your carefully laid plans. Yet, if you squint hard enough through the frustration and embarrassment, you'll see that failure often leaves behind an oddly useful parting gift: perspective.

Take hiking, for example. Imagine you're enthusiastically trekking through the woods, confident you'll reach the summit in record time. Suddenly, your toe catches on an inconveniently placed root, and down you go—face first into a pile of leaves and your own wounded pride. While brushing off the dirt and mumbling choice words about the root's ancestry, you notice something unexpected. Just beyond where you fell, there's a break in the trees revealing a breathtaking view—a panorama you'd have missed entirely if you hadn't been forced to pause.

This is the curious value of failure in entrepreneurship. It trips you up, yes, but it also offers a new vantage point, one that often leads to unexpected insights. Maybe your product launch flopped, but in the process, you discovered a niche market you hadn't considered. Or perhaps a partnership fell apart, only to clear the way for a better one that aligns more closely with your goals.

The key to embracing failure lies in reframing it not as the end of the road, but as a particularly bumpy stepping stone. Sure, it's annoying—and occasionally painful—but it's also part of the natural terrain of growth. Every entrepreneur worth their salt has stories of things that didn't go as planned, from cringe-worthy marketing missteps to supply chain disasters that would make a logistics expert weep. What sets the resilient ones apart is their ability to look past the tumble and focus on what the experience can teach.

The next time you trip over a metaphorical root, take a moment to stop, look around, and see what new perspectives you've gained. That stunning view just beyond the fall? It's the kind of lesson that sticks with you long after the dirt has been brushed away and the path forward becomes clear again.

Conducting a Post-Mortem (Without the Drama)

Setbacks, while unpleasant, are like overly dramatic theater performances—you dread them while they're happening, but they often provide valuable lessons if you're willing to sit through the second act. And that's where the post-mortem comes in. Don't worry, there's no actual drama (unless someone insists on reenacting the event), just a thoughtful look back at what went awry and, more importantly, what you can learn from it.

Imagine you've just wrapped up a team retreat, and against your better judgment, you decided to include a late-night karaoke session. What began as a lighthearted attempt at team bonding ended in a spirited but unfortunate rendition of *Bohemian Rhapsody*, complete with a botched air guitar solo and a broken office chair. The retreat wasn't a total disaster, but let's just say it didn't hit the harmonious note you'd envisioned. How do you unpack this without triggering PTSD for everyone involved?

Step one: Identify what went wrong. Was it the choice of activities? The timing? Or maybe the fact that no one thought to remove the more fragile furniture from the karaoke zone? This isn't about pointing fingers but spotting the potholes you tripped over so you can avoid them next time.

Step two: Highlight what went right. Yes, the karaoke machine might have been a questionable addition, but perhaps the breakout sessions during the retreat were a huge hit, fostering genuine collaboration and generating exciting new ideas. Acknowledge the wins—it's not all doom and gloom.

Step three: Pinpoint what *definitely* shouldn't be repeated. This is where you make peace with the fact that not every experiment is a keeper. Team karaoke, for instance, might best be relegated to the "never again" pile, at least until your office invests in sturdier chairs.

The goal of a post-mortem isn't to wallow in mistakes; it's to distill them into actionable insights. By objectively examining what happened, you can turn even the most awkward mishaps into a roadmap for better decisions. And who knows?

With the lessons learned, your next team retreat might just hit the high note—no Queen covers required.

Applying the Lessons

Learning from setbacks is all about turning hindsight into foresight—because while the phrase "live and learn" is comforting, it's much more satisfying to "learn and improve." Think of it as upgrading your toolkit after discovering the hard way that your hammer couldn't quite handle the job. Sure, it got the nail in, but it also left you with a slightly bent nail and a bruised thumb.

Imagine you've just completed a major product launch, only to realize afterward that your marketing campaign was about as effective as shouting into a void. The emails didn't hit the right notes, the social media posts felt flat, and your audience responded with a collective shrug. Ouch. But rather than wallowing, this is your chance to turn it into an upgrade opportunity.

Start by reviewing the specifics. Maybe the messaging didn't resonate, or the timing clashed with a bigger industry event (looking at you, competitor's surprise launch). Did your ads miss their mark? Did your target audience see the campaign at all? Break it down to uncover what went sideways.

Then, integrate those lessons into your future strategy. For the next launch, you might hire a copywriter to finesse the messaging or invest in a scheduling tool to ensure you avoid major conflicts. Perhaps you'll conduct audience surveys to fine-tune your targeting. These aren't just fixes; they're enhancements—like swapping your flimsy hammer for a sleek, ergonomically designed model that gets the job done without collateral damage.

The beauty of applying lessons is that it ensures every misstep becomes a stepping stone. Each tweak, adjustment, and upgrade strengthens your foundation, making your future efforts more effective and less stressful. So, while failure isn't fun, it's often the catalyst for growth—and, with the right mindset, a better toolkit. Stepping back and saying; "Well, at least I won't do *that* again" might not go as far as being satisfying, but at least the thought might keep you from laying awake for a few nights fretting about it.

Celebrating Resilience

Celebrating resilience doesn't have to mean throwing a lavish party with confetti cannons and a DJ who misreads the room. Sometimes, it's as simple as taking a quiet moment to acknowledge, "I made it through that," with a cup of tea, a deep breath, or perhaps an impromptu victory dance in the office kitchen (bonus points if your team joins in).

Imagine you've just navigated a particularly rocky period—a product recall, a staffing hiccup, or one of those weeks where the universe seems intent on testing your patience. You've brainstormed solutions, weathered the storms, and somehow emerged intact, even if a little frazzled. That's no small feat. In fact, it's worth celebrating.

Take a moment to reflect on the journey—how you adapted, the lessons you learned, and the strength you found in the process. Maybe you were creative in solving a seemingly impossible problem, or perhaps you simply managed not to lose your sense of humor when everything felt like it was on fire. These are wins, and they deserve acknowledgment.

Your celebration doesn't have to be elaborate. It could be as understated as treating yourself to your favorite snack or as spirited as cueing up your go-to playlist for a mini dance break. If you're feeling generous, share the moment with your team—because resilience often takes a village. Gather everyone, pop some sparkling water (or something stronger), and toast to the collective effort that got you all through.

The act of celebrating resilience reinforces its importance. It's a reminder that setbacks don't define you—your ability to rise, adapt, and carry on does. So, don't skip this step. Whether it's a quiet smile of gratitude or an exuberant jig near the office fridge, take the time to honor your resilience. You've earned it.

The Resilient Entrepreneur's Playbook

The entrepreneurial journey, much like climbing a mountain, isn't exactly what anyone would call a leisurely stroll. It's filled with rocky trails, moments where you lose your footing, and patches of dense fog where you're not entirely sure if you're still on the path—or just stubbornly scaling a sheer cliff. But here's the thing: it's all worth it. Not just for the spectacular view at the summit (though that's certainly a perk) but for the sense of accomplishment that comes from tackling something genuinely challenging and emerging stronger on the other side.

Resilience, in all its scrappy glory, is what makes this journey possible. It's not about sidestepping every obstacle or somehow avoiding all the storms that come your way. Instead, it's about facing those storms head-on—sometimes with creativity and courage, other times with nothing more than sheer stubbornness and a deep sigh. It's about getting back up when the world knocks you down, dusting yourself off, and muttering, "Well, that could've gone worse," as you forge ahead.

Think of resilience as your entrepreneurial superpower, the secret weapon that allows you to weather downturns, adapt to changes, and turn those inevitable lemons into something resembling lemonade—or at least a passable lemon tart. It's not a one-size-fits-all skill, either. For some, it might mean leaning on a network of supporters; for others, it's finding humor in the chaos or stepping back to recalibrate before charging forward again.

And let's not forget the laughter. Resilience doesn't mean taking yourself so seriously that you forget to enjoy the ride. Yes, there will be challenges—probably more than a few—but there will also be moments of triumph, unexpected joy, and the occasional story that's so absurd it's destined to become legendary among your peers. Embrace those moments. They're what make the climb worth it.

So, here's the nudge you've been waiting for: resilience isn't just a strategy for survival; it's your golden ticket to navigating the wild, wonderful rollercoaster of entrepreneurship with grace, grit, and maybe even a few chuckles along the way. Keep climbing, keep laughing, and remember—there's always room at the top for those who refuse to quit.

Chapter Twelve

Legacy Beyond Profits

What Will They Say About You at Your Retirement Party?

IMAGINE FOR A MOMENT, if you will, the grand affair of your retirement party. There you are, the guest of honor, perched on a rickety fold-out chair while someone gives a speech about your years of service. Now, the speaker clears their throat, adjusts their tie, and declares with great solemnity, "We'll always remember [insert your name here] for... the coffee machine." Specifically, the way it dispensed lukewarm sludge that defied the laws of taste and physics. Or perhaps you're fondly recalled for your filing system, which to this day remains an unsolved mystery, equal parts Da Vinci Code and local escape room challenge.

If this scenario feels a touch anticlimactic, you're not alone. The idea of legacy can be a daunting thing to ponder. It's one thing to leave behind a business that hums along like a well-oiled machine, and quite another to consider the ripples of your influence on people, relationships, and the world at large. After all, you want to be remembered for more than a sticky coffee pot or a baffling penchant for Post-It notes.

Legacy isn't just about the tangible—though a thriving business and a nicely framed portrait in the office lobby wouldn't hurt. No, it's about something far more profound: the impact you've made on the lives around you, the values you've instilled, and the way your vision continues to shape the future long after you've stepped away from the proverbial desk.

This chapter isn't here to preach about creating a perfect legacy—because, let's face it, perfection is overrated (and exhausting). Instead, we'll explore how to craft a legacy that feels meaningful to you. One that aligns with your values, supports the people you care about, and maybe, just maybe, leaves the world a little better than you found it.

So, let's set aside the coffee machine anecdotes and dive into what really matters. Whether it's fostering a culture of kindness in your business, inspiring the next generation of leaders, or simply making sure no one ever has to decipher your filing system again, your legacy is yours to shape. Let's make it a good one—sticky coffee and all.

Redefining Legacy: Moving From the Bottom Line to the Bigger Picture

Legacy is a curious word, isn't it? It conjures up grand notions of statues, plaques, or perhaps a bustling building bearing your name. But for most of us, the concept feels a bit slippery, like trying to hold onto a handful of jelly. What does legacy mean in the day-to-day reality of running a business, where the immediate goal is often just making it to next Friday without losing your sanity?

Here's a hint: it's not about the bottom line—or at least, not *just* about the bottom line. Sure, profits are lovely, and they keep the lights on, but they're hardly the kind of thing that makes people tear up during your retirement party speech. A legacy, a true one, is less about the balance sheets you left behind and more about the lives you touched, the values you championed, and the way you made people feel.

Picture this: decades from now, someone's reminiscing about their time working with you. Do they recall quarterly earnings reports with misty-eyed fondness? Unlikely. More likely, they'll remember the time you encouraged them to take a risk, showed empathy during a tough time, or made a decision that put integrity over profit. They'll remember the way you made them feel like more than just a cog in a machine.

Legacy is about moving beyond the numbers to the bigger picture. It's about asking, "What am I building here that will last beyond me?" Is it a business that operates with kindness and purpose? A team that feels empowered and supported? A vision that inspires others to do better, be better, and—if we're feeling ambitious—make the world a better place?

The beauty of redefining legacy is that it's entirely yours to shape. It doesn't have to be grand or dramatic; it just has to matter. And while the bottom line keeps the engine running, the bigger picture is what gives it direction. After all, no one remembers the car that drove the longest—they remember the one that went somewhere extraordinary.

What Legacy Really Means

Legacy, at its heart, is one of those deceptively simple ideas that's remarkably difficult to pin down. It's not about financial success alone—though let's not pretend a tidy profit margin doesn't help. Nor is it about leaving behind a bronze bust of your likeness to gather dust in a lobby. Legacy is, in essence, what lingers after you're gone, like the scent of freshly baked cookies in a kitchen long after the baker has taken off their apron.

Think of it as planting a garden. You don't tend a garden just for today. You plant seeds knowing full well you might not be around to see all of them bloom. Legacy works much the same way. It's the values, lessons, and influence you cultivate over time, which continue to grow, inspire, and provide nourishment long after you've moved on to other ventures—or to a well-earned retirement hammock.

The beauty of legacy lies in its quiet resilience. A legacy doesn't need fanfare or gold-plated plaques. It's in the gratitude of a team member who learned from your mentorship, the community that benefited from your generosity, or the way your business stood as a beacon of integrity when others faltered.

Sure, financial success is a piece of the puzzle—it keeps the soil fertile, after all—but a true legacy is about more than the harvest. It's about leaving behind a patch of earth (metaphorical or otherwise) that's better for having had you there. And while the idea might seem grand, it's often built in the small, everyday acts: a decision made with integrity, an extra moment of encouragement, a choice to do what's right even when it's inconvenient.

So, as you contemplate what legacy means to you, remember: it's not the size of the garden that matters—it's the seeds you choose to plant.

Shifting Focus to Values and Impact

Legacy, as it turns out, isn't about how much you amassed or the size of the corner office you vacated. It's about what you stood for—and, more importantly, what you left behind that reflects those values. Think of it this way: If your legacy were a painting, would it be an inspired masterpiece, or one of those questionable abstract works that leaves everyone tilting their head and murmuring, "I don't get it"?

Aligning your legacy with your personal values is what gives it resonance, depth, and meaning. Maybe you've always been a quiet champion of innovation, the person who encouraged ideas to flourish even when they were still half-baked and a bit lopsided. Or perhaps equality has always been your North Star, and you've worked tirelessly to create a workplace where everyone—no matter their background—feels empowered and respected.

And let's not underestimate the profound impact of simply being a boss who wasn't terrifying. You know the type—the leader who inspired more admiration than dread, who could give feedback without making employees reconsider their career choices, and who had the uncanny ability to turn the most stressful of days into something almost enjoyable.

Legacy, at its core, is less about the "what" and more about the "why." It's about what you valued and how you infused those values into your work, your team, and the lives you touched along the way. Were you the kind of person who prioritized fairness, kindness, and growth? Did your decisions reflect a commitment to something bigger than profits—something that made a real difference to the people and communities around you?

The good news is, you don't have to have it all figured out just yet. The act of building a legacy starts with small, intentional steps, aligning your everyday choices with the impact you hope to leave behind. And remember: no one's asking for perfection—just authenticity, and maybe a little humor along the way. After all, a legacy worth remembering is one that's as human as it is inspiring.

The Trap of a Wealth-Only Legacy

Ah, the allure of the wealth-only legacy. It's the stuff of glossy magazine covers and Hollywood clichés—leaving behind vaults of cash, towering skyscrapers with your name emblazoned across the top, and perhaps a yacht or two christened in your honor. But here's the rub: while a bulging bank account might impress your peers, it's unlikely to make anyone misty-eyed at your retirement party or funeral service.

Picture it: a heartfelt eulogy that starts with, "Well, he sure was loaded," and ends with an awkward pause as everyone tries to come up with a second redeeming quality. It's not exactly the legacy most of us aspire to leave behind. Being remembered solely for your net worth is like being known for owning the fanciest lawnmower on the block—technically impressive, but not exactly endearing.

Sure, wealth can be a powerful tool. It can build schools, fund charities, and support loved ones long after you've exited stage left. But if that's all there is—no relationships nurtured, no values shared, no moments of genuine human connection—it risks becoming as impersonal as an ATM receipt.

Let's face it, no one gathers around decades later to reminisce about how spectacularly you nailed your quarterly earnings reports. What people cherish, what lingers in their memories, are the intangibles: the encouragement you offered during a tough time, the generosity you showed when it wasn't expected, the laughs you shared over coffee (or something stronger).

The truth is, being the wealthiest person in the cemetery isn't much of an accolade. But being remembered as someone who used their resources—financial, emotional, and intellectual—to make life a little better for others? Now, that's a legacy worth leaving. So, while wealth can certainly be part of your story, let's make sure it's not the entire plot. After all, nobody ever built a statue for someone just because they had a really nice checking account.

Reflection Exercise: Pondering Your Eulogy Virtues

Now, take a moment—yes, even you, the one rolling your eyes at the word "virtues"—and imagine this: the scene is your farewell party, or perhaps the unveiling of a statue dedicated to your life's work. People are gathered, murmuring about your legacy, and someone steps up to deliver a speech. What do you hope they'll say?

Would you want them to talk about your uncanny knack for nailing pivot tables in Excel? Or would you rather hear them reflect on the way you made their lives better—whether by mentoring them through a tough patch, fostering a business culture that didn't make Mondays unbearable, or funding a community project that still thrives today?

This is your chance to consider your "eulogy virtues," those qualities and contributions you'd like to be remembered for beyond the bottom line. What values have you lived by? What kind of ripple effect do you want your actions to create?

For some, it's about nurturing relationships and being a source of encouragement. For others, it's about innovation, advocacy, or simply making people laugh when the coffee machine broke down for the third time that week. Whatever it is, write it down. Let your imagination run wild, and don't hold back.

And for a bit of fun, picture what might appear on your statue plaque—because, naturally, there will be a statue. Would it say something like, *"Changed lives, shared laughs, and always paid for pizza on Fridays"*? Or maybe, *"Visionary leader, compassionate mentor, and undefeated in trivia night"*?

The point isn't to be somber; it's to inspire a moment of reflection. After all, a legacy isn't built in sweeping gestures but in the small, consistent ways you show up for others. And if nothing else, let's agree on this: "Excel Wizard" does not belong on the plaque. Unless, of course, you also happen to be an Excel Wizard who built a school, mentored future wizards, and always remembered to laugh along the way.

Embedding Purpose Into Your Business Culture

Let's talk about embedding purpose into your business, which sounds lofty but is, in reality, a lot like teaching a child to tie their shoes: it takes patience, some creative thinking, and a bit of backtracking when someone gets frustrated and declares they're never wearing shoes again.

Purpose isn't about slapping an inspiring quote on the office wall or adding "integrity" to the company mission statement and calling it a day. It's about ensuring that what you do and how you do it reflects something meaningful—not just for you, but for everyone involved. It's the secret sauce that transforms a workplace from "just a job" into something people care about, remember, hopefully, take pride in.

Take a moment to think about the businesses or leaders you admire most. Odds are, they've embedded a sense of purpose into everything they do. Maybe they champion sustainability, promote inclusivity, or genuinely believe in treating employees like actual humans instead of productivity machines. Whatever their mission, it seeps into their culture, shaping decisions big and small.

This isn't just about being noble—it's about making sure your business stands for something that lasts. After all, would you rather be remembered as "the boss who always scheduled meetings at lunchtime" or "the leader who made coming to work feel meaningful"?

Embedding purpose into your culture starts with clarity. What do you, as a business, value most? Is it innovation? Community impact? Empowering your team? Once you've nailed that down, let it guide your actions. If you say you value teamwork, for instance, don't turn around and reward cutthroat competition. If you claim to prioritize work-life balance, don't email employees at midnight asking for "just one quick update."

Purpose also thrives in the little things—those daily, often-overlooked moments that quietly define your culture. It's in how you handle mistakes (do you scold, or do you support?), how you recognize achievements (with heartfelt thanks or a generic email blast), and even in the tone you set during Monday morning meetings (uplifting or soul-sucking?).

By embedding purpose into your business, you're not just creating a legacy of profits and products. You're creating a legacy of positive change—a workplace where people leave better than they arrived, a business that contributes to something larger than itself.

And who knows? Maybe, just maybe, you'll end up as the leader who isn't remembered for a sticky coffee machine but for creating a culture that made people believe in the power of purpose. That's a legacy worth tying your shoes for.

Building a Purpose-Driven Business

Creating a purpose-driven business is a bit like tossing a pebble into a pond: even the smallest, most unassuming pebble can send ripples far beyond its initial splash. Granted, if your pond happens to be the office koi pond, those ripples might lead to some grumpy fish and a disgruntled facilities manager, but you get the idea.

The point is, when you embed purpose into the very DNA of your business, its effects stretch far beyond your immediate team or customer base. A purpose-driven company inspires people, fosters innovation, and creates a positive impact that radiates outward—like ripples in the proverbial (and hopefully non-koi-infested) pond.

Take, for instance, companies known for championing sustainability. It's not just about offering eco-friendly products; it's about creating a culture where every employee, partner, and customer feels part of a greater mission to do good. The company's values seep into hiring decisions, vendor choices, and even how they design their office spaces (hopefully with lots of natural light and fewer fluorescent flickers of despair).

This ripple effect doesn't just change the world outside your company; it transforms the world inside it, too. Employees who believe in the purpose of their work are more engaged, more loyal, and—surprise, surprise—happier. Purpose has this magical ability to turn a job into a calling, which is particularly helpful if you want to be remembered as a visionary leader and not just the person who sent out relentless emails about synergy.

To build a purpose-driven business, start with clarity. What's the big "why" behind what you do? Is it to create life-changing products? To revolutionize an industry? To make workspaces less about beige cubicles and more about creativity and connection? Whatever it is, your purpose should act as your guiding star, steering decisions from the boardroom to the breakroom.

Then, ensure that purpose is not just a lofty statement framed on the wall but a lived experience. If you claim to prioritize community, show it by volunteering, donating, or partnering with local organizations. If innovation is your mantra, give your team the tools and freedom to experiment—even if it occasionally leads to ideas like kombucha-flavored chewing gum (which should probably stay in the idea phase).

And don't underestimate the power of small gestures. A purpose-driven business is just as much about grand missions as it is about everyday interactions—encouraging collaboration, celebrating contributions, and ensuring everyone feels part of the bigger picture.

Remember, even the tiniest pebble has the power to create ripples. And when your business is purpose-driven, those ripples might just turn into waves—waves of innovation, impact, and legacy. Just try not to aim them at the office koi pond.

Choosing Causes That Matter

Identifying the right causes to champion as a business is a bit like choosing a new hobby: it has to resonate with your personality, align with your values, and ideally, not be something you pick up just to impress people at dinner parties. After all, there's only so much mileage you can get out of saying, "Our company is deeply committed to promoting artisanal cheese appreciation," before everyone realizes you're just angling for better charcuterie boards at events.

The key to selecting causes that matter lies in authenticity. Start by looking inward. What issues or initiatives genuinely align with your personal and business values? If sustainability is your thing, consider environmental efforts—perhaps reducing waste, planting trees, or switching your office coffee cups from disposable to something that won't outlive humanity. If education resonates, maybe you can offer scholarships, mentorship programs, or resources for underserved schools. The point is to choose something that feels like an extension of who you are as a business rather than something picked out of a "Top 10 Trendy Causes" list.

A great way to narrow this down is to think about what your business already stands for. If your company produces eco-friendly products, sustainability might be a natural fit. If you're a tech entrepreneur, supporting STEM education could align beautifully. Or, if your business thrives on local community support, why not reinvest in that same community? Causes that complement your mission tend to integrate seamlessly into your operations, making them more impactful and less performative.

And here's a tip: steer clear of causes you know little about or don't feel strongly connected to, no matter how impressive they might sound at networking events. Nothing undermines credibility like someone who claims to be passionate about ocean conservation but struggles to differentiate between a whale and a manatee.

It's also worth involving your team in the decision. Often, employees have incredible ideas about initiatives that could align with the business's goals while making a meaningful difference. Plus, giving them a say can make the effort more collaborative, ensuring everyone feels invested in the impact.

Most importantly, remember that choosing a cause is not about scale—it's about sincerity. Even small actions, like sponsoring a local cleanup drive or donating supplies to a nearby school, can have a significant ripple effect. The goal isn't to save the entire world (unless you're particularly ambitious); it's to make a positive, lasting difference in a way that feels true to you and your business.

So pick a cause that matters—not because it looks good on paper but because it feels good in your heart. And if that cause happens to involve better charcuterie boards, well, who's to judge?

Making an Impact Through Small Actions

When it comes to leaving a positive legacy, many entrepreneurs fall into the trap of thinking it has to involve grand gestures—endowing a university library, building a hospital, or funding a space telescope. While those are lovely ideas (and if you're in a position to do them, more power to you), meaningful impact doesn't always have to come with fireworks and a commemorative plaque. In fact, some of the most profound legacies are built on the back of small, consistent actions that make life just a little brighter for the people around you.

Take, for instance, the humble act of mentoring an intern. Sure, you're not solving world hunger or developing a vaccine, but to that intern, your guidance might just be the difference between a bewildering career start and a lifelong trajectory of confidence and success. Sharing a little wisdom—how to navigate tricky client meetings, avoid the pitfalls of reply-all email disasters, or simply how to organize their calendar—can ripple out into something far greater than you'd ever imagine.

Or consider hosting a local community event. It might not make national news, but a well-planned networking night, a charity bake-off, or even an open house at your business can create connections and goodwill that linger long after the last cupcake is eaten. (Just remember to be gracious when someone shows up with oatmeal raisin cookies and tries to pass them off as chocolate chip.)

The magic of small actions lies in their accessibility. They don't require massive budgets or complex logistics—just a little effort and a lot of heart. And their impact? It's like baking cookies for your neighborhood. Sure, it's a small gesture, but the smiles it generates have a way of spreading, making everyone's day just a bit sweeter.

Small actions also allow you to engage more personally. It's one thing to write a check for a cause; it's another to roll up your sleeves and contribute in a way that's visible and immediate. These moments of direct interaction—teaching a skill, supporting a team member, lending a hand to a community project—create lasting memories and build a legacy that's not just about what you gave but how you made people feel.

The beauty of these smaller-scale efforts is that they can add up over time. A business that consistently invests in small, meaningful actions will eventually create a cumulative impact that's anything but small. It's the entrepreneurial equivalent of planting wildflowers along a well-traveled path: each seed might seem insignificant, but together, they transform the landscape into something vibrant and memorable.

So, start small. Mentor that eager intern. Host a community event. Bake those metaphorical (or literal) cookies. You don't need a Nobel Prize-worthy initiative to create a legacy. Sometimes, it's the little things—done with consistency and care—that leave the biggest smiles in your wake.

Case Studies of Impact

When it comes to integrating purpose into a business, the possibilities are as varied as the businesses themselves. Some companies embrace large-scale initiatives that redefine their industries, while others create meaningful change through small, heartfelt gestures that resonate deeply with their employees, customers, and communities. Both approaches can leave lasting legacies, provided they're rooted in authenticity rather than gimmickry. After all, while sponsoring a skywriting ad might grab attention, it doesn't exactly scream "meaningful impact."

Take, for instance, a small coffee shop in a bustling city. Instead of simply slinging lattes and keeping the Wi-Fi running, they decided to create a scholarship fund for local students pursuing environmental science degrees. Each cup of coffee sold contributed a few cents to the fund, and within a few years, they'd helped dozens of students afford tuition. It wasn't a splashy move, but it was deeply aligned with their mission to promote sustainability—and their customers appreciated knowing their caffeine habit had an added benefit beyond staying awake during morning meetings.

Then there's the story of a mid-sized marketing agency that decided to make mentorship part of their DNA. They partnered with local high schools to offer internships and workshops, giving students a hands-on introduction to the world of branding and design. Not only did this create opportunities for young people who might not have considered marketing as a career, but it also energized the agency's team, who found new joy in sharing their expertise and watching their interns' confidence grow.

On the larger end of the spectrum, consider a tech company that committed to hiring and training veterans transitioning to civilian life. Their initiative wasn't just about adding diversity to their workforce—it was about recognizing the unique skills veterans bring to the table and providing them with meaningful career paths. The company's leadership discovered that this initiative not only strengthened their team but also earned them a deeply loyal customer base, as people rallied around their purpose-driven approach.

Of course, not every attempt at embedding purpose lands perfectly. Take the well-meaning (but misguided) bakery that decided to raise awareness for endangered species by baking panda-shaped cookies... with charcoal to represent pollution. Unfortunately, the cookies were about as palatable as an actual lump of coal, leaving customers perplexed and bakers scrambling for a new idea.

The lesson here is simple: successful purpose-driven initiatives resonate because they align with a business's values, its strengths, and the needs of its community. They don't have to be enormous or perfect; they just need to be genuine.

Whether it's a small shop funding scholarships, an agency mentoring the next generation, or a tech firm championing veterans, the impact comes from connecting actions to values in a way that feels meaningful. And if you can do it without accidentally poisoning your customers with charcoal cookies, all the better.

Mentorship and Knowledge Sharing: Passing the Baton (Without Dropping It)

Mentorship and knowledge sharing are the entrepreneurial equivalent of passing the baton in a relay race—except in this version, the baton is a wealth of experience, and the track is littered with the occasional pothole of questionable decisions. The goal is to hand over your hard-earned wisdom without accidentally tripping the next runner (or, worse, losing the baton entirely).

Think about it: every great leader, in some form or another, has been shaped by mentors—people who offered guidance, shared lessons, or simply gave a much-needed nudge in the right direction. And yet, when it comes time to do the same for others, it's easy to feel a bit hesitant. What if you don't have all the answers? (Spoiler: you don't, and that's okay.) What if your advice sends someone in the wrong direction? (It won't, as long as you steer clear of suggesting they invest in pet rocks.)

Mentorship, at its core, isn't about having all the answers—it's about being willing to share what you've learned, stumbles and all, to help someone else find their path.

Why Mentorship Matters

Passing on knowledge is one of the most enduring ways to create a legacy. It ensures that the lessons you've learned don't fade into obscurity but instead ripple outward, shaping the next generation of leaders, innovators, and adventurers.

Take the example of a seasoned restaurateur who spends time mentoring aspiring chefs. Sure, they teach them knife skills and how to make a perfect hollandaise sauce, but they also share the less glamorous realities of the industry—how to handle an unruly customer, why you should never scrimp on quality, and the importance of taking deep breaths when the oven breaks mid-dinner rush.

Or imagine a tech founder who dedicates a few hours a month to mentoring startup entrepreneurs. Through their guidance, they save these bright-eyed newcomers from repeating the same mistakes, like launching a product before checking if anyone actually wants it.

Mentorship is more than a transfer of skills—it's an act of hope and belief in the potential of others. And it's not just good for the mentee; it's incredibly rewarding for the mentor, too. After all, there's nothing quite like the warm glow of realizing someone actually benefited from your advice (and didn't just nod politely while secretly Googling something else).

The Joy of Knowledge Sharing

If mentorship feels like a big commitment, think smaller. Sharing your expertise doesn't have to involve formal programs or grand gestures—it can be as simple as hosting a lunch-and-learn session for your team, offering advice during coffee chats, or writing a blog post about lessons learned in your field.

Think of knowledge sharing as a way to leave breadcrumbs for those following behind you. And, if you're lucky, some of those breadcrumbs might even circle back to you as fresh ideas and insights from the people you've helped.

The key is to approach it with authenticity and humility. You're not here to play the all-knowing guru atop a mountain—you're here to be the friendly guide who admits they've taken a few wrong turns but eventually found the scenic route.

Passing the Baton

As you share your knowledge and mentor others, remember that the goal isn't to mold someone into a carbon copy of yourself (one of you is quite enough). Instead, focus on equipping them with the tools, confidence, and resilience they need to carve their own path.

Legacy isn't just about what you achieve—it's about what you inspire in others. So pass that baton with care, encouragement, and maybe a little humor. Because when the next runner takes off down the track, fueled by what you've shared, you'll know you've left a mark that truly matters.

The Joy of Mentorship: A Lighthouse on Solid Ground

Mentorship isn't just a gift for the mentee—it's a surprising source of joy and fulfillment for the mentor, too. There's something deeply satisfying about sharing your hard-won wisdom and watching it light the way for someone else. It's like being a lighthouse: you stand firm on the shore, steady and grounded, while your light helps others navigate their journeys.

Think about the beauty of this role. You're not steering their ship, barking orders through a megaphone. You're simply casting a guiding light, offering direction and reassurance to those venturing into the often unpredictable waters of business and life. And as they find their way, you get the quiet satisfaction of knowing you've played a part in their success—not by holding the wheel, but by helping them see the path ahead.

Mentorship as a Two-Way Street

What many mentors discover is that the experience is far from one-sided. While your mentee gains insight and perspective, you gain something just as valuable:

a fresh outlook, a renewed sense of purpose, and perhaps even the occasional brilliant idea you hadn't considered before.

It's like walking a familiar trail with someone who's seeing it for the first time. Their excitement and curiosity can remind you of why you started the journey in the first place. They might even spot a shortcut or a hidden view you've missed all these years.

Professional and Personal Fulfillment

Professionally, mentorship lets you see your knowledge and skills ripple outward, shaping the next generation of leaders, creators, and innovators. Personally, it's an opportunity to connect, to reflect on your own growth, and to find meaning in the experiences that have shaped you.

And let's not overlook the moments of humor and camaraderie that often come with mentorship. Guiding someone through their first big challenge—or watching them navigate the same potholes you once stumbled over—can be both humbling and oddly entertaining.

Lighting the Way

As a mentor, you're not expected to have all the answers. (Sorry: no one does, not even you.) What matters is your willingness to share what you've learned, to listen, and to encourage others to trust their instincts.

Like a lighthouse, your purpose isn't to steer the ship—it's to remind the sailors that they're not alone, that the shore is within reach, and that even in the foggiest moments, there's a way forward.

So, shine your light. Share your stories, your lessons, and even your missteps. Because there's a unique joy in knowing that your experiences—good, bad, and occasionally absurd—can help someone else chart their course with a little more confidence and a lot more hope.

Identifying Future Leaders: Spotting Potential Without Rose-Tinted Glasses

Identifying future leaders within your team—or among those you mentor—is a bit like prospecting for gold. There's a lot of shiny enthusiasm out there, but not every glint in the pan is the real deal. It's about recognizing the qualities that hint at future brilliance while gently nudging aside the more, shall we say, overly ambitious folks who might just be spinning in place.

Beyond Enthusiasm

Now, don't get me wrong: enthusiasm is a fine quality. It's the engine that drives curiosity and initiative, and without it, you're left with the professional equivalent of a soggy sandwich—functional, but not inspiring. That said, enthusiasm alone doesn't guarantee stellar leadership potential.

You've likely met someone whose eagerness outpaced their judgment. (Think of the intern who enthusiastically volunteers to run a meeting but ends up scheduling it at 3 a.m. because "that's when they're most productive.") Keen enthusiasm is a good starting point, but it needs to be paired with other, more substantial qualities to indicate true leadership potential.

The Hallmarks of Future Leaders

So, what should you be looking for? Let's start with adaptability—a willingness to embrace challenges and pivot when things go awry. A potential leader isn't someone who panics when the PowerPoint crashes; they're the one who calmly cracks a joke and switches to a whiteboard without missing a beat.

Next, there's empathy. This doesn't mean they have to bake birthday cakes for the entire office (though points if they do), but a great leader understands people—their motivations, their challenges, and occasionally, their need to vent about the mysterious sticky spot on the breakroom counter.

And of course, there's the ability to take initiative. This isn't about hogging the spotlight or barking orders. It's about stepping up when needed, suggesting solutions, and taking ownership of outcomes. A true leader doesn't just ask, "What should we do?" They propose, "Here's what I think we can try."

Spotting the Spark

Future leaders often reveal themselves in subtle ways. Maybe it's the quiet team member who consistently delivers thoughtful insights in meetings or the employee who finds creative solutions to everyday hiccups. Leadership potential isn't always flashy; sometimes, it's the steady glow rather than the burst of fireworks.

That said, don't discount those who might still be rough around the edges. A good leader can be polished over time, but their core qualities—resilience, curiosity, and a dash of courage—should already be there, waiting to shine.

Cultivating Potential

Once you've identified someone with that spark of leadership potential, your role shifts to cultivating it. Offer opportunities to stretch their skills, provide constructive feedback (minus the sugarcoating), and cheer them on as they grow. Just be prepared: sometimes, their growth will surprise even you. The goal here is to guide them to become the best version of themselves—a leader with their own unique style, quirks, and hopefully, a few brilliant ideas that even you didn't see coming.

Because, in the end, identifying future leaders isn't just about spotting potential. It's about believing in people, nurturing their talents, and then stepping back to watch them thrive. And if they bake a birthday cake or two along the way? All the better.

Sharing Wisdom Without Sounding Like a Know-It-All

Passing on wisdom is one of the great joys of mentorship. It's a chance to reflect on what you've learned, share the lessons, and hopefully spare someone else from making the same mistakes you did—like trying to schedule meetings without time zones or underestimating the sheer havoc a misused "Reply All" button can wreak. But here's the thing: sharing wisdom is a delicate art. Too much, and you risk coming across as a sanctimonious windbag. Too little, and your mentees are left floundering, wondering why you even agreed to mentor them in the first place.

Striking the Balance

Think of sharing wisdom like seasoning the chili: you want just enough to enrich the flavor, not so much that everyone's gulping water to recover. This means balancing personal anecdotes with actionable advice and tailoring your pearls of wisdom to what the person actually needs at the moment.

Personal stories can be great—who doesn't love a tale of triumph over adversity or a "learn from my epic failure" moment? But if every interaction begins with "Well, back in my day..." you might start losing your audience to glazed-over eyes and strategically timed coffee refills.

Actionable Advice

What makes wisdom stick? Actionable advice. Instead of waxing poetic about how you single-handedly saved a product launch, share the steps you took to do it. Offer frameworks or tips that can be applied in real-world scenarios, like how you learned to delegate effectively or calm a tense client with the charm of a diplomat and the patience of a kindergarten teacher.

Be honest about what worked, what didn't, and what you'd do differently if given the chance. And always, always leave room for questions. There's nothing quite like realizing your mentee heard your entire story and still has no idea how to apply it to their situation.

Avoiding the "Back in My Day" Trap

The "back in my day" mentor often has good intentions—they genuinely want to help. But here's the problem: the world is always changing. What worked for you might not work now, and what seemed cutting-edge in 1998 is probably a museum relic by 2024.

Instead of harping on the past, connect your experiences to current realities. For example, instead of recounting the glories of cold-calling in the pre-internet era, discuss the universal principles of connecting with clients and how they might translate to today's tools, like email campaigns or social media outreach.

Humor: The Great Equalizer

Finally, don't forget humor. A well-timed quip or self-deprecating anecdote can lighten the mood and remind your mentees that even the most seasoned mentors were once clueless beginners. Share the time you accidentally sent an invoice to the wrong client or flubbed an important presentation—and how you recovered. Laughter breaks down barriers, builds trust, and makes your wisdom infinitely more relatable.

In the end, sharing wisdom is less about impressing your mentees with how much you know and more about empowering them with what they need. Give them the tools, insights, and confidence to succeed, then step back and let them shine. Because ultimately, the mark of a great mentor isn't the stories they tell but the stories they help others create. And if you can do all that without a single "back in my day"? You've truly mastered the art.

The Legacy of Leadership

Mentorship isn't just about passing along a few handy tips or sharing tales of your most spectacular blunders (though those certainly help). It's about planting seeds that will grow into something far greater than you could ever accomplish alone. It's about creating a ripple effect, where the lessons you share inspire someone else to do the same for others—long after you've stepped away from the conference room or, dare we say it, the stage of life.

Imagine this: years down the road, a mentee of yours solves a problem, lands a deal, or pioneers a brilliant idea. In an interview or a toast, they casually mention, "I learned this from [your name here]." There's your legacy—not etched on a plaque or commemorated with an office plant in your honor, but alive in the work and actions of others.

Carrying the Torch

Leadership, when done right, is less about telling people what to do and more about lighting the path so they can navigate it themselves. The lessons you pass on—whether about handling failure, staying adaptable, or simply keeping a sense of humor when the Wi-Fi crashes during a critical meeting—equip others to face their own challenges with confidence and creativity.

What's remarkable about mentorship is that it's not confined to a single moment or relationship. When you teach someone how to weather a storm or seize an opportunity, they take that knowledge with them. They pass it on, adapting it to their own experiences, and in doing so, extend your influence far beyond what you could ever achieve alone. It's the leadership equivalent of planting a tree whose shade you might never sit under but knowing someone else will.

A Legacy Beyond the Bottom Line

Perhaps the greatest gift of mentorship is the chance to shape not just careers but lives. You help foster innovation, resilience, and kindness in a world that sorely needs them. You encourage others to dream boldly, to laugh at their mistakes, and to keep going when the going gets tough.

And yes, if you do it right, you might even leave behind a bit of wit to go along with the wisdom. After all, what's a legacy without a touch of humor? Whether it's the mentee who remembers your advice to "never skip lunch before negotiations" or the one who still laughs at your joke about managing clients being like herding cats, you'll have left a mark that's both practical and personal.

So, as you guide the next generation, remember this: leadership isn't about standing at the front—it's about empowering others to take the lead. And if you can do it with generosity, humor, and just a dash of charm, your legacy will shine brighter than any award or title ever could.

Keeping the Flame Alive After You've Moved On

A legacy isn't a one-time act; it's more like a campfire. Sure, you can light it, stand back, and bask in its glow, but if no one tends it, you'll eventually be left with ashes. Sustaining your legacy requires a bit of effort, a touch of foresight, and the occasional poke with a stick to ensure the embers stay alive.

Let's start with the most obvious hurdle: stepping away. Whether it's retiring, selling the business, or just transitioning into a less hands-on role, moving on from something you've poured your heart into can feel like handing over your favorite sweater to someone who doesn't know the delicate wash cycle. But here's the thing—if you've built something truly meaningful, it can thrive without you.

Building Continuity

A sustainable legacy hinges on continuity. This means putting systems in place, training successors, and ensuring your core values are so deeply embedded in the business that they remain intact even after you've moved on. It's not unlike teaching someone to care for a prized houseplant. You wouldn't just hand it over with a vague, "Good luck." You'd leave clear instructions: how much sunlight it needs, how often to water, and why it appreciates a little classical music on Tuesdays.

The same principle applies here. Whether it's a detailed handbook, a mission statement etched into the hearts of your team, or simply mentoring a successor who "gets it," you're ensuring the spirit of what you've built endures.

Staying Involved Without Interfering

There's also an art to letting go gracefully. You don't want to be the ex-boss who haunts the office like a well-meaning but exasperating ghost, popping in with unsolicited advice and rearranging the coffee mugs. Instead, find ways to stay connected that add value without undermining the new leadership.

Maybe you take on an advisory role, offering insights from a safe distance while letting the team chart their own course. Or perhaps you focus on broader impact—mentorship programs, speaking engagements, or initiatives that extend the reach of your values and ideas beyond the company walls.

The Ripple Effect

The beauty of a well-sustained legacy is its ripple effect. When you invest in people, they carry your lessons forward, influencing others in ways you may never see. A piece of advice you gave to one person might inspire a whole new way of thinking in a different corner of the world. That's the kind of magic no title, plaque, or end-of-year bonus can replicate.

A Legacy That Lives On

Sustaining your legacy isn't about being remembered; it's about making a lasting difference. It's knowing that the principles, culture, and impact you've cultivated will continue to thrive and evolve, even without your direct involvement.

So, whether you're handing over the keys to your business or simply stepping into a quieter chapter, take comfort in this: a legacy worth sustaining isn't tied to one person—it's a flame that keeps burning, warming and inspiring those who come next. And if you've done it right, it might even burn a little brighter after you've moved on.

Creating Systems for Long-Term Impact

Creating systems for long-term impact is much like crafting a fine clock: it's about precision, foresight, and ensuring that all the gears keep turning smoothly long after your hands are no longer setting the time. In a business context, this means embedding your values and initiatives so deeply into its framework that they become self-sustaining, ticking away reliably without your constant intervention.

Take, for example, a company culture initiative. It's one thing to tell your team, "Be collaborative and innovative," but quite another to build processes that actively encourage and reward those behaviors. You need systems—clear guidelines, structured mentorships, or even something as simple as a recognition program—that reinforce the values you hold dear. Think of these as the gears in your business clock: each one playing a part to ensure the entire mechanism runs seamlessly.

And then there's the matter of leadership succession. Handing over the reins isn't about finding someone who can do things exactly as you did. (In fact, that's probably the last thing you want.) It's about finding someone who understands the core principles behind what you've built and can adapt them to a changing landscape. It's the difference between winding a clock and crafting a self-winding one—a leader who doesn't just carry on the tradition but evolves it, ensuring it stays relevant and vibrant.

Let's not forget about documentation. Yes, it sounds dull—like organizing your sock drawer—but it's essential for long-term impact. Documenting the "why" behind your initiatives is just as important as the "how." Why did you prioritize customer relationships over quick profits? Why does your company invest in community programs? These whys are what transform a mechanical process into a meaningful legacy. They're the instructions that help future leaders wind the clock without losing sight of its purpose.

Finally, consider how you communicate these systems to your team. This isn't a one-time handover but an ongoing process of education and reinforcement. It's sharing your vision not just as a directive but as a story—something that inspires and engages others to keep the clock ticking long after you've stepped back.

By creating systems with clarity, purpose, and adaptability, you're ensuring that what you've built doesn't just last—it thrives. Long after your part in the story has ended, the clock will still chime, marking time with a rhythm you set but a legacy that belongs to everyone who continues to wind it forward.

Investing in People Over Processes

Investing in people over processes is the cornerstone of sustaining a meaningful legacy. Processes, while useful, are like scaffolding—they provide structure, but it's the people who bring the building to life. After all, no amount of policy writing can replace the impact of a passionate team that truly believes in the vision you've cultivated.

Imagine passing your business to a successor. You could leave behind a manual thicker than a Tolstoy novel, detailing every single procedure. But without a team that understands the heart of your mission, it's just words on paper. Investing in people means identifying and nurturing those who not only grasp the "how" but also embrace the "why." These are the ones who will infuse your legacy with fresh energy, ensuring it evolves rather than stagnates.

This doesn't mean processes are unimportant—far from it. It's just that a great process in the hands of an unmotivated or disconnected person is like giving a Stradivarius violin to someone who doesn't care for music. Focus on mentoring and developing individuals who can wield those processes with passion and creativity. Teach them the values and principles that guide decision-making, so they're equipped to adapt when the inevitable curveballs of business come their way.

And let's talk about traditions, shall we? Maybe you've started something quirky, like "Hat Day Fridays," where everyone wears their most eccentric headgear to spark creativity. Or perhaps there's a beloved team outing or charity initiative that holds special meaning. The key to passing on these traditions is ensuring your successor and team genuinely enjoy them. Otherwise, you risk leaving behind something that feels like a duty rather than a joy.

Investing in people also means fostering an environment where they feel empowered to grow into leadership roles. Share your knowledge, encourage curiosity, and—perhaps most importantly—create a culture where mistakes are seen as stepping stones rather than cliffs. After all, the best leaders are those who've stumbled, learned, and risen stronger.

So, when the time comes to hand over the reins, trust in the people you've nurtured rather than clinging to rigid processes. Your legacy isn't a checklist or a binder of protocols; it's the inspiration, innovation, and humanity you leave behind in those who carry the torch forward. And if they decide to keep Hat Day alive? Well, consider that a bonus.

Balancing Legacy With Adaptability

Balancing legacy with adaptability is like planting a grove of trees—not just for shade today, but for future generations to climb, picnic under, or perhaps even turn into a quirky treehouse. The trick lies in choosing trees that can withstand storms, thrive in shifting climates, and maybe even surprise you with the occasional unexpected bloom.

Your legacy, much like that grove, isn't meant to be a rigid monument. It's not a stone statue engraved with "Thou Shalt Never Change." Instead, it's a living, breathing thing that evolves with the times. Businesses grow, societies shift, and the people who inherit your vision will bring their own ideas and innovations to the table. That's a good thing—it means your legacy has roots strong enough to support new branches.

Imagine the alternative: a perfectly preserved but utterly irrelevant artifact, like an untouched room in a museum where the furniture is roped off and visitors murmur, "Why did they need this many doilies?" A legacy that doesn't adapt risks becoming just that—stagnant, out of touch, and more of a historical curiosity than a meaningful influence.

To strike the balance, think of your legacy as a set of guiding principles rather than an unyielding roadmap. Focus on the values and impact you want to leave behind but give the people carrying it forward the freedom to adapt it to their era and circumstances. Maybe you started with a commitment to innovation and community impact. In 50 years, that could mean anything from embracing cutting-edge technologies to tackling global challenges you can't even imagine today.

And let's not forget the importance of flexibility in your own lifetime. Times change faster than ever, and what feels like a groundbreaking initiative today might seem quaint tomorrow (looking at you, fax machines). By staying open to new ideas and adjusting your vision as needed, you ensure that your legacy remains relevant and vibrant, not a relic of "how things used to be."

Ultimately, the goal is to leave something that lasts but doesn't feel like a straitjacket for those who come after you. Whether it's a company culture that champions creativity, a community project that evolves with local needs, or even just a tradition of leaving things better than you found them, the beauty of your legacy lies in its adaptability.

And who knows? One day, someone might be sitting under the proverbial tree you planted, reading a book about how you built something enduring and meaningful—and maybe laughing at a story about your Hat Day Fridays. That's a legacy worth leaving.

Long-Term Contributions Beyond Business

Long-term contributions beyond the walls of your business are where legacy truly stretches its wings. It's like stepping out of your office and realizing that the world beyond your carefully curated desk setup is ripe for a touch of your brilliance—or at least a thoughtful donation to the local library's book repair fund.

Philanthropy is a classic way to leave a lasting mark. Whether you're funding scholarships, supporting environmental conservation, or simply ensuring the local coffee shop never runs out of beans, these acts of giving ripple outward in ways you might not even realize. It's less about the size of the check and more about the intention behind it. Are you improving lives, sparking innovation, or at the very least, ensuring the community's yearly pancake breakfast doesn't go under? If so, you're on the right track.

Thought leadership is another delightful way to extend your influence. Sharing your wisdom—whether through speaking engagements, blog posts, or the occasional LinkedIn rant—can inspire a whole new generation of entrepreneurs to dream big, act boldly, and perhaps learn from your missteps before they make their own. Just remember, the goal is to sound insightful, not insufferable. Nobody likes a know-it-all, especially one who insists they invented email marketing.

And then, of course, there's the memoir. Ah, the sweet, self-indulgent joy of recounting your life story—preferably with the narrative flair of an epic saga. Feel free to embellish slightly; no one's counting the exact number of hours you spent single-handedly saving the company from financial ruin. After all, it's your story, and you are, naturally, the hero. Just keep it relatable—readers tend to glaze over during lengthy monologues about quarterly reports but will devour tales of scrappy beginnings and office escapades involving rogue printers or an unfortunate coffee spill.

But why stop there? Perhaps your legacy is about creating a lasting connection with the people and places that shaped you. Sponsor a local arts festival, plant a community garden, or mentor young dreamers who are as wide-eyed and clueless as you once were. These contributions might not come with plaques or press releases, but their impact will be felt in smiles, opportunities, and stories told long after you're gone.

Ultimately, legacy is about living beyond yourself, leaving the world a little—or a lot—better than you found it. Whether that means funding breakthroughs, sharing wisdom, or simply being remembered as the quirky genius who always had a kind word and a penchant for exaggerated storytelling, it's all part of the adventure.

And who knows? One day, someone might pick up your memoir, leaf through its pages, and say, "This person? They made a difference." (Even if the chapter on the coffee spill incident makes them chuckle more than tear up.) That's the magic of a legacy—uniquely yours and ever-reaching.

The Legacy You Leave Behind

As you step back to consider your legacy, let's put aside grand monuments and brass plaques for a moment—because, let's face it, no one is itching to read *Here Lies the Founder of Excel Wizardry*. Legacy, at its heart, isn't about what you leave behind but the ripples you create while you're still splashing around in the pool of life.

Think of your legacy as a quilt. Not the pristine kind you find on display at a museum, but a practical, well-loved patchwork of contributions, relationships, and values. Some stitches might be a bit crooked, a few patches mismatched, but taken as a whole, it tells a story—one of effort, care, and, hopefully, more laughter than unraveling threads.

The beauty of legacy is that it's not etched in stone. It's organic, evolving with each conversation, act of kindness, or moment of shared insight. It's the mentorship that gives someone their first break, the business practices that set a new standard, and the laughter shared over a botched PowerPoint presentation that turns into a team inside joke.

Remember, your legacy is less about the towering structures you leave behind and more about the lives you've touched along the way. It's in the intern who learns to dream bigger because of your encouragement, the colleague who starts tackling problems with a little more humor because of your example, and the community that feels a bit stronger because of your contributions.

In the end, legacy is about connection. It's about finding ways to make a difference—big or small—that ripple outward long after you've moved on. And let's not forget: it's also about sharing your story, wisdom, and quirks with those who'll carry them forward. After all, the world could always use more colorful patches to stitch into its quilt.

So, go ahead—build something meaningful, share your wisdom generously, and leave the world just a bit better than you found it. If you can manage that, you won't just leave a legacy; you'll create a life worth celebrating, one joyful stitch at a time.

About the Author

Roger Best

MEET ROGER BEST

Roger Best is a seasoned entrepreneur who's navigated the wild ride of building multiple successful businesses. With years of battle scars and triumphs, he knows firsthand the relentless grind of entrepreneurship—those long hours, high-stakes decisions, and the relentless chase for success that can sometimes steal the joy out of life.

But Roger isn't just a survivor; he's a thriver. After his own transformation from a business owner burning the candle at both ends to a man who's mastered the balance of work and play, he's on a mission to help others break free from the chains of the endless hustle. In this book, he lays out practical, no-nonsense strategies to reclaim your time, achieve financial freedom, and craft a life packed with purpose, adventure, and a healthy dose of leisure.

When Roger's not in the trenches with one of his ventures, writing, or mentoring fellow entrepreneurs, you'll find him living life on his terms—spending quality time with family and friends, exploring new terrain, or just kicking back and enjoying the satisfaction that comes from running a successful business that doesn't dominate every moment.

Roger's been married to his soulmate for just over 45 years, a proud dad to two grown kids, and a devoted grandfather to two little princesses. In 2021, he and his wife decided to turn their island dream into reality, moving to Puerto Rico, where they now run their businesses while soaking up the hammock life.

Roger's mission is straightforward: to inspire and empower entrepreneurs to build thriving businesses without sacrificing their happiness, health, or freedom.

Also by Roger Best

EXPLORE A COLLECTION OF inspiring and practical reads designed to empower entrepreneurs and business owners. From reclaiming your time to building a business that truly serves you, these books offer actionable insights to help you create a successful and meaningful life and business.

From Hamster Wheel to Hammock: A Guide to Taking Your Day Back*(Available on Amazon – ebook, paperback and Audible)*

Escape the relentless grind and rediscover the freedom you dreamed of when you started your business. This practical and empowering guide offers actionable strategies to help you break free from the hamster wheel, reclaim your time, and build a balanced, fulfilling life. Whether you're overwhelmed by long hours or stuck in the cycle of constant hustle, this book will show you the path to a life of purpose and peace.

Personal Growth for Entrepreneurs: Your Time, Your Way*(Available on Amazon – ebook and paperback)*

Take a deeper dive into aligning your business and life with your values and passions. This book focuses on developing habits, mindsets, and systems that not only support your professional goals but also nurture your personal growth. Learn how to create meaningful success that feels true to who you are while finding fulfillment in every step of the journey.

The Liberated Entrepreneur: Building a Business That Works for You (Available on)

Running a business doesn't have to mean sacrificing your life. In this transformative guide, you'll learn how to build a business that aligns with your values, supports your dreams, and works *for* you—not the other way around. Discover strategies for streamlining operations, empowering your team, and creating a sustainable work-life balance. This book is for entrepreneurs ready to escape burnout and reclaim the joy and freedom they set out to achieve.

Purpose-Driven Entrepreneurship: Reclaim Your Why for Lasting Success *(Available on)*

Discover the power of reconnecting with your purpose and unlock the clarity and passion needed to thrive. This book offers practical exercises, journaling prompts, and reflective tools to help you rediscover your core motivations, make aligned decisions, and build a life and business that truly matter. Perfect as a companion to *From Hamster Wheel to Hammock* and *Personal Growth for Entrepreneurs*, this book is essential for anyone seeking deeper connection, fulfillment, and long-term success.

Protecting Your Business in the Digital Age: A Non-Technical Guide to Cybersecurity for Small Business Owners

Cybersecurity doesn't have to be overwhelming or overly technical. In this straightforward guide, you'll learn how to protect your business from digital threats, safeguard your financial resources, and ensure your customer data stays secure. Designed specifically for small business owners, this book breaks down the essentials of cybersecurity into practical, easy-to-understand steps that anyone can implement. Whether you're a tech novice or simply want peace of mind, this guide will help you secure your business and its future.

Each of these books offers unique insights into different aspects of entrepreneurial life. Whether you're seeking to break free from burnout, deepen your personal growth, reconnect with your purpose, or protect your business in a rapidly changing digital landscape, these reads are your guide to a more intentional, successful, and resilient journey. Explore them today and take the next step toward the life and business you've always envisioned!

www.ingramcontent.com/pod-product-compliance
Lightning Source LLC
Chambersburg PA
CBHW061551120626
46550CB00004B/1446